When You Are Down to Nothing, God Is Up to Something

Also by Robert A. Schuller

Leaning into God When Life Is Pushing You Away
Walking in Your Own Shoes

Available from FaithWords wherever books are sold.

When You Are Down to Nothing, God Is Up to Something

DISCOVERING DIVINE PURPOSE AND PROVISION WHEN LIFE HURTS

ROBERT A. SCHULLER

with William Kruidenier

New York   Boston   Nashville

Contents

ACKNOWLEDGMENTS   *vii*

INTRODUCTION   *ix*

PART I

WHAT GOD IS UP TO IN
YOUR RELATIONSHIPS

1 God Is Always with Me (Presence)   *3*

2 What You Can't Live Without (Love)   *17*

3 Being Together Is Better (Community)   *27*

4 You Are Your Own Best Friend (Identity)   *37*

5 How to Be Set Free (Forgiveness)   *47*

PART II

WHAT GOD IS UP TO IN
MEETING YOUR NEEDS

6 God Is Never Lost (Guidance)   *61*

7 You Are Totally Gifted (Gifts)   *71*

8 When You Need to Talk to Someone
   (God's Availability)   *80*

9 Nobody Has More Money than God (Provision)   *89*

10   Living Old, Dying Young (Health)   *98*

11   The Mythical Get-Out-of-Pain-Free Card
     (Suffering)   *107*

PART III

WHAT GOD IS UP TO IN
YOUR EMOTIONAL LIFE

12   Nothing to Be Afraid Of (Security)   *119*

13   What Goes Up Must Come Down (Disappointment)   *128*

14   The Greatest Feeling in the World
     (Freedom from Guilt)   *138*

15   How to Re-Joice (Joy)   *148*

16   The Rest of Your Life (Peace)   *158*

PART IV

WHAT GOD IS UP TO IN
KNOWING AND TRUSTING HIM

17   It's Not as Hard as You Think (Knowing God)   *171*

18   Who's in Charge Here? (Sovereignty)   *182*

19   Cancel Your Accident Insurance (Purpose)   *192*

20   You Have to Trust Somebody (Trust)   *202*

21   There Is a Good Reason to Hang On (Hope)   *212*

22   I'm Sorry, I Have No Recollection of That (The Past)   *223*

23   Living on a Need-to-Know Basis (The Future)   *233*

24   The Never-Ending Story (Eternity)   *242*

NOTES   *251*

Acknowledgments

Of the dozen or so books I have written, this one was the most challenging. Not the writing of it, but the living—living and retelling the story on which the book is based. As does anyone who goes through a difficult transition period in life, I stood up on the other side and realized I survived because I didn't journey alone. I am grateful to those who have been friends, counselors, and supporters in recent days:

Father, Son, and Holy Spirit were true to their Word: keeping their promises, shining light on my path, and keeping me from harm.

My new vocational family at ComStar Media (especially my son-in-law, Chris Wyatt) is helping to shape my vision of the future with skill while helping me see new ways to build on the past.

On a logistical level, telling a challenging story was made possible by my cowriter William Kruidenier, Joey Paul and his team at FaithWords, and my literary agent Sealy Yates.

Finally, it is the loves of my life—my wife, Donna, and my four wonderful children, their spouses, and my new grandbaby, Haven—who always make life worth fighting for and make every outcome a victory.

Introduction

Saint John of the Cross (Juan de Yepes Álvarez) was a sixteenth-century Spanish friar—a member of the Roman Catholic Carmelite order. Today he is perhaps best remembered for his classic work *Dark Night of the Soul* (*La noche oscura del alma*), a poem that describes the trials and suffering the soul goes through in this life. Because of his work as a reformer, John was arrested by his superiors, imprisoned, and tortured before he escaped nine months later. Dying before he reached the age of fifty, his writings have been a comfort to many who have endured their own "dark night of the soul."

While I in no way compare myself to Saint John of the Cross in spirituality, in insights, in suffering, or in contribution to Christendom, the title of his classic poem serves me well as I introduce this book—as do the circumstances under which he wrote. John used his own strained relationship with his superiors to write of the journey of the soul through the difficult darkness of trouble in this life—as do I. My dark night of the soul can in no way be compared to his except in this way: Trouble is life's wisest teacher; suffering is the schoolmaster that leads us to humble submission; trials are the tutor that explains the difference between life as we would like it and life as we are given it—and how the latter is the gateway to a deeper knowledge of God. In short, trouble teaches us that God is always up to something in our life.

My own dark night began in July 2008 when my superiors—specifically, my parents and other extended family members involved in leading "the family business," decided I was not the right person to continue in the positions they had asked me to fill two and a half years earlier: Senior Pastor of the Crystal Cathedral church and pastoral host of the international *Hour of Power* television broadcast. My sun set, and the dark night began, in July and lasted through October of 2008. It was like an eclipse—something that occurs in a matter of minutes with little or no warning. And the four months of darkness that followed were like a school in which I discovered that when we are down to nothing, God is always up to something.

This book is not about me and what I experienced. It's about God and what He does when we are in the dark corners of life. What happened to me is what has happened to millions of other people: the loss of a job, the death of a dream, the confusion about what to do next, the questioning of one's value, the questioning of God, and all the rest. I won't insult you by saying, "*If* you've been through something similar..." because I know you have. We are "born to trouble as surely as sparks fly upward" the book of Job tells us (5:7). If you have a pulse, you've seen trouble. And if you're reading these words, you've apparently lived to tell about it.

Or perhaps you're in trouble right now. You may feel you are down to nothing in one or more areas of life. Maybe you have lost a job or a marriage or an important relationship. Or maybe you've lost the faith and hope and confidence you need to pick yourself up and continue the journey. In truth, it doesn't matter so much *why* you feel you are down to nothing—the reasons are as innumerable as the people who name them. What matters is that you know what I learned in my own time of trouble: God is always up to something good in your life.

Yes, trouble can make us think we're down to nothing. But when we get to that lowly place we find what the point of trouble is: our ongoing growth in grace leading to a place of deeper maturity.

I've done lots of hiking in the California mountains, and this image comes to mind when I think of what I've been through—and what you may be going through: It's as if we're standing on a mountain peak. The view is great, the weather is fine, and we can't imagine wanting or needing to be anywhere else. But then God speaks to us out of the clouds (a true biblical image!) and says, "I know you are content on this mountain, but if you will cast your eyes over that way you'll see a peak that is slightly higher; a peak where I know you'll be wiser and happier and more mature than where you are." Taking God's word for it, you say, "Fine—put me over on that peak. If you say that's better, I'm willing to be moved."

"Sorry," God says. "To get there you need to move yourself. You need to go down into that valley and climb up the other side to reach the place I want you to be." One look down into the valley gives you reason to reconsider. You can't even see the floor of the valley because storm clouds and dark fog obscure your view. But you can see flashes of lightning and hear the low rumble of thunder from your place on the peak—and it looks none too inviting. It's sunny on your peak and it looks sunny on the peak God has picked out for you. But the path through the valley is a path of trouble for sure. You wonder whether you can trust God on the way. You don't know how long the trip will take or what you'll encounter in that dark valley.

Life, of course, doesn't look like that. God doesn't map our journey out in a "Point A to Point B" fashion. Indeed, we often don't even know the journey has begun until we find ourselves in the valley, surrounded by darkness and trouble. Only then do we realize we're down to nothing and wonder what God is up to.

I went through that valley for four months in 2008. I am far enough up the side of the distant peak to be able to look back and see what God was up to in the days when I thought I was down to nothing. I haven't arrived—do we ever arrive?—but I have traveled far enough to extend a hand to you as others farther along have extended a hand to me. I want my journey to count not only in my life but in the life of at least one other person who finds themselves down to nothing in a valley they didn't choose to enter.

I have divided this book into four parts that summarize the categories of comfort and change I experienced: Relationships, Needs, Emotions, and Knowing and Trusting God. When I thought I was down to nothing, all four were critical in realizing what God was up to:

- Relationships: with God, with self, and with others.
- Needs: "down to nothing" means we have serious needs.
- Emotions: fear, disappointment, guilt, search for peace—a roller-coaster ride.
- Knowing and trusting God: God is always there, always up to something good.

There are twenty-four chapters allocated among these four parts, and each part begins with a vignette about an aspect of my own transition out of leadership at the Crystal Cathedral and the *Hour of Power* television broadcast—just enough to set the stage for that chapter's theme in light of my own experience. The chapters themselves are about your life, my life, and how God works in our circumstances to prove Himself faithful regardless of why we find ourselves in need.

Even though my trouble at the Crystal Cathedral involved being on opposite sides of key decisions from my parents and other extended family members, in no way do I mean to cast aspersions on their character or motives. Even though I disagree with the decisions they made, they are my brothers and sisters in Christ whom I honor for their desire to be used by God to do the best for the ministries under their oversight. The days of our dialogue and disagreements, and their ultimate decisions, were difficult, and writing about them has surfaced old emotions. But more than anything, it has reminded me of where I am now—called of God to pursue a new vision and ministry for His glory and thankful He would give me a new task, on a new mountain peak, on the far side of the valley through which I have come. The dark night of my soul—at least *this* dark night—has seen the rising of the Son in my own sight.

May God use this book—the telling of parts of my story and much of His—to remind you as it has reminded me: When you are down to nothing, God is up to something.

PART I

WHAT GOD IS UP TO IN YOUR RELATIONSHIPS

Every person has three kinds of relationships in life:
With God
With others
With self
And God is always up to something in all three areas of life.
Chapter 1 speaks to our relationship with God.
Chapter 2 talks about love, life's indispensable factor.
Chapter 3 covers the benefits of living in community.
Chapter 4 addresses the importance of proper self-identity.
Chapter 5 delves into forgiveness as a source of freedom.

1

God Is Always with Me

(Presence)

"Be strong and courageous. Do not be afraid or terrified because of them, for the LORD your God goes with you; he will never leave you nor forsake you." Then Moses summoned Joshua and said to him in the presence of all Israel, "Be strong and courageous, for you must go with this people into the land that the LORD swore to their forefathers to give them, and you must divide it among them as their inheritance. The LORD himself goes before you and will be with you; he will never leave you nor forsake you. Do not be afraid; do not be discouraged."

Deuteronomy 31:6–8

My Story

In spite of what I knew to be true theologically, I felt alone—completely alone. To this day, I marvel at how one's feelings can take precedence over one's true convictions. But it happened to me. What I had preached to thousands of people—"God is always with you"—I began to question. Intellectually, I knew I was loved by my wife, my children, my church's congregation, the worldwide audience of the television broadcast on which I appeared weekly, and many good friends. And yes, I knew God loved me and was with me. But I still felt alone.

If you have ever been in that "alone" place, you know how I felt—and what a scary feeling it is.

The story of how I arrived at such a lonely place is a complicated one, the details of which I won't go into. Besides, the details aren't really that important. They are just another verse in the long song of human drama that has been written through the ages, a song that tells of conflict, hurt, power struggles, betrayal, and not always successful attempts at closure and reconciliation.

When these dramas play out in corporate boardrooms around the world, we're not surprised. But when they happen in Christ's church, our hearts are broken—and we wonder why God allows it. That's what I wondered during the latter half of 2008 as I struggled to make sense of what was happening around me—to me and to my family.

I pastored an internationally known church in California that was founded by my father. When I was invited to become the senior pastor of the church, and the speaker on the church's worldwide television broadcast, I gratefully accepted the call, honored to follow in my father's footsteps which had been laid out for me my entire life. But after thirty-two years of being affiliated with the broadcast, and several years of fruitful ministry as senior pastor of the church, my family members, and some other board members loyal to them, felt it would be appropriate for me to drastically curtail my responsibilities and activities. (There were differences concerning vision and governance.) In spite of having the support of the congregation and television audience, I was told that my role was to be greatly reduced in the church and the television ministry.

I was stunned by this decision and spent August through October 2008 wrestling with what to do. It was during those three months that I had to consciously remember that "the Lord is my shepherd" who promises to walk with me "through

*the valley of the shadow of death." The shadows were huge
and pitch black in the valley where I walked, and I have never
felt so alone.*

*I was confused and frustrated. And yes, I was angry.
Every fiber of my flesh wanted to fight for what was legally
and ethically "mine"—the right to continue a ministry that
was bearing fruit. But to make a three-month-long story short,
I resigned in November realizing that I couldn't fulfill my
responsibilities to the church and the broadcast under the new
restrictions. Positioning myself in a protracted battle with my
own parents and other associates would have only sullied the
name of Christ further. I didn't know why God allowed things
to happen as they did, I only knew it was not God's fault. If
removing myself from the situation would allow wounds to
heal more quickly and allow the family and board to do what
they felt was necessary, then that was what I needed to do. My
prayer became the second half of the prayer of Jabez, "Oh . . .
that You would keep me from evil, that I may not cause
pain!"(1 Chron. 4:10 NKJV).*

*If I had felt alone from August through October, in
November I was alone! Not literally, of course—the support
of my wonderful wife, Donna, and my four grown children
(and that of many, many friends) was never failing. But my
entire vocational support structure—that which I knew how to
do and was good at doing—was gone. I had no job, no pros-
pects, and only modest amounts of hope. But my confidence in
God's presence began to return. I regained my trust in what the
Bible says, that He never leaves us nor forsakes us; that He
causes all things to work together for good to those who love
Him and are called according to His purpose.*

*What I had learned many times in the past began to echo
in my heart: "When you're down to nothing, God is up to
something!"*

Like the man described in the famous Footsteps poem,[1] I can look back now and know that when I thought I was alone in that dark valley, I really wasn't; that the single set of footprints in the sands weren't mine, walking alone, but His as He carried me through that period. God hadn't abandoned me. Rather, He was with me all along—something I see more clearly today than ever before; something I want you to see as well.

My "nothing" was all too plain to me in November 2008, but it wasn't long before God's "something" began taking shape as well. I'll tell you some of that story in this book to encourage you to believe with me—that when we're down to nothing, God is always up to something. And that something is always good!

In a perfect world, you would never be alone or feel alone. You would enjoy the psychological satisfaction that comes from being in the physical, emotional, or spiritual presence of another person who you know cares for you. Note: physical *or* emotional *or* spiritual presence. Loneliness is not just the absence of another body; it is also the absence of a spiritual or emotional connection.

In a perfect world, even if you found yourself physically alone for a time, you would not *feel* alone. Whether you were in the presence of no one, one person, or a crowd, you would feel "accompanied" in life. If you were physically alone, you would enjoy the security of trust, knowing that others on whom you depend were faithful or loyal to you in your absence; that their love, companionship, and mutual care was not defined by physical location. Trust alone can be as reassuring as the physical presence of the person you long for. Indeed, any healthy person would rather be alone with trust than be in the presence of suspicion.

In a perfect world, you would receive constant affirmation of your existence and value. Being physically, emotionally, or spiritually alone makes it difficult, if not impossible, to receive the feedback that matters to us all. The presence of others—their physical, emotional, and spiritual presence—is a way of us hearing life's most important words: "I want to be where you are. I have come to this place because of you. If you were not here, I would not be here. That's how important you are to me." While that sounds like something romantic lovers might say and feel, that kind of affirmation is not limited to romantic love alone. Affirmation is a human need, not just the need of lovers. Affirmation is an antidote to loneliness.

God created a perfect world for His creatures, human and non-human, to inhabit. He created pairs of creatures to solve the need for physical presence and created "soulish" bonds for creatures that they might enjoy emotional presence. But for those created in His image, He created a higher dimension of togetherness—the presence of spirit. That presence allows us to live securely in God and securely in one another—in a perfect world.

But God's perfect world, in which no one should ever feel alone, is not the world in which we live. So we have to address the needs that arise when physical, emotional, and spiritual presence is broken. We have to discover how not to be alone in a world that sometimes feels very lonely.

Proof of God's Presence

Fortunately, we have (almost) the entire Bible to draw upon for insights into God's presence. Only the first two chapters of Genesis and the last two of Revelation are based on God's perfect world (plus some visions of perfection by the Old Testament prophets). Everything in between is the world we live in—the world where loneliness is a reality.

One of the great ironies of the biblical story of creation is that God said to Adam, "It is not good for the man to be alone" (Gen. 2:18)—when God and man had been partners in the Garden from the beginning. God saw there was no one to tend His creation, so He formed man "from the dust of the ground" (Gen. 2:7) and put him in the midst of the Garden as a steward over it all (Gen. 1:28). As usual, science continues to corroborate God's design—in this case, why it is not good (healthy) to be alone. A new study published in the journal *Psychology and Aging* has proven that loneliness can dramatically increase blood pressure. "Loneliness behaved as though it is a unique health-risk factor in its own right," one of the primary researchers noted, increased blood pressure being a risk factor for heart attack, stroke, and kidney disease.[2] No wonder God said it's not good to be alone!

The very nature of stewardship involves relationship and interaction between master and steward. When Potiphar, the Egyptian official, made young Joseph steward over his house and property, that assignment involved instructions and interaction: "Potiphar put [Joseph] in charge of his household, and he entrusted to his care everything he owned" (Gen. 39:4). Potiphar and Joseph were not face-to-face continually; indeed, as Potiphar's trust in Joseph grew, "he left in Joseph's care everything he had; with Joseph in charge, he did not concern himself with anything except the food he ate" (v. 6).

And therein is an illustration of why physical presence is not the only ingredient in combating loneliness. The element of trust is central—the bond that says, "Our relationship carries us forward even when you are absent. My trust in you, and yours in me, affirms our relationship." Whether Potiphar and Joseph were in the same room was not an indication of the level of trust they shared, which Joseph validated in Potiphar's absence by resisting the temptations of Potiphar's wife (vv. 11–20).

Back to the Garden of Eden: God and Adam had a master-steward relationship in which Adam no doubt felt affirmed as a person. In spite of being in a close, affirming relationship with God, Adam was still, in God's opinion, alone. Did Adam feel lonely as the only human on earth? We don't know—but it's obvious God wanted Adam to know that there was another dimension to his humanness.

As an object lesson, an illustration in loneliness, God assigned Adam the task of naming the animals (Gen. 2:19–20a). As the animals paraded before Adam—in pairs, no doubt—he gave them a name. At the end of the process, it must have been painfully obvious to Adam that he was the odd man out in the world: "But for Adam no suitable helper was found" (v. 20). He now understood why God had said that it wasn't good for him (man) to be alone. God solved Adam's problem by creating Eve, the first woman.

So man was created with the capacity for togetherness (the opposite of aloneness) in two dimensions: vertical and horizontal. Adam had the vertical relationship but was still alone until Eve joined him in the Garden, supplying the horizontal. The biblical implication is that human beings need vertical and horizontal togetherness in order not to be lonely. The person who says, "I don't need God" or "I don't need you" (to another person) is denying the essence of humanity: the need not to be alone. On the other side of the coin, the person who experiences a profound or debilitating sense of aloneness is manifesting a disruption of one or both dimensions of togetherness. The Catholic monk and author Hubert van Zeller wrote, "The soul hardly ever realizes it, but whether he is a believer or not, his loneliness is really a homesickness for God."[3]

That disruption may or may not have been intentional; the person may or may not be aware of how to remedy his or her aloneness. But at the basic level, there is a vertical reason and a horizontal reason for aloneness—and there is a priority between the two.

Though I can't prove it scientifically, I am going to say in this chapter that the cure for aloneness begins with restoring one's relationship with God. And that is not difficult to do because God is always there and willing. (More on that in a moment.)

Obviously, establishing togetherness with another person or persons is not easy. When imperfect human beings attempt to establish a relationship that satisfies the security, togetherness, and affirmation needs, the attempt is fraught with peril. People are imperfect, undependable, immature, unfaithful, and they change over time. And therein lies the reason that beginning with God is a better course of action. To put it simply, everything that makes human relationships hard—the imperfection of people—makes a relationship with God easy. It is God's perfection that allows us to come to Him and never be disappointed. God is perfect, dependable, mature, faithful, and He never changes.

In later chapters, I'll talk more about what God promises and advises about relationships with others. But for now, it's important to know that Step One in not being alone is to put yourself in Adam's shoes: God created Adam and wanted a relationship with him; God created you and wants a relationship with you. He wants you to have a relationship with "Eve" (with others) as well, but He wants you to start with Him.

Here's the simplest reason I know for beginning with God: In order to have a meaningful togetherness with another person, you must know who you are. And to know who you are, you must know who you were created to be. And to know who you were created to be, you have to know your Creator-God. If life should ever deposit you on a desert island to live for the rest of your life, you should be secure in that future simply because you know who you are and that God is always with you. That fate is unlikely, of course, and your life would be diminished for lack of the horizontal dimension. But knowing God means you would not be alone.

In a famous sermon preached at the Metropolitan Tabernacle in London on June 10, 1880, pastor Charles H. Spurgeon began his sermon with a desert island illustration:

Were you ever in a new trouble, one which was so strange that you felt that a similar trial had never happened to you and, moreover, you dreamt that such a temptation had never assailed anybody else? I should not wonder if that was the thought of your troubled heart. And did you ever walk out upon that lonely desert island upon which you were wrecked and say, "I am alone—*alone*—ALONE— nobody was ever here before me"? And did you suddenly pull up short as you noticed, in the sand, the footprints of a man? I remember right well passing through that experience—and when I looked, lo, it was not merely the footprints of a man that I saw, but I thought I knew whose feet had left those imprints. They were the marks of One who had been crucified, for there was the print of the nails. So I thought to myself, "If He has been here, it is no longer a desert island. As His blessed feet once trod this wilderness- way, it blossoms now like the rose and it becomes to my troubled spirit as a very garden of the Lord!"[4]

When I was on my own desert island a few years ago, I began to see signs—footprints in the sand that meant I was not alone. I began to believe again that God had been with me all along.

Even though it feels like God is billions of miles away in heaven and we are on earth, if our relationship with God is strong and mature, then the trust factor—the love, loyalty, and promises factor—takes the place of His physical presence. When lovers part for a time with professions of love for one another, it is that intan- gible promise of love that keeps them company, that keeps them secure, until they are reunited. Love, loyalty, and friendship almost become personified, so powerful are their effects in keeping lone- liness at bay.

But how do we know that God is always with us? Because He has said as much to many people just like you and me through the ages, and those conversations are recorded in Scripture. One can choose not to believe what the Bible says, of course. But for someone who is at all inclined to accept the reliability of God's revelation of Himself to humankind as recorded in the Bible, there is plenty to go on.

Take Joshua, for instance—the man whom Moses groomed to take over the leadership of Israel as they entered the Promised Land of Canaan. Joshua certainly wasn't physically alone. He was surrounded by hundreds of thousands of Israelites and a group of lieutenants and aids. Yet it would have been a perfect time for Joshua to think, "It's lonely at the top."

Think about his task—leading an entire nation of people into a land populated by people who would be none too hospitable. It's no wonder that Moses said to Joshua, "The LORD himself goes before you and will be with you; *he will never leave you nor forsake you*. Do not be afraid; do not be discouraged" (Deut. 31:8; italics added). Moses died, and it was time to enter the land. This time God spoke directly to Joshua: "As I was with Moses, so I will be with you; I will never leave you nor forsake you.... Do not be terrified; do not be discouraged, *for the LORD your God will be with you wherever you go*" (Josh. 1:5, 9b; italics added).

This is such a profound promise from God—so direct, so undeniable—that nearly fifteen hundred years later the early Christians were repeating and depending on that promise. Not that they were going into military warfare, like Joshua. Indeed, they were wrestling with a battle much more akin to the ones we fight: contentedness—the temptation to resort to the world's solutions to meet their needs instead of God's solutions. The writer to the Hebrews wrote to his readers, "Keep your lives free from the love of money and be content with what you have, because God has said, 'Never will I leave you; never will I forsake you'" (Heb. 13:5).

Now if those followers of Christ in the first century could look back to God's promise to Joshua and rely on it in their battles against insecurity and fear of the future, why can't we depend on that promise in our battle with loneliness?

Hebrews 13:5 wasn't some kind of religious talk designed to placate lonely, insecure people. These Christians lived a life-and-death existence in their day. They had to depend on what was true about God—or else. As I heard an African bishop say once, "You Christians in America put your faith in blessed insurance, but in Africa all we have is blessed assurance!"

Same with the recipients of the letter to the Hebrews in the mid-first century. They had nothing but God. They really needed to know if God was with them or not. The writer could just as easily have quoted the words of Jesus himself when He commissioned His disciples to take the gospel into all the world: "And surely I am with you always, to the very end of the age" (Matt. 28:20). And we have confirmation that Jesus kept that promise in Mark 16:20: "Then the disciples went out and preached everywhere, and the Lord worked with them and confirmed his word by the signs that accompanied it."

The Bible is so clear about God's presence that the onus shifts to us in this matter: Do we really believe He is present?

Parting from God

I will be the first to admit that feeling and trusting in the presence of someone we've never seen or met is a stretch. There are more than two thousand years of history to bridge between us and Jesus Christ. It's one thing to trust in the love and security of someone who is absent after having spent three years with that person, as the disciples did with Jesus. It's quite another to live with the security of His presence having never spent time with Him physically.

The apostle Peter anticipated this disconnect when he wrote to people (who had never spent time with Jesus) who were experiencing severe persecution for their faith: "Though you have not seen [Jesus], you love him; and even though you do not see him now, you believe in him and are filled with an inexpressible and glorious joy, for you are receiving the goal of your faith, the salvation of your souls" (1 Pet. 1:8–9).

Sometimes people lose their sense of God's presence in times of stress—yes, the stress of loneliness. The thought process is, "God must not be with me or I wouldn't be experiencing this stress." But that suggests God's presence eliminates all trouble. The disciples almost drowned in a storm on the Sea of Galilee with Jesus right there in the boat with them (see Matt. 8:23–26)! Yes, in that case, Jesus stilled the storm. But the lesson is not that Jesus rescues us *from* the storm, but that He is with us *in* the storm.

If you are going through a period of loneliness in your life, there are many variables to consider. But the first one is the one I'm talking about in this chapter: Do I have a relationship with God, and do I believe He is with me? If you answered yes and yes, but still feel alone, there are some things you can do that will help you experience God's presence.

Practicing His Presence

First, be honest with God. Tell God that you believe what the Bible says but that you're not experiencing His presence. Tell Him that you want to grow in your confidence of His presence and His love for you, that you need His assurance that He is with you. Ask Him to show you little things that will increase your faith—ask Him to show you His footprints in the sand so you will know you are not on your island alone. Ask Him to confirm in your heart the promises of His presence. God Himself said, "Call to me and I will answer you and tell you great and unsearchable things you do not know" (Jer. 33:3).

A young couple in full-time Christian ministry was considering an opportunity to move to Thailand to serve in an orphanage. They had moved a number of times before, and the mother thought their current home, in beautiful Colorado, was a place they could stay for a long time. Her life had never been more full. Her three young children were happy, they had lots of friends, and their ministry was bearing fruit. But then came the call from Thailand—she really needed to know it was from God. So she opened a Bible commentary and turned to Luke 5, the passage where her husband had found the assurance she lacked. The passage involves Jesus calling Simon Peter while he was busy hauling in a great catch of fish. The commentator wrote that Jesus' call came at the very moment when Peter was experiencing his greatest success as a fisherman. And she felt that was the confirmation she needed from God—that God sometimes calls people to something different at the height of their fruitfulness, a seemingly illogical time to make a switch. (I can identify!) Another person, not needing what the young wife needed, might have read the same passage and not received that application. But God was there when she needed Him and answered her prayer for assurance.[5]

Second, talk to God. Before the digital revolution, people who were separated had to write letters or send telegrams to stay in touch. Today we see people talking out loud to seemingly no one in particular until we realize they have a Bluetooth earpiece and they're talking on their cell phone. Some people spend hours each day talking, texting, and tweeting those with whom they are in relationship. You should treat your relationship with God the same way. Back in the days of leather scrolls, the apostle Paul put it simply: "Pray continually" (1 Thess. 5:17). People today stay in touch with their friends—they might be a block away or on the other side of the world—by talking and texting continually. It's as if they never left the person's presence. And it's the same with God. The more you talk to God about all the affairs of your life, the more real His presence will become.

Brother Lawrence, author of the classic book *The Practice of the Presence of God*, wrote, "There is not in the world a kind of life more sweet and delightful, than that of a continual conversation with God. Those only can comprehend it who practice and experience it."[6]

Third, spend time with God and with others who know Him. How contradictory is it to never spend time with someone you say you want to be close to? That doesn't work in the horizontal dimension, and it doesn't work in the vertical either. Yes, God is with *you*, but you need to want to be with *Him*. Wherever you sense the presence of God best—church, nature, a personal devotional time, reading the Bible, prayer—pursue it. The famous British writer and apologist G. K. Chesterton once said, "When I fancied that I stood alone I was really in the ridiculous position of being backed up by all of Christendom."[7] The more you are involved with others who depend on God's presence, the more you'll realize you are not alone.

Finally, assume (believe) that what God says is true. The heart of this issue is found in 2 Corinthians 5:7: "We live by faith, not by sight." You have to incorporate into your belief system the truth that God is with you. That means the battlefield is your mind. When your emotions tell you God is absent, you "take captive every thought to make it obedient to Christ" (see 2 Cor. 10:3–5). You may *feel* lonely, but in truth, you are not. God is with you, just as He promised.

The longer you walk with God, and the more time you spend with Him, the more confident and secure you will become in His presence. You will be living your life by faith rather than by feelings. Once you are secure in the vertical dimension of your relational life, you will know who you are. Regardless of what happens in the horizontal realm, you will know you are never alone.

2

What You Can't Live Without

(Love)

And now these three remain: faith, hope and love. But the greatest of these is love.

1 Corinthians 13:13

My Story

As I left my leadership role at the Crystal Cathedral and the Hour of Power *telecast, I engaged (many times) in self-talk that sounded something like this:*

"Am I in pain?" (Yes.)

"Does God love me?" (Yes.)

"Is pain consistent with the love of God?" (Yes. Think of all the people, including Jesus Christ Himself, who have undeservedly suffered pain while in the will of God.)

"What does it mean to be in pain yet still be loved by God?" (It means God has a purpose in my pain; God has a reason for my experience; because God loves me, He has not abandoned me; God is with me; therefore, there is hope for the future.)

"How would the absence of God's love make my pain different?" (I would have to conclude my pain was the result of bad luck, "karma," or an unfortunate, arbitrary confluence of circumstances. That is, there would be no purpose in my pain.)

*"How does knowing God loves me make my pain differ-
ent?" (God is shepherding me through my experience. God is
going to birth something good out of my pain. God loves me
enough to allow me to experience a measure of pain to accomplish the promise of conforming me to the image of Jesus Christ.)*

*"Is God's love meaningful enough in my life to make me
willing to lose everything else except that love (which I know
I can't lose)?" (Yes.)*

*I have had that mental conversation with myself many
times during the last few years, reminiscent of the self-soul-
talks the psalmist David had with himself (see Ps. 42:5, 11;
43:5). Actually, those mental meditations were prompted by a
conversation a friend of mine had years ago with a counselor
who helped him through his own dark valley—a conversation,
at the core of which, caused me to fight my way back to the
central reality of healthy human existence: the love of God.*

*Steve was an Episcopal rector (pastor) who, in 1971, in
the second year of his marriage, heard these words from his
wife: "I want a divorce." The day his wife left, Steve met with
the bishop of his diocese to talk about what had happened and
what he should do. Steve poured out his heart while the bishop
listened quietly to the young pastor's doubts about whether he
could, or should, continue in ministry.*

*And here is what the bishop told Steve that changed not
only his life, but would change mine as well: "There are two
things you can do, Steve. You can fulfill the ministry and call
God has given you, or you can quit and walk away. It's that
simple."[1]*

*When my father told me this story during a previous dark
time in my own life, the words were like a lightbulb turning
on: "the ministry and call God has given you!" In other
words, God loves me not because I'm perfect and sinless. He
loves me in spite of the reality that I'm not. And His love
includes a call to be of service to Him, blemishes and all! Even*

if a ministry organization asks me to leave, nothing changes the fact that God loves me and has called me into His service.

Having confessed and corrected anything for which I am at fault, I am left with two things: a clear conscience and the love of God. Reflecting on the bishop's words to my friend, I decided God had not stopped loving me, that His call on my life was still in place, and that my only response was to prepare myself to respond anew to His leading. Because I know God loves me and has a purpose and plan for my life, I chose not to respond to pain by walking away.

How powerful is the reality of the love of God when we are down to nothing! At times like that, when it is only God and us...the love of God is enough! During my recent transition out of leadership at the Crystal Cathedral, I would sit and meditate on a piece of art several times each day—actually, at the Bible verse inscribed on it: "And Jabez called on the God of Israel saying, 'Oh, that You would bless me indeed, and enlarge my territory, that Your hand would be with me, and that You would keep me from evil, that I may not cause pain!' So God granted him what he requested" (1 Chron. 4:10 NKJV). God hears our cry; He blesses us; He can enlarge our territory even when it is shrinking in around us; His loving hand will be with us; He will keep us from harm. And he will keep our pain from debilitating us.

That's why I've gotten through every difficult period in life I have faced—because I know God loves me. And I know He loves you. If you are down to nothing today—maybe you're down to your last ounce of feeling loved—know that the something God is up to begins with His love for you. With it, you can live through anything.

You may not be familiar with Harry Harlow's name, but you have probably heard about the results of the psychological study he conducted and reported on in 1958. He titled the report on his study "The Nature of Love" and delivered it at the annual meeting of the American Psychological Association.[2]

As a young psychologist at the University of Wisconsin, Harlow set out to study the IQ of rhesus monkeys. He began to notice the strange attachment of baby monkeys, in the absence of their mothers, to the terry cloth materials covering the bottoms of their wire cages. They would lay on the cloth, cuddle with it, and throw fits if the terry cloths were removed from their cages. This led Harlow to revise his study to consider the impact of nurture on the lives of the infant monkeys. He created wire figures with heads to represent monkey mothers, covering some with terry cloth while others were left bare. He discovered that the infant monkeys preferred a soft, cuddly, cloth-covered wire "mother" that offered no food to a plain, hard wire monkey with a bottle attached at which the baby monkey could nurse.

Prior to Harlow's studies, it was thought that babies love their mothers first and foremost because their mothers feed them. After Harlow's studies, the power of touch—love and nurture—was seen to be more highly valued by infants than food. As long as Harlow allowed the infant monkeys to cuddle with the cloth-covered "mothers," he could take their food away without a fuss ensuing. But if he tried taking their terry cloth "security blankets" away from the wire frames, the infant monkeys would have none of it. Harlow concluded that the benefit of an infant nursing had as much to do with the nurture of cuddling as with nutrition.

Similar findings were made with human babies. When the Soviet Union fell and access to Soviet bloc countries was granted to Westerners, visitors, and then researchers, were shocked to discover orphanages in countries like Russia and Romania where infants were warehoused by the thousands. The only human contact many of them had was to be fed and have their diapers changed—no holding, rocking, or cuddling. And many developed poorly, mentally and physically, and many died from sheer emotional neglect—from the lack of love.[3]

Harry Harlow had it right when he stated in his study: "Certainly, man cannot live by milk alone." And certainly John Watson, a behavioral psychologist who wrote on childrearing in the first half of the twentieth century got it wrong when he counseled against showing too much love to children: "Do not overindulge them. Do not kiss them goodnight. Rather, give a brief bow and shake their hand before turning off the light."[4] I thank God my parents (apparently) never read Dr. Watson's books!

The Centrality of Love

Thankfully, we have better ideas, biblical ideas, about love today. But they are not new ideas. The first use of the word "love" in our English Bible refers to the love Abraham had for his son, Isaac, several thousand years ago (see Gen. 22:2). From beginning to end, the Bible is a book about love—the subject is mentioned more than five hundred times and displayed in multiple stories and accounts.

But that is to be expected because God is love (see 1 John 4:8, 16). "Love" is the only noun used to describe God in the form, "God is...." Love is the essence of who God is. The greatest act of sacrifice in human history is said to have been prompted by God's love: "For God so loved the world that he gave his one and only Son..." (John 3:16). And the apostle Paul wrote that, while faith and hope are noble virtues, love is the noblest of all (see 1 Cor. 13:13).

You and I were created to begin, live, and end our lives in a "sea" of love. Love was meant by God to surround us, to be the air we breathe. I can say with confidence that all the insecurity and dysfunction that leads to hurtful acts and wounded people in the world can be traced back to the absence of love. Like orphaned babies or baby monkeys, we can live without a lot of things, but we cannot live without love.

Do you remember the character Tristan Ludlow in the movie *Legends of the Fall*? I can't recall more positives and negatives about love arising from the life of a single character. He loved his younger brother, Samuel, passionately, but wrongly held himself responsible for Samuel's death in World War I. Unable to forgive (love) himself after Samuel's death, he couldn't accept the love of the woman he wanted to love, but couldn't. So he left her and traveled the world looking for peace. Returning, he fell in love with another woman and married her, seeming to find peace and love in his new family. Then, when she was killed in a freak accident, he again blamed himself. He retreated into the wilderness and ended his torment in a hand-to-hand battle with a giant grizzly bear, a battle he lost. Tristan Ludlow is a portrait of the tormented soul who is loved by others but cannot love himself. Unable to understand that love includes forgiveness, that love does not require perfection, he ended his life when he could not reconcile love and loss.

The Two Sides of Love

Dividing the Bible into its Old and New Testaments, we find the two enduring qualities of love that characterize God's love for man and should characterize our love for one another.

The Old Testament's idea of love is expressed by the Hebrew word *hesed*—loving-kindness or loyal love. It reflects the kind of love that God had for His covenant people Israel. Loyalty, or long-loving, is the idea of *hesed*. God's love is not a fair-weather love or a sometimes love—it is a loyal love. God told His people that as long as the heavenly bodies in the sky—the sun, moon, and stars—continued in their paths, that His love for them would endure. As long as the extent of the heavens and the foundations of the earth remained immeasurable, He would love them. In other words, He would love them forever; He would be loyal to them (see Jer. 31:35–37).

At the human level, this loyal-love was expressed between the young, anointed king David and his friend Jonathan. Jonathan knew David had been anointed to replace his (Jonathan's) father, Saul, as king, and Jonathan chose loyalty to David over loyalty to his father. When Saul was trying to kill David in order to keep his throne, Jonathan pledged his loyal-love to David by saying, "Whatever you want me to do, I'll do for you" (1 Sam. 20:4). And Jonathan kept his word, protecting David from the murderous advances of Saul.

In the Old Testament, love was loyal. It could not be distracted by a better offer. It could not be terminated because of "irreconcilable differences." It could not be negated by unloving acts.

If love was loyal in the Old Testament, it was unconditional in the New. The well-known word for unconditional love in the New Testament is *agape*—a quality of love not known in the culture outside of biblical revelation. All we need to understand unconditional love is to meditate on its dimensions as listed in 1 Corinthians 13. Negatively, love is not envious, boastful, proud, rude, self-seeking, angry, doesn't remember wrongs suffered, and doesn't elevate darkness over light (evil over truth). On the positive side, love is patient and kind, and it protects, trusts, hopes, and perseveres. In short, love never fails.

When relationships fail, or break down, in life, it's almost always because a condition wasn't met somewhere in the murky middle ground between hurt and blame. But if there are no conditions, there can be no failure to meet them. That's why *agape* love never fails—because it's unconditional. Imagine a husband coming to a wife to admit to something hurtful he has done that he is sure will cause a rift in their relationship:

HUSBAND: "I need to confess something to you. I..."
WIFE: "I don't care what you've done."
HUSBAND: "But it's worse than you think. I..."
WIFE: "No, I've thought of everything. And I don't care what you've done. I love you. I forgive you."

Granted, this is unrealistic in human relationships—but in the divine it is not. When there are no conditions for love, there is no violation egregious enough to cancel out love. That's what "unconditional" means. (The above scenario is simplified. I wrote it that way to make a point. Husbands and wives may talk through offenses for the sake of unburdening the offender's soul, but still arrive at the same conclusion: "My love for you is unconditional.")

When we love by forgiving unconditionally, we take away any excuse for retaliation ("If you really loved me, you would forgive me!") Only love that is loyal and unconditional can defuse an angry heart, humble a defensive heart, and soften a hard heart.

God knows that's the kind of love we needed when we were separated from Him. So He sent His Son into the world to demonstrate that love and meet our need to be loved back into a relationship with Him. And He then asks us to love one another the same way: "As I have loved you [loyally, unconditionally], so you must love one another" (John 13:34). "My command is this: Love each other as I have loved you" (John 15:12).

Lost and Found

Like everything in life, there is a gap between God's ideal and our execution of the idea, especially when it comes to love. I don't have to guess or wonder about you—I know you have experienced "love" that was neither loyal nor unconditional. And probably from both sides of the equation. You have undoubtedly not been loved loyally or unconditionally at times by others, and you have likely been guilty of the same shortcomings yourself. Personally, I have been guilty on both counts.

Note: Love that is not loyal and unconditional, biblically speaking, is really not love at all. Can we stop doing something that is, by definition, loyal and unconditional? Many people mistake hormonal "like" for willful "love." Then, when dislikes begin outweighing likes, they conclude, "I don't love that person any-more." The truth is, unbeknownst to themselves, they likely never did love. We are so used to hearing, "I fell out of love with him/her," that we have adopted the mentality that drives such an erro-neous conclusion. Likes can change with the seasons; love is for a lifetime.

But note: Because love is loyal and unconditional, that doesn't mean it is always compliant. A spouse in an abusive relationship may have to walk away from a marriage. In fact, doing so may be the most loving thing to do for the sake of the abuser. Giving someone the opportunity to continue sinning is not a loving choice.

The more I experience the bitter fruit of substandard love, the more challenged I am to love better. Through the difficult times in my life I have described to you (and others that I haven't), I have found that sustainability in life is ultimately a function of love—either someone loving me in spite of my failures, my choosing to love others in spite of theirs, my choosing to love myself, or most importantly, my choosing to love God and the life He is orchestrat-ing for me.

I've been around "religion" my entire life—the Christian variety. And I can tell you that there is often a deficiency of love (including times when I have not loved as I should have). But if we are going to call ourselves followers of Jesus, we have to gain God's perspective on love. Jesus said, at a time before the New Testament was written, that the entire Old Testament can be summed up in one word expressed two ways: love—for God and neighbor (see Matt. 22:37–40).

Later, in his writings, Paul echoed that thought, saying, "Love is the fulfillment of the [Old Testament] law" (Rom 13:10). He said the obligation we have to love one another is a never-ending debt (see Rom. 13:8-10). We can never love too much or too long. Just when we think we have discharged our debt to love another person, one who is particularly unlovely in our eyes, Paul says, "Sorry. Love is a never-ending debt. You are never free to stop loving." (Loving the *person*, that is—not loving everything a person does.)

Yes, only God can love nonstop, loyally, and unconditionally. It's not in our human nature to love that way. But if God is alive and well in you, through your faith in Christ, then you have the Holy Spirit, the first fruit of whom is love (see Gal. 5:22). It is the Holy Spirit (Christ in you) who will convince you that you are loved by God and who will give you the power to love others.

When you reach the "down to nothing" points in your life, take it from someone who has been there. God's promise to always love you is real. The most important lesson you can learn in those down days is that you are loved by God, loyally and unconditionally. And if there is a person in your life—a spouse, a child, a friend—who is down to nothing, the thing they need more than any other is love. They need God's divine love and your divinely inspired love as well.

Please remember: Love is the most important reality in human life. When you're down to nothing, God is up to something that will show you how much you are loved. As someone has well said, "The true measure of God's love is that He loves without measure." Receive that never-ending love yourself and then give it away in full measure to others.

3

Being Together Is Better

(Community)

Two are better than one,
because they have a good return for their work:
If one falls down,
his friend can help him up.
But pity the man who falls
and has no one to help him up!
Also, if two lie down together, they will keep warm.
But how can one keep warm alone?
Though one may be overpowered,
two can defend themselves.
A cord of three strands is not quickly broken.

Ecclesiastes 4:9–12

My Story

I told you in the previous chapter about Steve—a pastor whose wife divorced him after two years of marriage. I mentioned the powerful counsel he received from his bishop—words that helped him remain on God's path and helped me, many years later, when I was in need of similar guidance. But I didn't tell you the rest of Steve's story.

After meeting with his bishop, Steve spent the rest of the week pondering the counsel he had received. With a not-totally-resolute heart, he prepared for the upcoming Sunday services. When he took the pulpit at the 8:00 a.m. service, who did he immediately see sitting in the front row of his church but the bishop and the bishop's wife. They were not members of his congregation, but they had come that morning to say to Steve, "We are with you. We love you and believe in you. We want to see you continue in the path to which God has called you."

It was a small, silent gesture, to be sure. But what a powerful signal it sent to a discouraged soul! It was a perfect example of how desperately we need to live in context with others who can come alongside us when we're down to nothing; people who can help us see what God is up to in our lives.

I have talked about the feeling of aloneness I experienced when leaving the Crystal Cathedral. Fortunately, it was more a feeling than a reality. (Be on guard: feelings can trump reality in life if we are not careful.) In addition to my wife and children, there were many people in my life who did for me what Steve's bishop and his wife did for him.

I've been part of a small group Bible study for most of my life. The group I was with in 2008 became "the body of Christ" for me more than any other group. I have a history and vulnerability with these friends that runs deep. Given my schedule, I occasionally miss a few meetings. But whether it's been a week or a month or longer since being with them, I know these friends have my back when trouble comes. They will pray, counsel, listen, share a meal, meet a practical need—and I will do the same for them—because we are "the physical body of Christ"; we are "the church of Jesus Christ."

One of the hardest things for pastors to do when they leave a pastoral assignment is find a new church home—for all the obvious reasons. And not a few pastors have found it easy to stop attending church. Donna and I were not going to let that happen to us when we left the pastorate of the Crystal Cathedral—it is simply unhealthy (and unbiblical) to live an isolationist lifestyle. Fortunately, my son is the pastor of a young church near where we live and it was easy for us to find a place there on Sunday mornings.[1] He is an excellent preacher with a shepherd's heart—God is using my son in significant ways to "restore my soul."

Associates, friends, spouses, sweethearts, children, small group members—all these and more make up the community(s) of our life. God never intended for us to live alone. Whether we are married or single, we still have a human need to be part of a network of souls—especially during the times when we're down to nothing.

I n the introduction to my book *Leaning into God When Life Is Pushing You Away,*[2] I suggested a label for the first decade of the twenty-first century: the Decade of Reaching Out. The Sixties were the (alleged) Age of Aquarius, the Seventies were the Me Decade, the Eighties were the Decade of Greed, and the Nineties were the Dot.com Decade. And frankly, those of us who lived through all four of those decades arrived at the doorstep of the twenty-first century a little exhausted and a lot disconnected—especially from the Dot.com Decade of the Nineties.

Computers were supposed to make life fun! Easier! Efficient! Enjoyable! Well, let's just say that vision got off to a rough start. Seemingly, the Internet saved us from the frustration of crashing computers. But it only allowed us to withdraw further into the soft glow of our own isolated, digital world. The Internet helped us learn a lot about people living on the other side of the planet while we became detached from those in our own homes. Family members curled up with their laptops instead of with each other. So by the time the first decade of the new millennium arrived, we were ready to be resocialized; we were hungry for relationships; we were craving to connect. And you know the rest: Myspace,

Facebook, Twitter, social networking, smartphones, iPhones, the iPad—we are connecting again. Instead of physical "face time" with other humans, a lot of connecting is via Skype, Video Phone and Face Time. But it's a mouse click in the right direction. We are gradually learning that the English poet John Donne had it right:

> No man is an island, entire of itself; every man is a piece of the continent, a part of the main; if a clod be washed away by the sea, Europe is the less, as well as if a promontory were, as well as if a manor of thy friend's or of thine own were; any man's death diminishes me, because I am involved in mankind, and therefore never send to know for whom the bell tolls; it tolls for thee.[3]

Like it or not, you and I are us. What happens to one, happens to all. *Leaning into God* was about staying close to God when life tries to push you away. This chapter is about the other variable in life's connection-equation: staying close to people. And why God promises benefits if we will conform to His design.

Planned Community

There is a simple and clear reason why human beings gravitate toward living in "community": because God is a community and we are created in His image.

God is a community? There are several places in the Old Testament where God speaks and refers to himself in first-person plural: "we" or "us." When God is about to create man, He says, "Let *us* make man in *our* image, in *our* likeness" (Gen. 1:26). Later, God is talking about Adam and Eve and says, "The man has now become like one of *us*" (Gen. 3:22). Much later, when God plans to interfere with the building project known as the Tower of Babel, He says, "Come, let *us* go down and confuse their language" (Gen. 11:7; italics mine in the above verses).

Scholars debate the meaning of these plural pronouns, whether they are to be taken literally or editorially. They certainly could be taken literally based on what the New Testament confirms: the biblical Godhead is plural—Father, Son, Holy Spirit (see references to all three as distinct persons in Matt. 3:16–17; 28:19; 2 Cor. 13:14; 1 Pet. 1:2). The Christian doctrine of the Trinity was settled in the earliest centuries of the Christian church and has represented orthodox belief ever since. It is the position I take in this chapter: God is a community of three divinely distinct, equal, and cooperative persons while remaining one God.

It is no wonder, then, that human beings—those created in God's image—naturally prefer what He prefers: life in community, human warts and all. Community is hardwired into our DNA. Even animals seem to require community for protection, food acquisition, and sharing of parenting responsibilities. Words like pack, herd, flock, pride, and covey are evidence of even the animal kingdom living in community.

We humans, however, seem to *need* community even more. Studies show we are healthier and live longer when we live in community—even in a community of two—than when we live alone. And we, distinct from the animal kingdom, seem to find ourselves—establish our self-identity—better through the lives of others than through looking in the mirror. (No lion or tiger ever spent an afternoon wondering, "Who am I?") It is the feedback we get from others—emotional and spiritual—that gives us something to think about at the end of the day. It is the cumulative rewards and reproofs from those around us that encourage us to "do it again" or invite us to change our ways. How would we know who we are becoming without the backboard of community off which bounce our best and worst moments? If those moments went unreflected into the void we would spend a lifetime giving but never receiving—and no way to gauge our progress.

The sinless state of community didn't last beyond the lives of our first parents in the Garden of Eden, so we don't know the role community was intended by God to play beyond the domain of the nuclear family. But in the sin-scarred, post-Eden world, in which our best efforts at life often fall far short of perfection, we need community and relations more than ever.

Living in the Plural

Within the framework of the decades I outlined at the beginning of this chapter, it is not surprising that a book was published in 2001 that served as a wake-up call to American culture: *Bowling Alone: The Collapse and Revival of American Community* by Robert Putnam.[4] Putnam's original thesis was set forth in an essay in 1995 in which he cited numerous examples of the decline of "social capital" in America—relationships, civic organizations, social intercourse, the family, even recreational events that drew groups of people together in past decades. He used "bowling" as a metaphor for the decline: Though the number of people bowling in America had increased in the two decades prior to his book, the number of people who bowl in leagues had declined. People were choosing to "bowl alone."

> Television, two-career families, suburban sprawl, generational changes in values—these and other changes in American society have meant that fewer and fewer of us find that the League of Women Voters, or the United Way, or the Shriners, or the monthly bridge club, or even a Sunday picnic with friends fits the way we have come to live. Our growing social-capital deficit threatens educational performance, safe neighborhoods, equitable tax collection, democratic responsiveness, everyday honesty, and even our health and happiness.[5]

While all these negative impacts in our society are noteworthy, it's the last two—health and happiness—with which I am most concerned. From my exposure within the sanctified walls of Christendom, I'm not sure that Christians have remained insulated against the "bowling alone" disease. At the same time, we have more reason than anyone not to let the world squeeze us into its mold in this area of life.[6] We believe differently than others when it comes to our origin and our heritage. If we are the product of evolution, then what difference would it make whether we lived in relationships or lived alone? We could live however we want without reference to any grand design.

But such is not the case. We serve a Lord who, when He came to earth and lived for three years, lived in community with others. Jesus didn't call one disciple, He called twelve. He didn't have one close friend with whom He enjoyed special occasions, He had three—Peter, James, and John. He didn't send out one emissary to share His good news with people, He sent out the Twelve and then a group of seventy-two. When the early church needed to handle administrative details, they didn't select one person, they selected seven (deacons). Everything Jesus did was in the plural—and He assumed we would live our lives that way as well: "For where two or three come together in my name, there am I with them" (Matt. 18:20).

Unfortunately, too many followers of Jesus have adopted the ways of the "bowling alone" world. They have retreated into gated communities, literally or figuratively, and shut themselves off from the relationships that God intended us to enjoy and benefit from. The vast majority of most Christians on Sunday morning attend a church service but don't attend a class or community group meeting either before or after the worship service. And an even smaller number are part of a small group of couples and individuals who meet regularly for study, fellowship, and accountability. Worship is fine, but worship is a vertical experience, focusing on God, not a horizontal experience, focusing on relationships with others. If the world bowls alone, Christians "believe" alone—to our detriment.

The Missing Ninety Percent

The brilliant British author and apologist C. S. Lewis conducted no scientific survey on which to base this observation, but I would not argue with his conclusion. He wrote in *The Four Loves*,

> If [what I have written] leads anyone to doubt that the lack of "natural affection" is an extreme depravity I shall have failed. Nor do I question for a moment that Affection is responsible for nine-tenths of whatever solid and durable happiness there is in our natural lives.[7]

I'm taking Lewis's word "Affection" as a metaphor for close, intimate relationships—the kind I'm talking about in this chapter. Let's not quibble over the percent. Rather, let's go with his broader idea: It is in giving and receiving affection in loving relationships that human happiness is realized. No wonder Jesus didn't say, "Wherever one of you is gathered together..." He promised to be in our midst when two or three are together! God wants us to be blessed and fulfilled, and the path to that goal entwines us with the lives of other people.

Jesus' promise to be in the midst of His people is amplified by the apostle Paul in his teaching on the spiritual unity of all believers in Christ. Jesus is head of the body of Christ, and we are the members (the ears, eyes, arms, legs, and so on—1 Cor. 12–14). Without pressing Paul's analogy too far, we can easily say that our presence in the lives of others is not optional—no more optional than if your eyes sent you a text message one morning saying, "I'm taking the day off—maybe two or three. I'll check in when I'm ready to start showing you things again. Good luck!"

The New Testament says if you belong to Christ, you belong to His body—to everyone else who belongs to Him. I don't think most Christians think of this "relationship" thing that way. But if the New Testament is correct, living in a connected way with others is better than living alone. We must believe this is true and take the necessary steps to integrate ourselves into relationship circles that will accomplish the "iron on iron" sharpening that God intended them to have (see Prov. 27:17).

Though C. S. Lewis wrote several decades ago, he would be pleased to find new scientific evidence emerging to support his idea of happiness coming through affection. Researchers are learning more and more about the power of oxytocin, affectionately called the "cuddle chemical." (Not to be confused with a brand-name opioid pain reliever, Oxycontin.) Oxytocin is a chemical hormone that serves as a neurotransmitter in the brain, released most abundantly in women during childbirth. Oxytocin is greatly elevated during labor, stimulating contractions and the letting down of mother's milk for the newborn—and stimulating the bonding effect between mother and baby. Men also release oxytocin, but after childbirth—greatly increasing their desire to hold and bond with the infant. But oxytocin is released by other human contact— touch, hugging, caressing, and, not surprisingly, sex. The result is greatly elevated human feelings of warmth, connectedness, esteem, and security. In other words, oxytocin makes us happy:

> The pieces of the puzzle are falling together. Oxytocin, whether it's released by friendly human contact or various chemical agents, can make us smarter, calmer, friendlier, healthier, even more attractive.[8]

But the "cuddle chemical" is only released within the bonds of meaningful relationships: human to human and human to animal. It's just another sign of God's design at work: We are happiest when we are relating to others in His creation—other people as well as animals. (We've all read about the powerful therapeutic effects of dogs and cats in nursing homes and hospitals. Contact with other living, breathing "souls" releases the "cuddle chemical" in us.)

Strength in Numbers

It's so easy, in life's difficult moments, to retreat into our own shell and cut off others—even those who care deeply about us. Sometimes we're ashamed of the trouble we're in; sometimes we're tired of being down to nothing yet again. Don't buy it! That's a lie by the enemy of your soul to keep you thinking that life is over.

Remember Job? When he was down to nothing, three judgmental friends showed up, and then a fourth, whom he allowed to rake him over the coals, thinking it was his unconfessed sins that had caused him to be sitting on the ash heap, stripped of everything he'd worked for in life. But Job didn't send them away. He allowed them into his space, to speak their minds. He didn't agree with their assumptions, and he told them so. But it was the *process* of those interactions that led to Job's interview with God and the healing of his soul. What if Job had excluded his friends from his life—told them to take their attitudes somewhere else? I don't know. I only know that the painful process Job went through, in the context of four other people, led ultimately to him seeing God more clearly than he ever had. Perhaps God sent those people to Job to play a role in his healing. We never know what God is up to in our lives.

If you are down to nothing today, you will have a better chance of discovering what God is up to if you allow people into your life than if you don't. It's His plan. It's His design. But it's your responsibility to open the door to others and let them in. Where two or three of you are gathered together, He promises to be in your midst.

4

You Are Your Own Best Friend

(Identity)

For you created my inmost being;
you knit me together in my mother's womb.
I praise you because I am fearfully and wonderfully made;
your works are wonderful,
I know that full well.

Psalm 139:13–14

My Story

In the months-long process of leaving my position at the Crystal Cathedral and the Hour of Power *broadcast, I was involved in countless hours of conversations—with the leadership of both organizations, with my parents and siblings (for better or worse, since its founding the Crystal Cathedral has been "the family business"), with my wife and children, with friends, with attorneys (on both sides), and with counselors. In most of those meetings and conversations, there was one primary topic of conversation: me!*

I don't say that egotistically—it is just the fact of the matter. Since I was the senior pastor of the church and the television host of the Hour of Power, *and since I was being asked* to step down from both responsibilities (a request I was not eager to embrace), most of the conversations revolved around me: my present, my future, and my opinions, performance, decisions, gifts, and abilities. It didn't take long for me to grow tired of hearing others, and myself, talk about me—whether in a positive or not-so-positive light.

This went on for months. Slowly I began to realize how easy it is to have our identity shaped by what others think and say. Don't get me wrong—I wasn't hearing negative or attacking comments apart from my family. For the most part, the meetings and conversations were cordial and focused, in spite of the large disagreement on the future of both ministries. But what I was hearing was a lot of opinions about who Robert Schuller is or should be. A lot of "data" was flowing about my calling, my gifts, my abilities, my strengths and weaknesses, and how I might best reinvest myself for the future.

I'm as happy as anyone to receive counsel from people I trust when life-changing decisions need to be made. But the environment I was in had become emotionally charged. It was becoming harder and harder to think clearly about who I believe I am and what I sensed God was saying to me about the present and future. That's why I eventually chose to end the conversations—shut down the data stream—by submitting my resignation.

Somewhere in that process I realized I was going to have to live with myself for a long time; I needed to be completely comfortable with myself, my relationship with God, and what I thought He wanted me to do. I needed to have a clear conscious and to act with conviction. So I respectfully stepped out of the data stream about Robert Schuller. I needed to clear my mental cupboard of every negative thing I was beginning to think about myself—doubts, criticisms, disappointments, embarrassment—and get back to my identity in Christ. I *needed God to speak clearly to me and tell me again who He created me to be.*

That didn't happen overnight. In fact, it took a little over a year for me to separate fact from fiction; to give myself permission to feel about me the same way God feels. I remember the day I broke through—my birthday—as if the cloudy windowpane I'd been squinting through for a year had suddenly been wiped clean. It was a huge, and necessary, step that God had orchestrated. I suddenly found myself excited about the future because I believed (again) that God was excited about me.

When a Christian gets down to nothing, you discover there are only two things left: who you are and the God who made you who you are. But that's a lot. In fact, it's all you need to get refocused, reenergized, and recommitted to the fact that God is up to something good in your life.

I have discovered through the years that many people are not comfortable talking about themselves, even thinking about themselves. For many people, a mirror is a thing to be avoided. It puts into plain view something we are not altogether comfortable with: ourselves.

To be sure, we all know there are people who love to talk about themselves. As someone has said, "The only thing good about being seated next to a narcissist at a dinner party is that there'll never be a lull in the conversation." When you meet someone like that—someone who talks and talks about themselves—you're really hearing about someone who, out of insecurity, is painting a verbal picture of who they *want* to be, not who they really are.

I'm talking about something different here. I'm talking about the person who is comfortable in his or her own skin; a person who is going through life on his or her own terms; a person who has come to grips with the past and is okay with its effect on the present; a person who thinks neither too high nor too low about who he or she is. And, as a Christian, I say all that within the context of acknowledging that God is the primary source of our identity since He is the one who created us.

I don't know where the custom started, but it seems to have been solidified in the Middle Ages when guilds of craftsmen in Europe began leaving their mark on their creations. Even today you can look on the bottom of a fine piece of sterling silver tableware and often find the imprint of the craftsman. It was a way for the craftsman to say, "I made this, and I am proud to identify myself with it. If anything ever happens to this piece, I am the one who can best repair it—because I am its creator."

In Westminster, California, up the coast from where I live, a builder of fine acoustic guitars named Kevin Ryan does something few instrument makers do. Because he invests so much time and talent in creating each instrument (they are *very* expensive), he warrants them for a lifetime against structural defects. While many instrument makers offer that initial warranty, Kevin goes a step further. If one of his guitars comes back to him on a trade—an owner is moving to another of Kevin's guitars—Kevin will offer the pre-owned guitar to his limited universe of buyers with the original lifetime warranty still intact. Once he, the creator of the instrument, examines it and makes any tweaks needed, he continues to stand behind it when it moves to a new owner. In other words, he is extremely confident in his original craftsmanship. He knows the instrument better than anyone and stands behind its integrity. It's not an overstatement to say that Kevin *loves* his instruments and wants the best for them—and expects the best from them.

In a similar fashion, God is like a master craftsman who creates *individual* human beings—each one different, each one valuable, each one good for a lifetime of joy and service. The Bible says that He makes us in His image (see Gen. 1:26–27)—He puts His seal of uniqueness and authenticity on us and is prepared to stand behind us for a lifetime. No, we don't have an imprint on the sole of our foot or the back of our neck with the date of our birth and a "maker's mark" engraved. Rather, *we* are His image. From the top of our head to the soles of our feet, we are the image of God. Our unique personality that sets us apart from the rest of creation—the ability to laugh, question, plan, ponder, confess, praise, and all the rest—is a self-certifying image that God has made us new, different, and unique.

That sounds good, of course—warm and fuzzy and all the rest. And I fear that is just how far it goes with many people who confess to believe in God as their creator. But I want to challenge you to move beyond hoping that's true to believing it's true. In Psalm 139, David, the psalmist, puts this about as plainly as it can be said:

> For you created my inmost being;
> you knit me together in my mother's womb.
> I praise you because I am fearfully and wonderfully made;
> your works are wonderful,
> I know that full well.
> My frame was not hidden from you
> when I was made in the secret place.
> When I was woven together in the depths of the earth,
> your eyes saw my unformed body.
> All the days ordained for me
> were written in your book
> before one of them came to be.

> *Psalm 139:13–16*

Here's the question: Do you really believe that God "knit you together in your mother's womb," that you are "fearfully and wonderfully made," that what God has made—*you*—is "wonderful," that God "ordained" for you the days of your life "before one of them came to be"?

If a maker of a fine guitar or a sterling silver tea service or a beautiful gold bracelet can be excited about what he or she has made, is it too much to expect that God is excited about what *He* has made—that He is excited about you? And just as those artisans could probably identify their own creations by touch if blindfolded, so intimately do they know the works of their hands, is it too much to think that God can pick you out of the crowd of six billion souls on this planet at any moment, night or day?

I believe that! I believe God's love for me translates, in human terms, to excitement about me. I want to press this point with you (you may think this sounds egotistical) because I want you to believe that God is excited about you. You are so unique and special in His sight that you bring joy to His heart when He finds you fulfilling the purpose for which you were created.

This is no more far-fetched than to believe that if I put my faith in Jesus Christ for the forgiveness of my sins, God will forgive. The same Bible that tells me about salvation also tells me about how I was created, about the image of God I bear, about my uniqueness in His sight. I choose *not* to be selective about which parts of the Bible to believe. I believe the parts of the Bible about God, and I also believe the parts of the Bible about me—and about you.

Believing what God says about you is the only way to quiet the data that the world is constantly streaming through your senses. If you have confidence in who you are, you won't need the world or any other person to force you into a mold that you don't fit. You'll be able to say, "Yes...no...no...yes...no...yes..." and so on to the messages that come your way about who you are, what you should do, and how you think about yourself. *But if you don't know who you are, you won't know whether to say yes or no to what you hear.*

One way I do this is to continually meditate on who the Bible says I am in Christ. The Bible study group I've been part of for years gave each member a card containing all the New Testament

promises pertaining to the believer in Christ. Continually review-
ing this small card is a way to constantly tell myself the truth about
who I am as a new creation in Christ (see 2 Cor. 5:17).

Finding Our True Self

In spite of God making us so intimately and uniquely, it takes many
bumps and curves in the road of life before we get a glimpse of our
destination: true self and identity. To continue with the biblical
version of the story, it's because we walked away from our Creator—our original ancestors did in the Garden of Eden—and
chose to identify ourselves with new names. To put it in the words
of the apostle Paul, ever since we lost our true identity "we see but
a poor reflection as in a mirror [a polished piece of tin in those
days]" (1 Cor. 13:12). It's why, when we look in a real mirror, we
aren't sure who is looking back at us or if we like what we see. Our
lifetime goal, then, is to get closer and closer to the identity God
gave us—first as human beings, then as *unique* human beings.

Christian author and counselor Leanne Payne has a beautiful
way of describing our problem and the solution:

> Born lonely, we try hard to fit in, to *be* the kind of person
> that will cause others to like us. Craving and needing very
> much the affirmation of others, we compromise, put on
> any face, or many faces; we do even those things we do
> not like to do in order to fit in. We are bent (to use [C. S.]
> Lewis's imagery) toward the creature, attempting to find
> our identity in him.[1]

She goes on:

> Spiritually and psychologically, to use C. S. Lewis's tell-
> ing image of fallen man, man is "bent." The *unfallen* posi-
> tion was, as it were, a *vertical* one, one of standing erect,

face turned upward to God in a listening-speaking relationship. It was a position of receiving continually one's true identity from God. But fallen man is bent toward the creature and trapped in the continual attempt to find his identity in the created rather than in the Uncreated [God].[2]

It's moving from a "bent" position, leaning into the opinion of others about our self, to a "straight" or "vertical" position, leaning into God and what He says about us, that is our lifelong quest. The more spiritually erect we become, the more clearly we hear God's voice and the less significant become the voices of others around us.

Too often we define ourselves only by labels that this world offers: job, education, age, status, ability, or disability. But I like what Pastor Shane Stanford says about who he is:

I am Shane Stanford. To my family, I am a husband of 20 years and the boastful father of three. To my congregation of nearly 5,000, I am a pastor. To my readers, I am the author of nine Christian books. To my friends, I am one of the guys. And, to so many over the years who have known my story, I am a man in a race—a race against illness, against fear, against discrimination. A race against my own body. A race against time. A hemophiliac since birth, I discovered my HIV status at 16. It was life-changing news, the result of a contaminated blood supply. And, so, the race began.[3]

But he concludes with what is most important: "No matter how I try to describe myself, I am more than the sum of what I can say."[4] He refuses to be defined by "facts," be they positive or negative. He knows there is an identity that is beyond labels and categories.

The descriptions of who we are in this world are so limited! There is a divine dimension to our identity that is found only when we listen to what God says about who we are.

Listening to God

I don't want to give the impression that we are to be free agents, much less loose cannons, in this world, blithely ignoring the insights about our life that accumulate through those around us and our life experiences. We are not free to shout, "I want to be ME!" and run unfettered through this world. As a child of God, our identity is bound up first and foremost by our obligations to God and others. We are not free to break promises, to cancel vows, to break God's or man's laws, to use others for our benefit, or to live a life devoid of integrity and trust. Indeed, to live in such a way would be to lose a major part of our true self—the part that is most like God.

Assuming we have been careful not to leave loose ends that we haven't tied up—a frayed hem on the garment of our identity that could trip us up in the future—we get to the place where we are free to choose. There comes a time when we have to stand vertically in God's presence and make a decision. We have to evaluate, seek counsel, pray, weigh the options, and then do what we believe is the right thing to do. Many people don't—which is why they aren't as happy with the face in the mirror as they should be.

If you know who you are as a child of God and are making progress in straightening up toward Him, no circumstance in life, no label or category, will be strong enough to keep you from accomplishing your purpose. But if you are not sure who you are, you'll bounce from pillar to post in search of an identity that others will be more than happy to assign to you.

While scholars aren't sure who said it first, the phrase "Know Thyself" was engraved in the court of the Temple of Apollo at

Delphi. Unfortunately, the ancient Greeks didn't provide a manual on how to "know thyself." Many hundreds of years later, Shakespeare had Polonius say to his son, Laertes, "This above all: to thine own self be true."[5] Again, good advice—but how?

First, *know*. You must have an intimate relationship with the God who created you and knows you best. Start with His Word. Continue with prayer. As you read and pray, be in a continual state of "knowing." Ask, "Lord, show me who You created me to be. Open my eyes. Second, *be true*. Live with a clear conscious. Never violate the standards God has set for you and you have set for yourself. If you do, let God's forgiveness be the reason you forgive yourself—immediately. Then move ahead with faith and conviction.

A true life is the only life you will want to look back on—the only life you *can* look back on with peace and satisfaction. It is not arrogant to say, "I know who I am." It is a perspective born of truth that you will find only in God. You have to live with yourself. Make sure the self you are living with is the one God designed for you to be.

If ever you find yourself down to nothing again, you can be your own best friend; you will be in the best place life has to offer: standing with our Creator who is committed to telling you what He is up to in your life.

5

How to Be Set Free

(Forgiveness)

Blessed is he
whose transgressions are forgiven,
whose sins are covered.

Psalm 32:1

My Story

When something interrupts your life in a way that involves pain, there is an immediate danger of resentment. The greater the pain, the deeper the resentment. And from seeds of resentment, bitterness can spring up. Suddenly you realize you are in a full-blown spiritual crisis. You've been hurt, resentment is an internal way of fighting back, and you are forced to decide: When will I—or will I—forgive? If you are a Christian, forgiveness is not an option—a reality with which I was confronted in the summer of 2008.

From my perspective, there were reasons I could have rationalized resentment. The very people who had asked me to assume the leadership role in two large ministries were now asking me to relinquish those roles. What made it worse was that my immediate family—my parents and some siblings—were involved in that change.

It's ironic that those you know and love the most are often the hardest to forgive, the reason being that we know them intimately. It's easy to say, "How dare you pass judgment on me! I know all your faults!" We (hopefully) don't say those things to our family, but the thoughts arise nonetheless. The truth is, our family, or others with whom we are close, is probably no more sinful than anyone else. It's just that we happen to know them better because of our long-term exposure to them. So they seem like bigger sinners. But they're not. They're just people who are in the same halting journey through a broken world that we are on. They are making decisions, trying their best, not plotting to hurt us intentionally. But in the midst of a crisis it is a challenge to remember those truths.

As of this writing, it has been over three years since the summer of 2008 when my family and I were in a very strained setting. In retrospect, I've thought about who was "right or wrong" in the situation at the Crystal Cathedral and—no surprise here—I believe they were wrong. (There are no totally innocent parties in such complicated affairs. By "wrong" I mean their decision to hold on to control after asking me to assume leadership of the church and television ministry.) That has become, over time, a dispassionate conclusion on my part—the conclusion I believe that a judge would reach in a hearing having heard both sides. It took a while to release the passion attached to that conclusion, something I worked diligently to achieve, knowing it is passion that can fuel bitterness and become destructive.

And I realized my responsibility to forgive everything I perceived to be wrong on anyone else's part. I didn't go to them and say, "I want you to know I believe you were wrong, but I forgive you." That has always seemed to me a way to get in a final dig before laying a matter to rest. Instead, I decided to do three things: One, to forgive any and all actions or motivations that I perceived to be wrong. Two, to work toward rees-

HOW TO BE SET FREE

tablishing relationships with my family. (We are not completely there yet, but I hope one day we will be. Healing takes time.) And three, to learn from the situation regarding future associations or alliances; that is, not to make the same mistakes again in terms of business or ministry activities.

Many business consultants warn against family-run businesses where emotions can cloud decision making, where deep-seated parent-child issues can arise unbidden and unnamed. Perhaps that's where I was wrong—putting myself back under the authority of my parents (who ultimately still controlled both ministries) as an adult. But when the arrangement began in 2006, I didn't think of it that way. It seemed to be a collegial relationship, not a parent-child one, though it didn't work out that way. But that's life. We go through difficult experiences more often than not and constantly have to clear the air through forgiveness and reconciliation.

Sometimes we get down to nothing as a result of the actions or decisions of others. Sometimes we're the "innocent" party in a divorce or other broken relationship. And the way we feel in those moments makes us think we'll be stuck in that place forever. Until we realize that God is up to something, reminding us that forgiveness is the key to healing, reconciliation, and moving forward.

When pastor and author Ed Rowell was growing up, a neighboring family suffered a series of medical calamities—several of the children died and others suffered permanent brain damage. A long investigation led back to a load of seed corn the father had found, which he fed to the hogs on their farm. Unknown to the father, the corn was not intended to be used for animal or human consumption; it had been treated with a chemical to keep bugs from eating it and ultimately discarded.

When the farmer fed it to his hogs, there were no side effects. But when the hogs were slaughtered and the family began consuming the meat over many months, they were poisoned by the chemicals on the corn.

It turns out that many toxic chemicals and substances do not pass through the human digestive system. Rather, they lodge in the human body and build up over time. In very small doses, the chemicals are not toxic. But if enough of a deadly toxin is consumed, the results are deadly.

"That's what happens to many of us," Rowell wrote. "Every day we ingest minute amounts of conflict and disrespect. No big deal, we think. Just blow it off. But we don't. Instead, it gets buried in our [system] and 20 years later, we go ballistic over some kid skateboarding in the [church] parking lot and wonder, *Where did that come from?*"[1]

I know exactly what the author is referring to, and you likely do as well. We're trucking along through life, thinking we have everything under control, when something blows to the surface like a geyser erupting in Yellowstone National Park. And we wonder, *Where did that come from?* Jesus answered that question when a group of religious "experts" complained about His disciples being careless about following the laws and traditions of the elders when it came to eating food. Jesus said (I'm paraphrasing), "It's not what goes into a person that makes him unclean. It's what comes out from within." Specifically, Jesus said, "For from within, out of men's hearts, come evil thoughts.... All these evils come from inside..." (see Mark 7:20–23).

Like the toxic chemicals that were stored inside the children who died, we store up "stuff" in our hearts that comes out at the least expected, and least opportune, times. And it can be just as deadly, in a spiritual and relational sense. What do we store up? Anger, bitterness, resentment, unforgiveness, envy, dissatisfaction, frustration, discontent—call it what you will. It's all the stuff we don't deal with in life through one key decision or action: forgiveness.

From my own experience and from talking with multitudes of Christians through the years, and reading the stories of many more, I believe forgiveness is the most-needed act in all human experience. Forgiveness is like a tall mountain peak on which the rain of life falls. Like a wedge, forgiveness separates the rain. That which falls on the forgiveness side of the watershed leads to one result, and that which falls on the unforgiveness side leads to another. What falls on the unforgiveness side separates into separate streams called bitterness, resentment, distrust, anger, and all the other emotions that build up over time and poison the landscape of our life.

But when we forgive, we have no basis for anger or bitterness or resentment that leads to distance and separation between people. When we forgive, we experience release and freedom.

I read about a guy who went online to purchase an airplane ticket for his wife: one-way from Chicago to Dallas, where she was going to help her sister move. He had purchased tickets often, so clicked quickly through all the boxes: departing city, destination, date, one adult, one-way, coach, seat assignment, credit card—including agreeing that the ticket was nonrefundable and nontransferable. Click, click, click—he was done. But when the e-mail confirmation arrived—yikes!—he had purchased the ticket in his name, not his wife's! Apparently, because of his prior use of the website, his name had been entered automatically. It was totally his fault; he had failed to type in his wife's name. Panicked, he called the airline and was told there was nothing they could do. The ticket was nonrefundable and nontransferable. But the agent suggested he call Travelocity, the Internet booking agent he had used, and see what they could do. After ten agonizing minutes of listening to elevator music while on hold, an agent named Jacob came on the phone and the man explained what he had done, assuming he would have to eat the $152 he had spent and purchase another ticket for his wife.

"No problem," Jacob said. "I'll delete your transaction here and you can go online and redo your reservation in your wife's name."

"Really, Jacob? Just like that? No penalty or anything?"

"No problem."

"Jacob, you are a gift from God! You made my day," the man exclaimed. He later wrote that if Jacob had been there in person, he would surely have hugged him.[2]

Who can't identify with that kind of mistake? We've all done things that fall into the "dumb" category. Even if it doesn't involve a lot of money, something far more precious gets spent: our self-image. What might have happened in the man's exchange with the agents? He took the first no in stride because there was still hope. But what if the second agent's answer had been no as well? He might have lost it. It might have been the third time that week he had done something dumb; he might have been mad as heck (at himself, at life, at the system) and decided he wasn't going to take it anymore. He might have unloaded on the agent named Jacob. And if Jacob had been standing there, he might have done something worse.

Instead he experienced euphoria! He had been released from the prison cell of his own carelessness. Someone in authority said to him, "No problem." That's the feeling of forgiveness.

The man mentioned something in his response that is central to this chapter: Undoing life's difficult events—even the dumb stuff we do—is "a gift from God." And that gift is called forgiveness. The sweet sense of relief and release and thanksgiving—experienced when something like an airline ticket mistake is cancelled—is what forgiveness is all about. But unlike the reversing of the man's airline ticket, there is a penalty to pay.

The Gift of God

God's gift to man is that He paid the penalty so we would not have to. It is important to remember that every time forgiveness is experienced—whether we are the giver or the receiver—there is a penalty involved. The one who pays the penalty is the one who forgives.

In the human plane, the penalty can take forms as varied as the situations in which forgiveness is granted. If a rambunctious child knocks a valuable vase off a table, shattering it into a thousand pieces, the parent forgives—but not without cost. First, there is the loss of the vase. Whether it is expensive or not, an heirloom or not, it is worth something. And that value is gone when all is forgiven. The parent doesn't say, "I'll forgive you when you replace the vase." He or she says, "I forgive you even though what I enjoyed is gone forever." Second, there is the cost of love, the cost being giving up the resentment or rage that wants to make the child feel guilty, that wants the child to pay if we have to pay. So the parent pays when the parent forgives—in dollars and the loss of vengeance.

The gift of God to us is His forgiveness for all the "vases" we break in His world, intentionally or not. The practical experience of His forgiveness is predicated, of course, on acceptance of the biblical story. What amazes me is how many people accept the biblical story of God's love through Jesus Christ but have a hard time accepting and applying the whole notion of forgiveness.

Perhaps it's the cost thing that isn't clear. In the Old Testament, there was always a cost for forgiveness. Tens of thousands of God's innocent animals were sacrificed, their throats slit and their carcasses burned, in order to cover the sins of the people. The gruesome nature of those sacrifices said to the Israelites, "This could have been you. God has forgiven you by giving up one of his lambs so you don't have to be killed." But then, as the New Testament book of Hebrews explains in great deal, God put an end to the repetitive sacrifices of bulls and sheep and goats by offering up His own Son, the "Lamb of God, who takes away the sin of the world!" (John 1:29).

The blood of animals "can never take away sins" (Heb. 10:11), but when Christ "offered for all time one sacrifice for sins, he sat down at the right hand of God" (v. 12). The Old Testament sacrifices were a reminder and a covering of sin, but the sacrifice of

Christ was a permanent taking away of sin. Anyone God has ever forgiven or will ever forgive will be forgiven on the basis of the blood of Christ. That price has been paid, never to be paid again.

If we accept the biblical story of forgiveness and redemption, we have to accept that God has paid the price for all our sins—period. There is nothing we can add to what He has done. Whether we sin once or one million times doesn't matter. The same price has provided forgiveness for all those sins. Once that fact gets settled in our heart, it will change how we feel about being forgiven and forgiving others.

God said, "I love you" when He sent Christ to die for our sins. Therefore we know we will always be forgiven. Likewise, if we say, "I love you" to a child or spouse or friend, that's like saying, "I will always forgive you." That doesn't mean we ignore the harm that might have resulted from someone's sin (see below). But it does mean we forgive the sinner—we don't retaliate or seek vengeance.

Realms of Forgiveness

I've seen people struggle with forgiveness at four different levels, any one of which can derail a healthy spiritual and emotional life. They are somewhat interwoven with each other but I'll break them down as follows:

1. Be Forgiven

The ability to receive forgiveness from God is the starting place for experiencing forgiveness in all other realms of life. The words of the apostle John to those under his care in the faith are perfect in their simplicity: "I write to you, dear children, because your sins have been forgiven on account of His name" (1 John 2:12). It is for the sake of His Son that God forgives our sin. Otherwise, the suffering and death of Christ would have been for nothing. Colossians 2:13 says, "He forgave us all our sins." To know that forgiveness, we simply must receive it: "Yet to all who received [Christ], to those who believed in his name, he gave the right to become children of God" (John 1:12). Once we receive God's forgiveness of our sins, that fact becomes the basis for all other forgiveness. If God has forgiven us, how can we not forgive ourselves and forgive others?

2. Forgive Yourself

How often have we heard, or perhaps even said, "I could never forgive myself for that!" We get the idea that what we have done is so bad, so repulsive, that no one, including God, could forgive us. And if others can't forgive us, how can we forgive ourselves? The truth is, it doesn't matter whether others forgive us or not after we have sought their forgiveness. It only matters that God has forgiven us. No one else is judge over us. If God forgives you, it is an affront to Him not to forgive yourself.

3. Forgive Others

This is probably the hardest of all. We are called to forgive our enemies (see Matt. 5:43–48)—that is, anyone who has harmed us—and to do so an unlimited number of times, without counting (see Matt. 18:21–35). The basis for forgiving others is God's forgiveness of us: "Be kind and compassionate to one another, forgiving each other, just as in Christ God forgave you" (Eph. 4:32).

Wess Stafford, along with many other young children of missionaries, was severely abused by the proprietors of a missionary boarding school he attended for years in West Africa. So painful were the memories of his experience that he did not speak of them for thirty-five years. But in the May 2010 issue of *Christianity Today* magazine, he told the story of how God healed his wounds and gave him the ability to forgive his abusers.[3] His story provoked an outpouring of response from readers who wanted to know how he moved beyond what happened to him. (Stafford is today the president of Compassion International.) He responded in the July 2010 issue of the magazine:

> Ever since my story appeared in *Christianity Today*, the most common question I've heard is, "How did you move from pain to deliverance?" My reply to readers is a single word: *forgiveness*.
>
> At age 17, I realized that those who hurt me would never apologize. They weren't even sorry. But I could no longer bear carrying the pain of my past, so I chose to forgive them anyway. "Get out of my heart. Get out of my mind. Get out of my life!" I remember saying. "What you did to me will not define me. You stole my childhood, but you cannot have the rest of my life. Get out—I forgive you!"
>
> Since then I've learned that while God always requires us to forgive, forgiving isn't saying that what happened was okay. It doesn't release someone from the consequences of their actions. And it doesn't require letting someone back into your life. It does mean giving up the right to seek revenge.
>
> So, here is my counsel to those who have suffered: If you have never been able to forgive, you are allowing the person who hurt you to live rent-free in your heart. It's costing him nothing and costing you everything. Perhaps it's time for you to evict him through forgiveness.[4]

4. "Forgive" God

Hear me out—I'm not suggesting, much less saying, that God ever does anything that needs forgiving. God is holy and righteous and does not sin. But, even though God does nothing wrong, *we* sometimes have the idea that He has. It would not have been unusual for a child like Wess Stafford (above) to have turned his back on a God who would allow him to be painfully abused for years at the hands of "Christian" people. Many people blame God for the hurts and painful events in their lives or the lives of people they love. So they hold God responsible—and they stop worshipping Him because they don't believe a God who would do thus-and-so is a God worthy of praise. Trust me—there are many people who have become trapped in this line of thinking.

You don't need to literally forgive God as He has done nothing wrong. But you have to release Him to be God—to cause and allow everything that filters through the grid of His perfect and loving will. If you hold God hostage, the opposite happens: You hold yourself hostage. You become bound by your own anger and resentment and will never be free again. If God has allowed something painful to happen in your life, tell Him you accept His will. Forgive anyone who was involved in your pain, and believe that God will cause even your pain to work together for your good.

The Power of Forgiveness

The following story is told about president Abraham Lincoln. He reportedly purchased a slave girl at the auction one day, and she was shocked when he turned to her and said, "You are free to go."

"What do you mean?" she said.

"It means you are free," the president answered.

"Free to say whatever I want to say?"

"Yes, you can say anything."

"Free to be anything I want to be?"

"Yes, you can be whatever you want to be."

"And free to go wherever I want to go?"

"Yes, you may go anywhere."

"Then," she said, with tears streaming down her face, "I will go with you."

That is the power of freedom—especially the freedom granted by another. When God sets us free through forgiveness, we are drawn to Him, to follow Him. When you are forgiven by another person, you are drawn to that person. And when you forgive others, they will be drawn to you. Why? Because forgiveness is not natural—it is supernatural. It is "better than expected," and we want to be around those who have that kind of power and strength.

If you are down to nothing because of your choices, the choices of others, or an "act of God," the very first step is to forgive. When you forgive, you exercise a power that is not yours. And you realize you aren't down to nothing. You have the power of God at work in your life. And where His power is at work, He is always up to something.

PART II

WHAT GOD IS UP TO IN MEETING YOUR NEEDS

We have many kinds of needs in life:
Spiritual
Financial
Emotional
Relational
Personal
and more.
God is always up to unique ways of meeting our needs.
Chapter 6 talks about God's commitment to guide us.
Chapter 7 reminds us of the gifts and abilities God has given us.
Chapter 8 addresses God's continual availability to us.
Chapter 9 reminds us that money is never a problem for God.
Chapter 10 introduces the idea of health as a matter of stewardship.
Chapter 11 looks at how suffering is useful in our life.

God Is Never Lost

(Guidance)

The LORD will guide you always;
he will satisfy your needs in a sun-scorched land
and will strengthen your frame.
You will be like a well-watered garden,
like a spring whose waters never fail.

Isaiah 58:11

My Story

The spring of 2008 was in full swing in my life and ministry. I had no idea that by the coming October I would no longer be the pastor of the Crystal Cathedral or the host of the Hour of Power *telecast. We planned and celebrated the wedding of one of my children—a glorious event—and my days were filled with pastoral and family activity.*

A church as large and unique as the Crystal Cathedral— especially one with a worldwide television audience, especially one that is in tourist-heavy Orange County, California— attracts lots of visitors. It is a rare day at the Cathedral when there are not individuals, small groups, or large groups that drop in hoping to see the church and perhaps meet some of the people they have seen on television—especially tourists who are visiting the United States from foreign countries. We would do our best, of course, to accommodate everyone who came to the church to visit, tours and greetings being handled by some of the church staff.

But one day in June 2008—a month before the conversations began about my role at the church—I was told a group of Asian businessmen wanted to visit the church and meet with me specifically. I didn't know the men and had no idea what they wanted, but I was able to make room in my schedule to meet with them for a few minutes.

I didn't know it, but these men were associated with a cable television network that had a moderate-size, family-oriented audience in the United States—primarily featuring reruns of family-friendly sitcoms and dramas from past decades. They were familiar, of course, with the Hour of Power *broadcast and . . . well, after they left, I still wasn't totally sure why they had come to see me. It was a "meet and greet" of sorts—friendly and sociable. Interesting, but I quickly returned to my desk as soon as they left and didn't think further about the polite Asian men I had just met.*

I'll tell you later in this book why God sent these men to see me that day. But for now, let me make the point of this chapter: God is always guiding us, even when we think we know exactly where we are, even when the need for guidance is the farthest thing from our mind.

Remember: This was June 2008. In July, my life began changing forever. Unbeknownst to me, the men I met with in my office that day would, many months later, come back into my life in a very significant way. In June, I was not down to nothing—everything was fine. But God knew that by October, I would be down to less than nothing. And in June He was already putting things in motion to keep me moving in the right direction later that year—to guide me even when I didn't know I would soon be "lost."

Looking back, I am amazed at what God did. It has made me much more aware of every person I meet, every event I attend, every idea I have. It has made me live a more "present" life, knowing that God is always up to something in our lives; knowing that the next time I'm down to nothing, I can be confident that His promise to guide His children will always be kept.

For years my favorite diversion, for which there has been precious little time lately, is to leave the California coast behind and motor out into the Pacific Ocean in search of large game fish. There's something about getting out of sight of land that allows a momentary disconnect from the pressures of life. It's quiet, peaceful, and relaxing. The fish, if any are caught, are just icing on an already delicious cake created from sun, salt spray, and silence.

Before GPS systems became available, venturing too far out of sight of land was a different matter. One needed to be careful about keeping track of position with charts, maps, compass, the sun, radio, and common sense. When it is time to go home and you look in all four directions and see nothing but water, guidance is bit more challenging. But GPS has changed all that. With a GPS on the boat and thirty-odd satellites circling the globe talking to my GPS, I rarely give a thought about where in the Pacific I am. The "system" knows where I am and is ready to tell me whenever I ask and gives me the directions I need to get home.

I'm all for technology—I'm no Luddite when it comes to appreciating the benefits of high-tech advances. But let me offer this observation: It is very easy in our day to get so used to the benefits of technology in our physical life that we approach the spiritual life with the same expectations of immediate gratification. We have a half-dozen ways to reach people on the spot—starting with the lowly telephone—and get frustrated when we can't connect with them or if they don't respond to our IMs, text messages, voice mails, or e-mails (heaven forbid resorting to this antiquated tool!) within a few minutes. I wonder if we bring that same expectation into our communication life with God—expecting immediate answers to our prayers and solutions to our problems. We have been acculturated in a not-too-healthy direction, spiritually speaking.

And now we have GPS. With this tool increasingly present in our cars (and on our cell phones or handheld GPS units), we are in danger of losing the whole concept of being "lost." We can go anywhere on the globe and never not know where we are or how to find our way to a location. The whole concept of stopping and asking for directions is "so 1990s" ("And it's about time," say the husbands who are tired of having their pioneer spirit teased by wives and children who don't like being lost). But have we approached guidance from God the same way—expecting Him to say, "Turn here, turn there" every time we get a bit confused about our direction in life?

The story I told at the beginning of this chapter means this to me: God knew that in October 2008 I would definitely need guidance. I would be out of a job and not sure what my next steps in life and ministry were. So five or six months ahead of my need, God began orchestrating a process that would contribute significantly to providing the guidance I needed. A half year before my need became clear, God was putting together a "guidance package" for me. But the half year it took me to get from June to October/November? It was like being out of sight of the California coastland in a boat, in the middle of a dark, cloudy night, with no navigation tools whatsoever. As I once heard someone say, "I was as lost as an Easter egg in high grass." It was not a fun experience, from a feeling perspective. My mind (theology) debated daily with my feelings (experience) over where I was versus where I wanted to be.

But here is what I have learned through that experience: *In the final analysis, it's less important for me to know where I am than it is to believe that God knows where I am.* In other words, God is okay with me being (feeling) lost at times. Because I am really not lost if He knows where I am and plans on giving me directions when I need to receive them.

Lost People

The 2000 Tom Hanks movie *Cast Away*—that's what it means to be lost. Hanks's character, Chuck Noland, was a FedEx systems engineer who was marooned on an uninhabited South Pacific island when the plane he was on went down, he being the only survivor. Not only did he not know where he was, nobody else knew where he was either. He was presumed dead until he was rescued by a passing ship after four years on the island. Now that's lost. Even more "lost" was the television series *Lost*—the perfect name for a show in which I, like many people who watched faithfully, was completely lost throughout. Entertained, but completely lost.

The Bible is full of stories of people who thought they were lost but really weren't. And not just lost physically—they were mostly lost like us: emotionally and spiritually. But all the time God knew right where each of them was. Without their knowledge, He was guiding them to where they needed to be.

Moses

Moses was lost for forty years in a backwater region of the Middle East called Midian. He lived his first forty years growing up and serving in the royal house of Egypt's pharaoh. After killing an Egyptian soldier for mistreating a Hebrew slave, he fled for his life to Midian where he was taken in by a Midianite priest named Jethro, for whom he worked as a shepherd for the next forty years. The last forty years of his life he spent leading the Hebrew slaves through the wilderness en route to the Promised Land. The middle forty years were Moses' "lost" years.

I was without direction in my life for the better part of one year. Moses was "lost" for forty years!—lost *personally*. Not really, though, because God had a plan that Moses needed to grow into. When it was time for Moses to lead the slaves out of Egypt, God gave him directions for the rest of his life. For all Moses knew as a forty-year-old, he was going to die as a shepherd of sheep. But as an eighty-year-old, God needed him to shepherd a couple million Hebrew slaves. All those years in Midian when Moses felt lost, God knew right where he was.

David

While a teenager, young David was anointed by Samuel to be the next king of Israel (around 1030 BC). But he wasn't established as king in Hebron until 1010 BC. So what was he doing during the twenty-year interval between those two events? He wasn't lost geographically; he knew the rocks, hills, and caves of Judea as well as the next shepherd boy. You could probably have blindfolded David and carted him off in any direction from his home in Bethlehem and he would have been able to find his way back. No, geography wasn't David's problem.

He was lost *vocationally*. God had told him he was to succeed Saul as king, but David no doubt wondered if God had told Saul—because Saul spent the next twenty years trying to kill the young king-appointee. David was no doubt greatly confused: Am I king or am I not? "Yes," God said, "but not yet." So David spent twenty years growing up, learning patience, politics, and perseverance until it was time for him to take the throne. For twenty years, David felt lost. But God knew right where he was the whole time.

Solomon

If anybody strikes us as having it all together, surely it is King Solomon, David's son. He was the wisest man in the known world—

and the richest. He was an expert in the flora and fauna of Israel. He was the author of thousands of proverbs and wise sayings and two other books as well. And he expanded Israel's commercial and military interests exponentially. But, in spite of his apparent success, Solomon got lost in the mid-to-later years of his life—lost spiritually.

Solomon's three books may well represent three phases of his life. Song of Songs is a picture of his love life as a young, virile king. Proverbs reflects him at the height of his wisdom and focus on God. But Ecclesiastes pictures Solomon when he was lost *spiritually*. He began using his massive wealth to indulge his senses and his curiosity. He was bored with being a godly king, so he focused on pleasure, on architecture, on expansion, on commercialization—and found it all to be empty of meaning. For years Solomon searched for meaning in life apart from God, a pathetic shadow of his former powerful self. But God was guiding him through that period too, allowing Solomon to test and reject all the world had to offer until he came to his own conclusion: that meaning is found only in God and His Word. Solomon felt and acted lost, but he wasn't. Because God knew where he was and where he was going the whole time.

Peter

Who doesn't love Peter? If he ever did get lost, he's the kind of guy anyone would pick up and help on his way. We would laugh with Peter about his "lostness." After all, is the life of the party ever really lost? They give the impression they've got it all together, and that's what Peter did—even with Jesus. Peter wouldn't hear of Jesus' pessimistic predictions about going to Jerusalem and being killed. When Jesus warned that some of His followers might desert him, Peter boasted, "Not me, Lord!" Peter was passionate, full of emotional confidence—except when the stakes got higher and he got lost *emotionally*.

You know the story. The night of Jesus' arrest, being one of His followers became dicey. It appeared Jesus' followers might be arrested right along with Him. So Peter lost his passion and his courage and denied even knowing His Lord—three different times. When he escaped the crowds, he wept at his own weakness and fear. I doubt if anyone has ever felt as emotionally lost as Peter did that fateful night in Jerusalem. But what Peter didn't know was that God was watching Him and had a plan in place for new directions. After Jesus was raised from the dead, He met with Peter and some other disciples by the Sea of Galilee where all was forgiven. Jesus recommissioned Peter to be the shepherd of His flock. And Peter got back the direction he thought he had lost in a moment of weakness. God had a plan for Peter—it just took some soul-sad days for Peter to see it.

Paul

Paul was not the kind of man who ever seemed to be lost. He was the man with a plan—a plan to reach the entire non-Jewish world with the gospel of Christ. He was a Type-A decision maker who didn't tolerate weakness or indecision. But on his second missionary journey, when he made plans to enter a region called Bithynia, God said, "No." We don't know how that message was delivered, but Luke's writing makes it clear that their way was blocked. For a matter of hours, perhaps days, Paul was lost *ministerially*—he had no idea where to go with the gospel since God had said no to his plan.

Never one to sit idly by, Paul and his fellow ministers went to the nearest town, Troas, on the coast of Asia Minor. While there, in a vision during the night, Paul received the guidance he needed. A man, across the Aegean Sea in Macedonia, was calling for Paul to come over and help him and his people. Paul took that as God's guidance: "Take the gospel to Macedonia" (now Europe)—and he did. Paul hit a dead end in his ministry and probably felt lost and confused. But he wasn't lost. God was watching him the whole time. As soon as Paul was in the right place, God gave him the guidance he needed.

Jesus

I'm going to ask you for a little headroom in discussing this last "lost" soul. We are so focused on the deity of Christ (rightfully so), that we sometimes forget he was also a man, a human being with a mind, will, and emotions We're even told in the book of Hebrews that Jesus had to learn obedience through the things that He suffered (see Heb. 5:8). But I want to suggest that even Jesus got a little lost—just a little, in a human way we can identify with—*theologically*. On the night he was apprehended and arrested, He was praying alone in the Garden of Gethsemane. He knew what was coming: a barbaric, Roman cross. We're told that he prayed and asked God, if it was possible (theologically), that He might be spared the cross. He prayed so intensely that He perspired drops of blood!

He knew what He was asking was not possible. He knew there was no remission of sin without the shedding of blood. And He knew He was the Lamb of God that takes away the sins of the world. But what He was about to experience loomed so large in His human vision that He had to ask for a pass. And God answered by sending an angel to the Garden to minister to him. I wonder what was said? What do you say to the Son of God to give Him guidance in an hour of temptation? I don't know, but it was enough. Jesus concluded His prayer, back on the path, by telling God, "Not My will, but Yours be done." Jesus may have appeared to be lost for a split second, wondering if there was any other way besides dying to atone for the sins of the world. But He wasn't lost at all. God knew right where He was, knew what He was feeling, and knew what He needed to complete the purpose for which He came into the world.

Lost Can Be Good

Growing up, I spent a lot of time in the California mountains where my father and I built a small weekend cabin for our family to use. I quickly learned that it is possible to feel lost and not be lost—at the same time. If you're in a valley, surrounded by peaks on all sides, you could be less than half a mile from "people"—a store, a cabin, or a road. But if you can't see civilization from where you stand, it's very easy to feel lost. Like a hiker who stumbles through a black forest at night, falls down in exhaustion and sleeps, and wakes up the next morning a couple hundred yards from a cabin in a clearing. The cabin was there the whole time—he just couldn't see it until the light became adequate the next morning.

That's the way it is with us at times. *Feeling* lost, but not really *being* lost. A child of God is never lost because God always knows where His children are. And He is preparing a way to give His children the guidance they need to get back on track. As I wrote earlier, *in the final analysis, it's less important for me to know where I am than it is to believe that God knows where I am—and to believe that His guidance will be forthcoming.*

If you are God's child, and you feel lost and in need of guidance, look at it as a good thing—something to grow your faith, to draw you closer to God, to strengthen your character, to teach you not to give up. You may feel like you're down to nothing and have lost your way, but take it from someone who learned: God is up to something that He will show you when you, and He, are ready.

7

You Are Totally Gifted

(Gifts)

Just as each of us has one body with many members, and these members do not all have the same function, so in Christ we who are many form one body, and each member belongs to all the others. We have different gifts, according to the grace given us.

Romans 12:4–6a

My Story

Dry mouth. Butterflies. Weak knees. I had them all any time I was asked to speak in a public setting. That might come as a surprise to some who know my father, an eloquent and gifted speaker. I grew up watching him make preaching look easy. But when people began inviting me to speak—it began when I was in elementary school—I was completely intimidated by the prospect. If a teacher called on me, I would cower. When I was asked to share in a small group, my stomach would get tight. My "Schuller" pedigree was of no use. I was scared to death of public speaking.

But I accepted every invitation. Why? Because I knew that God had called me to preach. And if He called me, I knew that He would gift me accordingly with the spiritual gift(s) I needed to succeed. I believed God's calling and

God's gifts were a package deal. God would not have called me to do something for which I was not equipped. So, early on, I put many audiences through the uncomfortable experience of listening to me stumble and watching me sweat as I preached in spite of my fears.

I remember precisely the day God released my spiritual gift of preaching. During seminary I was invited to speak to a group of churchwomen (as always, I said yes automatically) and began to dread the experience. But that day something palpable happened. As I stepped onto the platform, the Holy Spirit of God touched my heart and my tongue in a way I didn't recognize. I didn't know what it meant, but I quickly learned. It was as if I had received the gift of tongues—the ability to speak in a new language. I actually felt this warmth flow over me, and I spoke with a power and presence that was completely new. I felt God was saying to me, "Welcome to your gift. Now use it to glorify Me. And don't ever forget where you got it."

I have tried to be faithful to use my spiritual gift of preaching ever since. That doesn't mean I'm the world's best preacher. Far from it! It simply means that God's Holy Spirit has chosen to work through me—through my personality, talents, strengths, and weaknesses—in this particular way. His gift of preaching was certainly consistent with my calling as a pastor. Or so I thought prior to the summer of 2008.

When it became clear that my calling to the Crystal Cathedral and the Hour of Power were over, I had no place to exercise my gift of preaching. But I was reminded of the apostle Paul's words in Romans 11:29: "God's gifts and God's call are under full warranty—never canceled, never rescinded" (The Message). While that verse was written with reference to God's covenant people, Israel, I certainly considered myself a covenant child of God. So I believed that while the venue might be changing, my call to encourage people to live a vibrant life in God through Jesus Christ was intact—and that my gift of preaching was still the means to fulfilling that call.

So I put aside thoughts of being finished as a proclaimer of God's truth and love. I chose instead to believe God's prom- ise that His gifts and calling are permanent, that His gifts are always to be used. I realized I wasn't down to nothing. I had the gift of God's Holy Spirit in my life. And because of that, I was confident that God was up to something.

I f you were the young child of one of the world's richest men— say, Mexico's Carlos Slim or America's Bill Gates or Warren Buffett—you might be living in anticipation of the gifts you would one day receive from your parents—or at least your future inheri- tance. But you would probably be surprised, if not disappointed, about what your parents chose to leave to you. Many very wealthy people leave precious little money to their children.

Take Warren Buffett, for example, the legendary investor. *Forbes* magazine's 2010 list ranked him as the third wealthiest per- son in the world with a fortune of around $47 billion.[1] But if you were one of Buffett's three children, gifts of money would be the last thing you could count on receiving from your father. When Buffett's son, Peter Buffett, was nineteen years old, he received an inheritance of $90,000—his share of a farm left to him and his sib- lings by his grandfather. Warren Buffett sold the farm and put the money into the stock of his investment company, Berkshire Hatha- way. If Peter Buffett, now fifty-two, had left the money invested, it would be worth around $70 million today. But as a college student, he wanted a career in music. So he used the money to purchase music equipment to jump-start his career—apparently not a bad move since he became a multiple Emmy Award-winning musician.

Things were as hard for this struggling son-of-a-billionaire musician as for any other. Peter approached his father once in his twenties for a loan to help him through a rough patch, and his father turned him down. Angry at the time, he now understands his father's reasoning. "I learned more in those [difficult] times about myself and my resiliency than I ever would have if I'd had a pile of money and I could have glided through life," he says. "I honestly feel that it is an act of love to say, 'I believe in you as my child, and you don't need my help.'"[2]

Warren Buffett and his late wife decided that money was the least important legacy they could leave to their children. Instead they chose to focus on bequeathing values, love, security, encouragement, counsel, and support—things money can never buy. The wealthy investor has given each of his three children a substantial sum for them to use in charitable work, but no financial inheritance for themselves. It's up to them to take the intangible gifts they've been given and create a life of their own.

I share that story because it so parallels how God gives to His children. I fear that some Christians view God's "cattle on a thousand hills" (Ps. 50:10) as belonging to them: "When do I get my share of the herd, Lord? I'd like to cash them in for a new house!" While God is concerned about our material needs, His primary gifts to us in this life are of a different sort—intangible gifts, spiritual gifts. Indeed, "spiritual gifts" is the very term the Bible uses to describe the most practical and valuable gift God gives to every one of His children.

Gifts of God

The New Testament mentions several gifts we have been given by God, all of which fall into the category of "Most Important." "Eternal life in Christ Jesus our Lord" is a gift from God (Rom. 6:23). The grace of God is an "indescribable gift" (2 Cor. 9:14–15). "Faith" to believe is a gift from God "so that no one can boast" about their salvation (Eph. 2:8–9). And the Holy Spirit himself is a "gift" given to everyone who believes in Christ (Acts 2:38). All of those gifts from God were given to unite us with Him, to restore our relationship with Him. We were separated from God by sin with no way to bridge the gap on our own. So God, as a gift, built the bridge for us. Christ, the Holy Spirit, grace—even the faith to believe in all the other gifts!—all were given as gifts.

Those gifts connect us to heaven. But there remains our need to be connected to earth, a way to "work out [our] salvation" (Phil. 2:12), a way to manifest our eternal gifts here on earth. And to that end, God has given every one of His true children—those who have received the eternal gift of His Holy Spirit through faith in Christ—another kind of spiritual gift. You didn't have to ask for it, and it is not optional. You have been given one or more spiritual gifts by the Holy Spirit to use in working out your salvation here on earth.

Here are a few summary facts to know about spiritual gifts:

- Spiritual gifts are not the same as natural, human talents or abilities.
- Spiritual gifts are given to Jesus' followers so they can manifest and continue His works. (The fruit of the Spirit [Galatians 5:22–23] manifest Jesus' character.)
- The gifts are discussed in four places in the New Testament: Romans 12; 1 Corinthians 12–14; Ephesians 4; 1 Peter 4.
- There is no "fixed" list of all the gifts of the Spirit. Each of the four letters in which they are mentioned has a different list with some overlap. That says to me that the labels are only for practical purposes of discussion. The gifts mentioned in the New Testament cover all the functional areas of ministry and service, but that's not to say the Holy Spirit cannot gift a Christian in a unique way not listed in one of the four passages.
- Gifts are given not for the individual's benefit, but for the purpose of strengthening the Church of Jesus Christ and serving others.

- The Holy Spirit distributes His gifts within the Body of Christ "just as he determines" (1 Cor. 12:11). Your gift is your "assignment," in a broad way of speaking.

Spiritual Prosthetics

God's promise to you about your giftedness is that you are gifted! You have been equipped by Him to play a unique role in His family. Your spiritual gift(s), coupled with your personality and natural abilities, make you unique in the entire world and in the Body of Christ. From my experience as a pastor, I don't think all Christians recognize what this means. And we pastors and leaders must share some of the blame for this for not emphasizing it more. The apostle Paul wrote extensively about spiritual gifts because they are so important.

How are they important? As important to the Body of Christ as your eyes, ears, hands, feet, and other limbs and organs are to your physical body. That's the metaphor Paul uses in 1 Corinthians 12 to emphasize the importance of the gifts. Unfortunately, some people do have to manage life without one or more limbs, sometimes even without an organ. But it is difficult. We're all too familiar with the soldiers returning from Iraq and Afghanistan, soldiers who no doubt would have died in previous wars. But military medical triage and trauma care on the battlefield is so outstanding that many soldiers are saved—but often at the expense of a precious part of their body. Fortunately, the science of prosthetics makes it possible for people who have suffered terrible wounds to have a productive life. Artificial limbs (and perhaps someday organs) can be used as replacements. They aren't perfect substitutes, but they are getting better all the time.

But here's the difference in physical body parts and spiritual gifts: There are no spiritual prosthetics. You—your spiritual gift, along with your natural gifts and abilities—are irreplaceable in the Body of Christ! If you are absent, the Church of Jesus Christ suffers just like a person who loses a limb in battle. The church is limping along trying to function without many Christians' gifts of teaching, giving, mercy, hospitality, administration, or whatever their gift from God is. That's how important you are. God promised to gift you, to equip you, because His people need you—*you*! God's family on earth is only as strong as its weakest member.

Think about the massive cables that are used to hold up gigantic suspension bridges like the Brooklyn Bridge or the Golden Gate Bridge. Those cables are made of thousands of tiny steel wires that are spun together to make up the main cables that hold the weight of the bridge roadway. If those individual cable wires began to break one at a time, the entire structure would grow weaker and weaker with the snap of every thread in the bundle. Eventually, with the breaking of one last thread, the bridge would come down. It's the "straw that broke the camel's back" idea. The load gets heavier, and the bridge gets weaker with the presence of one more straw or the absence of one more tiny thread. Eventually deterioration becomes dysfunction, and dysfunction becomes disability, and disability becomes death.

I'm sad to announce: There is no spiritual gift described in the New Testament called "Attending the Worship Service." I sometimes think that many Christians feel that is their gift—attending their church's weekly worship service. Don't get me wrong— that's an incredibly important part of our life as Christians. But because spiritual gifts are given to build up the Church (see Eph. 4:7–13), it's necessary to get involved in the Church to exercise the gift(s) God has given you. That can be done a myriad of ways, obviously. I can't say *how* you should be involved with the Body of Christ, but I can say that you *should be*. It's the reason God gave you your gift(s). There is no prosthetic version of you waiting to take your place if you decide not to participate in strengthening the Church. It's you or nobody.

Venues Change, Gifts Remain

I had to get comfortable with a spiritual reality as I transitioned out of the pastoral and television setting I had been part of for thirty-two years: *Venues for exercising spiritual gifts may change over a lifetime, but gifts remain constant.*

I'm not going to speak for God as to whether a person's spiritual gifts might change over time and in different circumstances. But I am repeating Romans 11:29: "God's gifts and his call are irrevocable." In general, we should expect that what God has gifted us to do is going to remain constant. What obviously can change is where and how you exercise your gift(s)—which is what I had to realize.

I know now that God has called me to a new venue (more on this later) to continue using the same gifts of preaching, communication, and encouragement that I have used fruitfully all my adult spiritual life. Not surprisingly, it will build on my background in television and will take full advantage of my love for speaking and teaching, encouraging people to experience the best God has for them.

When I began thinking about this, I was reminded of the apostle Paul's words to his young pastoral protégé, Timothy: "For this reason I remind you to fan into flame the gift of God, which is in you through the laying on of my hands" (2 Tim. 1:6). The better part of a year went by as I contemplated my own spiritual calling and gifts. And I realized: my gift is like a fire—the fire of the Holy Spirit. If I don't feed the flame, if I don't fan the flame, the Spirit in me is quenched. The fire will go out! (See 1 Thess. 5:19.) I don't mean God will take back the gift. I mean it will atrophy and grow weak and useless. As I saw God begin to open doors to a new venue for my gifts, I grew more and more excited. I began fanning the flame of my gifts and regaining confidence that God was going to use me in the same areas of giftedness, just in a different venue.

Fanning by Faith

Is it possible you need to stir up the fire of the Holy Spirit in you—to "fan into flame the gift of God, which is in you"? If you are not currently using your spiritual gift to strengthen Christ's Church by ministering to others the same way Jesus would, then I know the answer to that question.

You may not even know what your spiritual gift is. Remember: if you are a true follower of Jesus, having received the gift of the Holy Spirit, then you do have a spiritual gift. If you don't know what it is, it's a treasure in you waiting to be uncovered. Study the gifts of God in Scripture. Talk to your pastor or other spiritual leader. Ask God to help you discover the gift(s) He has given you. And then find a way to begin using it.

It's easy to come to the conclusion that God doesn't need us, that there isn't a niche for us. But that's wrong! God's people need you and your gift(s) desperately. And *you* need your gift(s). When you reach a point in your life where you feel you're down to nothing, you're not. You have the gifts of God alive and well in your life. One of the best ways I know to find out what God is up to in your life is to put your gift(s) to work.

Fan the flame. Feed the fire. And watch God reveal new directions and new chapters in your life story.

8

When You Need to Talk to Someone

(God's Availability)

He will not let your foot slip—
he who watches over you will not slumber;
indeed, he who watches over Israel
will neither slumber nor sleep.

Psalm 121:3–4

My Story

July 9, 2008, was a watershed day in my life. That was the day I was informed of the planned changes in the Crystal Cathedral's and Hour of Power's ministries, changes that would radically alter my role in both. For the next three-plus months, I labored in prayer with God and in counsel with trusted friends to assess my future—what these changes would mean for me and my family.

There were more than a few (very) late nights and (very) early mornings during those months. I could not sleep. My adrenals were pumping out so much adrenaline that I was non-stop from early morning calling the east coast or even Europe where we had offices that would be affected. Then I would be up till late at night consulting and examining all the different options that were available in an attempt to change the course that had been set. When that was all done, I would try to sleep—but would lay there with my mind moving a hundred miles an hour. I began to revel in the fact that, when everyone else in my world was sleeping, God was awake and waiting for me to appear with questions or concerns in hand.

And I had plenty of both. The summer of 2008 was a graduate-level course for me in the availability of God. I understood theological truths from textbooks, like the omnipresence of God (He is everywhere at once) and the immanence of God (He is within all parts of His creation). But I had never contemplated the availability of God—His willingness to treat me as if I were the only child He has. I learned that God was never on the phone, had never stepped out of the office, and was never otherwise occupied. I began to treat my thoughts as prayers—a continual stream of communication to God. Yes, I continued to pray in more formal and traditional ways. But I learned afresh that God knows my thoughts and my heart—that it's possible to live life in a never-ending conversation with Him. I knew that truth before. But there is nothing like a crisis in life to raise our awareness level and sharpen our focus on what is most important and most valuable to our survival. And I definitely felt like I was in survival mode during the summer of 2008.

And something else came out of my graduate course in God's availability: a new focus on being available to those who need me. Even with those we love most, it's easy to be only partially present in their lives. Even when my wife or children are conveying something to me that is heartfelt from their perspective, I confess—my mind can be entertaining other things: my reply to them, what I did earlier in the day, what I have to do next. I could be there with them and somewhere else at the same time.

But I have a new desire to be to others what God has become to me: completely present and available. I believe every encounter is a divine appointment. Therefore, if my wife or children, or a friend or even a stranger, needs me, I have learned it is God's will for me to be completely present in their life. I believe that is how God is to me and how I should be to others.

The more I thought I was down to nothing, the more I discovered I had: friends, my wife and children, God's purpose and plan for my life, God's gifts and guidance, and, now, His availability. The more I realized I had, the more confident I grew that God was up to something.

Never let it be said that humor, even sarcasm (in its pure form, irony), has no place in the spiritual life. Nowhere in Scripture is it more evident than in the account of the showdown between Elijah, the prophet of God, and the 850 prophets of Baal and Asherah, Baal's wife (the story is in 1 Kings 18:16–40).

Under the influence of Israel's apostate king, Ahab, and his pagan wife, Jezebel, Israel had incorporated the worship of Baal, the dominant pagan god of the day, into their worship life. Elijah had made a career out of attacking Ahab and Jezebel and calling on the nation of Israel to repent of their idolatry. To make the case that Baal was not a god, but just an idol carved from wood or stone, Elijah proposed a contest—a fire-off, if you will—to see who was the true God: Baal or Yahweh, God of Israel. Ahab accepted the challenge and summoned the prophets of Baal and Asherah to Mount Carmel—the high place where Baal was worshipped. Elijah took the fight right to the idol's front door.

Here was the challenge: both "teams"—the false prophets and Elijah and his helpers—would prepare a bull for a burnt offering. Each team would call upon their respective god to send down fire from heaven and consume the sacrifice. The team whose god answered the prayer and sent down fire from heaven would be declared the true God.

The prophets of Baal prepared wood for their altar and laid the pieces of their bull upon it, ready for the flames. Then from morning until noon, hundreds of prophets "danced around the altar they had made" (v. 26), calling on Baal to hear them and send down fire from heaven. Nothing. The bull was heating up, but it was from the noonday sun, not from any fire.

Elijah's team had been watching this display of pagan prophesying for several hours—and Elijah couldn't contain himself. It was obvious that Baal wasn't available just then; something had distracted Baal, or perhaps he was away from his desk at the moment. Here is the version of Elijah's taunt from The Message (v. 27):

> By noon, Elijah had started making fun of them, taunting, "Call a little louder—he is a god, after all. Maybe he's off meditating somewhere or other, or maybe he's gotten involved in a project, or maybe he's on vacation. You don't suppose he's overslept, do you, and needs to be waked up?"

Elijah shows his cultural understanding of the pagan pantheon. It was common for a pagan god like Baal to be involved in all manner of commercial ventures—things related to crops and trade, things related to his own survival and prosperity. So Elijah suggested that maybe Baal was on a business trip, that he wasn't available to hear the prophets' prayers.

But the prophets' barbs were likely even more pointed than The Message suggests. Here's the same verse from the second edition of the New Living Translation:

> About noontime Elijah began mocking them. "You'll have to shout louder," he scoffed, "for surely he is a god!

Perhaps he is daydreaming, or is relieving himself. Or maybe he is away on a trip, or is asleep and needs to be wakened!"

See the difference? Elijah was suggesting to the prophets of Baal that their god might be in the bathroom, relieving himself! That's an entirely legitimate translation of a Hebrew word that means to step away or withdraw for a moment—not like a trip, but just to turn aside temporarily.

Do you see what Elijah was doing? All the reasons he suggested to account for Baal's silence are the same reasons one would give for the silence (the unavailability) of a human person: "Shout louder—he can't hear you!" "He's daydreaming and isn't paying attention!" "Give him a minute—he's in the bathroom!" "Sorry—he's out of town on business!" "Ssshhhh—he's taking a nap!" He's trying to show them that they had created a god in their own image, a god with human foibles and weaknesses, a god who has no power, a god who can't be depended on to be there when they need him. Instead of worshipping the true God in whose image they were created, the prophets of Baal and Asherah were worshipping gods they had created in their own image! What a ludicrous religion: create a god like yourself, then get outraged when he is no more reliable than you are!

Elijah's sarcasm and irony fully infuriated the prophets of Baal. They began cutting themselves with swords and spears (customary in pagan worship) to please Baal with their bloodletting and danced and bled and called out for the rest of the afternoon: "But there was no response, no one answered, no one paid attention" (v. 29).

You may know the rest of the story. After the prophets of Baal fail to rouse their god, Elijah's team went into action late in the afternoon. They rebuilt the altar to God that had fallen into disrepair during Israel's apostasy. They laid on wood, the cut-up bull, and then soaked the entire thing with water three times just for good measure—to prove that when God sends fire, he sends *serious* fire. Then Elijah prayed one simple, thirty-four-word (in Hebrew) prayer. No yelling, no dancing, no flagellation or cutting, no bleeding, no pleading. Elijah expected God to be available and to answer.

And answer He did: "Then the fire of the LORD fell and burned up the sacrifice, the wood, the stones and the soil, and also licked up the water in the trench" (v. 38). Like I said, *serious* fire. And the crowds that had gathered to watch the fire-off fell down on their faces and proclaimed that Yahweh, not Baal, is God. Everybody except the prophets of Baal and Asherah, that is. They ran for their lives, but to no avail.

The moral of the story is obvious: It's far better to have a God who is always available to you than one who isn't. Of course, the latter kind are not gods at all, but human creations. They are no more a god than a volleyball with a face painted on it. Hope as you may that it will be there when you need it, it won't. Elijah's God, on the other hand, proved what the prophets knew by heart: "Call to me and I will answer you and tell you great and unsearchable things you do not know" (Jer. 33:3).

"Available"—especially to someone who is down to nothing—is definitely better. Elijah was down to nothing but a prayer and a short one at that. But that's all it took to reach his God.

The Variability of Availability

The same variability exists with theo-availability. But several things may make God more or less available to us:

First, sin in our heart can make God unavailable to us. Consider this testimony written by a psalmist:

> Come and listen, all you who fear God;
> let me tell you what he has done for me.
> I cried out to him with my mouth;

his praise was on my tongue.
If I had cherished sin in my heart,
the Lord would not have listened;
but God has surely listened
and heard my voice in prayer.
Praise be to God,
who has not rejected my prayer
or withheld his love from me!
Psalm 66:16–20; italics added

That's the testimony of a person who found God available to him—God "listened and heard [his] voice in prayer." But look at what else he understood: If he had cherished (nurtured, coddled, tolerated) sin in his heart, he knows God would not have listened. That's the testimony of a realistic person who knows how God works. I can't say that God would never make himself available to a person who at the same time was harboring sin in his or her heart. That's God's business, not mine. But I do know the Bible is pretty clear, in general, about the necessity for us choosing one or the other: God or materialism (see Matt. 6:24), God or other gods (any kind of idol; see Josh. 24:15), God or sinful habits and activities (see Ps. 66:18), and so on. God doesn't want to play second fiddle to anything else in our life, and certainly not to sin.

God doesn't ask that we be sinless or perfect. But He does ask that we be honest with Him. If He is not the most important thing in our life—or if that's at least not our desire—then His availability to us is going to be hindered.

Second, being insensitive to God can push Him away. The Bible talks about "grieving" the Holy Spirit (see Eph. 4:30) and "putting out the Spirit's fire" or "quenching" the Spirit—treating the things of God "with contempt" (see 1 Thess. 5:19). I think of this like I think of marriage. If I treat my wife unkindly or with contempt, how likely is it that she will be emotionally available to me? Not very. Relationships take cultivation and nurturing, and they can be easily wounded. When a spouse shuts down or backs off in a relationship, it's a sure sign he or she has been wounded in some way. And the more the wounds happen, the longer it takes to heal.

From the day a teenaged David was chosen by the prophet Samuel to succeed Saul as king, David's heart was the issue. In justifying his choice of David, the youngest and least of Jesse's eight sons, Samuel said, "Man looks at the outward appearance, but the LORD looks at the heart" (1 Sam. 16:7). God obviously saw something in David's heart that attracted Him to the young shepherd. Even though David had some serious lapses in judgment in his adult life, he was always known for being a man after God's own heart (see 1 Sam. 13:14; 1 Kings 15:3; Acts 13:22). That's all God wants—someone who wants to follow after Him, have a close relationship, and keep short, honest accounts in the process. Trying to live with God any other way will hinder His availability to us.

Third, not being available to God will hinder His availability to us. I've said, and I repeat, that God is always available to us. But I don't think the opposite is always true—that we are always available to Him. God is a seeking God, a relational God, a desiring God when it comes to having a relationship with us. There is no better example of that than God "walking in the garden [of Eden] in the cool of the day," calling out, "Where are you?" But Adam and Eve "hid from the LORD God among the trees of the garden" (Gen. 3:8–9). They weren't available to God when He wanted to be with them. They had their reason of course—they had sinned and become aware of their nakedness and couldn't bear the holiness of God's presence. So they hid—made themselves unavailable.

We have our reasons as well, all seeming as justifiable as Adam's and Eve's did to them. But there are no good reasons for hiding from God or failing to come when He calls us to spend time with Him. If we choose not to be available to Him, the net effect is His unavailability to us.

How Could We Say No?

God's availability is incomprehensible, isn't it? There is not a moment of our day, nor a season of our life, when God is unavailable to us. We should work at making the same thing true of ourselves—being just as available to God as He is to us.

We live in a connected age, but not necessarily an available age. We are connected to lots of people by phone, e-mail, and texts, and many more by social-networking sites. But being connected doesn't always mean contact. There are occasional delays when trying to reach even our closest friends.

But such is not true with God. British Bible teacher Major Ian Thomas once wrote, "When all that you are is available to all that God is, then all that God is is available to all that you are." How could we say no to a God like that?

In other words, when you think you are down to nothing, you really aren't because God is always available to you. And because His availability is active, not passive, He is always up to something—seeking you out, being in touch, leading and guiding you on.

9

Nobody Has More Money than God

(Provision)

The earth is the Lord's, and everything in it,
the world, and all who live in it;
for he founded it upon the seas
and established it upon the waters.

Psalm 24:1–2

My Story

I have already mentioned a group of Asian businessmen who came into my office at the Crystal Cathedral in June 2008. That was the month before I learned that my role at the church was being redefined. I didn't know it at the time, but that meeting was something God was up to in my life.

The men were part of the ownership team of a cable television network called ALN—American Life Network (now Youtoo TV).[1] ALN featured twenty-four hours of daily family-friendly programming: reruns of dramas and sitcoms from a previous era when many popular television shows supported family values. The network also featured lifestyle-entertainment features, cooking shows, documentaries, and a variety of other programs. They had more than eleven million subscribers nationwide.

But God was up to something, as He always is. By November of that year, I was without a job. I had resigned from my involvement with the Crystal Cathedral and the Hour of Power *broadcast and had no idea what I was going to do. But, as I have said previously in this book, I knew who I was and what God has called me to do. As far as I knew, only the venue for my life was changing, not the big picture. God has called me to preach a message of love and encouragement, based on the biblical gospel of Jesus Christ, to a world filled with people who need hope. All my adult life I had fulfilled that calling within the context of the local church—and the television broadcast ministry. I was no longer the pastor of a church, so how and where was I to continue fulfilling God's calling for my life?*

It's too detailed a story to relate here, but I reconnected with the ALN owners who had visited me earlier in the year—even flew to South America to meet with them and discuss buying their network. It was a perfect fit. They had a functioning television network with programming in place, the values of which I was comfortable with. It was a perfect infrastructure around which to build a new network over time that would incorporate the Judeo-Christian values found in the Bible. Since I had television experience already, it was a perfect medium through which I could continue to encourage individuals and families and help shape the moral and spiritual culture of our nation.

But do you remember what was happening in the last quarter of 2008 and first quarter of 2009? The bottom had dropped out of America's economic bucket. This was not the time to buy anything—except things that were on sale . . . things like ALN. A team was formed—people like my own son-in-law, Chris Wyatt, the founder of GodTube.com. Technical people, financial people, legal people—all gave it a thumbs-up. Providing, of course, we could come up with the money.

God provided the money to buy ALN and turn it into Youtoo TV.[2] *It didn't fall out of the sky—a lot of hard work went into preparing and presenting the opportunity to investors who agreed that it was a worthwhile venture, financially and spiritually. Without God's permission and blessing, I don't think the money would have been raised. Again, money is never a problem for God. He can provide it or withhold it as He sees fit and knows is best.*

In this case, when I thought I was down to nothing but a dream and a possibility with no money, I realized God was up to something. He showed me, yet again, that He is always at work to accomplish His will. And if that will involves money, He is more than able to meet the need.

Money. Nothing has been talked about more in the last two years. Actually, I can't remember anything in my whole lifetime that is discussed more frequently than money. It's the oxygen of the material world; it's what makes life possible on a day-to-day basis. And our nation, and now the whole world, has been consumed with the subject for the last two years. Even when another crisis hits that seems to take precedence—like the oil-well disaster in the Gulf of Mexico in early 2010—the conversation quickly gets around to money: how much it's going to cost to clean up the mess, how much fishermen and Gulf Coast commercial interests are going to lose in lost revenue, how much British Petroleum is going to have to pay in reparations, the value of the oil that is escaping out of the well on the seafloor, how much money British Petroleum stockholders are losing as BP's stock declines in value day after day—and on and on. Almost everything in life that lasts more than a day or two—eating, living, going, re-creating, socializing—depends on money.

The numbers associated with the money that is being lost, created, spent, and loaned in the current economic crisis are so big that they defy comprehension. Hundreds, maybe thousands, we can understand—those are the amounts we deal with on a monthly basis, the numbers in our checking or savings accounts. Tens of thousands we understand since those numbers relate to our salary or the price of a new car. Move beyond a hundred thousand and we're into the bracket that is the largest most of us will ever deal with—the cost of our biggest lifetime purchase: a home. We can handle a million by thinking of it as a half-dozen houses, but beyond that we begin to lose touch.

We knew we had entered a new world of money sometime during the 1960s when Senator Everett Dirksen (supposedly[3]) said, "A billion here, a billion there, and pretty soon you're talking about real money." Now we're talking about trillions of dollars, the number used to measure the U.S.'s increasing indebtedness. The average person begins to tune out when the numbers get that big—especially when he or she has lost a job or has a medical emergency to pay for. If the president of the United States loses sleep over trillions, you and I lose sleep over much, much smaller amounts. And we wonder if God knows what His children need.

Our biggest challenge in these days is not to get caught up in the hysteria and anxiety about money in our nation or our world. This is the time to step back and remind ourselves of who we are, what we need, and what God has promised.

Who We Are

If you are part of God's family through faith in Christ, then you are God's child. And that is the first thing to reckon with when it comes to thinking about money. You are the spiritual child of a God who owns everything. Nobody has more money than God, not even Warren Buffett or Bill Gates. In fact, God owns all of their billions and the rest of the money in the world as well. We would do well to remember the words of King David when he prayed a prayer of thanksgiving to God for supplying (through the Israelites) the money to build a temple in Jerusalem:

"But who am I, and who are my people, that we should be able to give as generously as this? *Everything comes from you, and we have given you only what comes from your hand.* We are aliens and strangers in your sight, as were all our forefathers. Our days on earth are like a shadow, without hope. O LORD our God, as for all this abundance that we have provided for building you a temple for your Holy Name, *it comes from your hand, and all of it belongs to you.* I know, my God, that you test the heart and are pleased with integrity. All these things have I given willingly and with honest intent. And now I have seen with joy how willingly your people who are here have given to you." (1 Chronicles 29:14–18, italics added)

David understood that, even after God has given money into our hands, it still belongs to Him. Possession of money or material things never passes from Him to us. Rather, God puts money in our hands for us to use as stewards (managers)—someone who is trusted by and accountable to an owner to use the owner's resources in a manner consistent with his desires.

The idea of stewardship is found throughout the Bible. Joseph, while a slave in Egypt, earned the position of steward over the property of Potiphar, a high Egyptian official. The Bible says Potiphar never gave a second thought to his money or possessions. He entrusted the management of it all to Joseph (see Gen. 39:2–6). Jesus told a parable using an owner and three stewards as the main characters (see Matt. 25:14–30). And the apostle Paul called leaders in the church stewards whose main responsibility is to be found faithful (see 1 Cor. 4:1–2; Titus 1:7).

In one sense, every human being is a steward of the gift of life given to us by our Creator-God. But in a more specific sense, those who have a faith relationship with God have been given even more of which we are to be stewards: salvation, grace, spiritual gifts, the Word of God, and our material provisions. So, in many different ways—money is only one—we are stewards of the gifts and graces of God.

That means, when it comes to money, that our first thought is not, "What do I want from God?" but "What does God want from me?" We are *His* stewards, not vice versa. The answer to the question, of course, is that God wants faithfulness and fidelity to Him and His purposes. He wants the money He has entrusted to us to be used as He would use it Himself. And therein lies the heart of the purpose of money in our life: to cultivate an Owner-Steward relationship, a Father-Child relationship. For us to know God and His purposes requires that we not "take the money and run" but that we discover how He would have us use what He has given us.

What We Need

This is no doubt the most difficult subject when it comes to money—at least living in the American culture. The line between "wants" and "needs" has become so blurred, and our lifestyles so rich compared to the rest of the world, that we have given ourselves permission to ask God for things we don't really need. We need them only in the sense that we are used to having them and would feel deprived without them.

In no way am I suggesting we should feel guilty for possessing what God's gifts, His grace, and our labor has provided. We should just hold those things lightly and keep them in context. When we think about what we need to stay alive—which is how much of the world counts "needs"—it is a far shorter list than what we think we need to live, work, dress, or play in a manner to which we have grown accustomed.

If we use the apostle Paul's standards for "needs," it is a short list indeed: "But if we have food and clothing, we will be content with that" (1 Tim. 6:8). He didn't even mention a place to live! But let's assume that, rather than a list, Paul used "food and clothing" to mean "the basics"—food, clothes, and shelter; whatever the very basics are. How could Paul suggest that we should be able to live a contented life with just those basic needs? Because he wrote that guideline in the context of warning about the temptation of seeking after riches for riches' sake. In other words, it would be better to live with just the basics in life than to fall into the trap of thinking money and material prosperity was a secret to happiness. Here's what Paul warned:

> People who want to get rich fall into temptation and a trap and into many foolish and harmful desires that plunge men into ruin and destruction. For the *love* of money is a root of all kinds of evil. Some people, eager for money, have wandered from the faith and pierced themselves with many griefs. (1 Timothy 6:9–10)

Paul didn't condemn rich people for being rich, but he warned people who weren't rich not to yield to the temptation to get there in a way that violated their spiritual priorities. And he warned all of us to remember that the basics—what we need in life—are few.

What God Has Promised

The Bible says a lot about money, but not so much that it's possible to promise that God is going to answer every prayer for financial help. Rather than His promises building our bank account, they build our confidence in God's character. Here are a few promises the Bible makes about money:

1. God takes care of what He creates. In the Sermon on the Mount, Jesus reminds His listeners that God is actively

involved in caring for creation—even the birds of the air and the flowers of the field. And we are more important than any other part of creation. Therefore, we shouldn't "worry about tomorrow" (see Matt. 6:25–34).

2. God has already given us His best gift, a sign that He knows what we need and will supply (see Rom. 8:32). Paul says since God did not hesitate to give up His own Son to meet our greatest need (forgiveness and salvation), we can expect Him to provide for our lesser needs as well.

3. God has warned us ahead of time about serving two masters—God and money. Anyone who has a divided heart toward God is probably bordering on presumption when expecting God to be generous toward him or her (see Luke 16:13–14).

4. God responds generously to those who are generous. One of the most famous promises in the New Testament is Philippians 4:19: "And my God will meet all your needs according to his glorious riches in Christ Jesus." Read that way, it seems like a blank check, doesn't it? Not so. Paul wrote those words to Christian believers who had sacrificially given of their meager resources to meet Paul's needs while he was imprisoned in Rome. So Paul was expressing confidence that God would repay their generosity by meeting their material needs. The implication is not that we should give in order to get, but give generously in order to be like God. As someone has said, the easiest hand for God to fill is one that is empty as a result of giving to others.

5. God wants us to be dependent on Him, not enslaved to others. The Old Testament warns that borrowing makes us a slave to the lender (see Prov. 22:7), and Paul exhorts his readers to owe nothing except love (see Rom. 13:8). Far too many people were put in dire circumstances in the current economic recession as a result of excessive indebtedness. I cannot say that debt is wrong. I can only say that

God wants us to be free of worldly encumbrances that "so easily entangles" us (Heb. 12:1). If we violate biblical principles of wisdom, there are consequences.

6. God says we will reap as we sow—in general (see Gal. 6:7) and with regard to finances (see 2 Cor. 9:6). We should look at our financial condition and see if the way God has given to us reflects how we have given to others.

God is God, and we aren't. If He makes exceptions to the above principles, that is His prerogative. It's His money. But, as in most cases, exceptions prove the rule. God is orderly and gives us guidelines in all areas of life because He knows our lives will be better for following them.

How God Uses Money

One thing I have learned in my life is that money is not nearly as important to God as it is to us. It is one of many things that God uses to accomplish His highest goal for us—conforming us to the image of Jesus (see Rom. 8:29). And He will use "all things" (v. 28)—even financial pressure or hardships—to accomplish that goal.

In this difficult economic period in which I am writing, I do not want to make light of any person's financial difficulties. They are widespread and often severe. If your finances are limited, or exhausted, you are not down to nothing. If you are God's child, He knows exactly what you have and what you need. You have a God who wants to prove Himself faithful to you and help you grow through this season of your life. So commit yourself to Him. Tell Him your needs, trust He has heard you, then look for Him to do something to prove that you are not down to nothing as long as you have Him.

10

Living Old, Dying Young

(Health)

Dear friend, I pray that you may enjoy good health and that all may go well with you, even as your soul is getting along well.

3 John 2

My Story

I'll spare you most of the gory details of the decline in health I experienced between July '08 and October '09. Suffice it to say that I was under a lot of stress—a lot—and the effects were becoming increasingly obvious. In fact, had it not been for my chiropractor's ongoing adjustment of my cranial plates and adrenal glands during that period, I'm confident things would have gotten worse.[1] Indeed, when he adjusted my cranial plates on my birthday, October 7, 2009—yes, stress can seriously affect the skeleton, even the skull—they popped as loudly as someone cracking their knuckles! My chiropractor said, "That was a good one." And indeed it was—I haven't required a cranial adjustment since.

My health did not immediately change for the better after leaving the Crystal Cathedral, but the change began. As I transitioned from being a pastor to a businessman, the stress of 2008 began to ebb. There were new stresses, of course, but they were of a different kind. In 2009, I was working with people

who were pulling together as a team in a new, exciting venture.
I was still tired at night, but it was a good kind of tired.

Being out from under the stress of the previous four months
was like receiving a new lease on life. Whoever said, "When
you have your health, you have everything" didn't get it com-
pletely right—but almost. When we think we are down to noth-
ing, we're not. If we've been careful to preserve our health, then
we are physically and emotionally able to move forward with
God. Health is like a savings account. If we consistently make
deposits in that account, we are able to draw upon those reserves
when going through periods of stress when we are not making
new deposits. I'm convinced that, from a physical perspective,
that's what got me through a difficult period—the attention I
have consistently given to a healthy lifestyle in my adult years.
If we have our health, we are never down to nothing.

*N*ew York Times best-selling author Geneen Roth has gained and lost more than a thousand pounds since adolescence. She'd tried every diet on the planet, and many religions, had been addicted and anorexic, and had a closet full of eight different sizes of clothes. But she's been healthy, and at a healthy weight, for a couple decades now and writes books and leads seminars for women on how to get the "crazy" out of their relationship to food. And it's a good thing. Unless you've been away from the planet for the last five years, you are aware that food, and therefore health, has become a major issue in the world vis-à-vis the obesity epidemic. Her latest book on women and food has been flying off the shelves since being released in March 2010. In it she says (referring to retreats she leads),

The retreat is based on a philosophy I've developed over the past thirty years: that our relationship to food is an exact microcosm of our relationship to life itself. I believe we are walking, talking expressions of our deepest convictions; everything we believe about love, fear, transformation and God is revealed in how, when and what we eat. When we inhale Reese's peanut butter cups when we are not hungry, we are acting out an entire world of hope or hopelessness, of faith or doubt, of love or fear. If we are interested in finding out what we actually believe—not what we think, not what we say, but what our souls are convinced is the bottom-line truth about life and afterlife—we need to look no further than the food on our plates. God is not just in the details; God is also in the muffins, the fried sweet potatoes and the tomato vegetable soup. God—however we define him or her—is on our plates.[2]

To be fair to you and to Ms. Roth, she doesn't mean "God" the way we are talking about God in this book. She honestly states in her writings and seminars that she doesn't mean God in a religious sense but in a sense of mystery and possibility—a higher power as you define it. But when I read the above paragraph and use my understanding of who God is—the biblical God, the Father of our Lord Jesus Christ—it works perfectly with what I want to say in this chapter about health.[3] In fact, I'll quote Geneen Roth: "How we eat is how we live." I'll expand it this way (because this chapter is about health, not food): Our relationship with food and other "consumables" in life—and therefore the health that results from our choices—is a mirror of the way we live, a mirror of who we are and how we perceive ourselves. If we are not healthy in our body (again, with regard to lifestyle choices), it's an indication that we are not healthy in our souls.

Pertinent to the discussion of health is this verse from the book of Proverbs: "Like a fluttering sparrow or a darting swallow, an undeserved curse does not come to rest" (26:2). That verse uses Old Testament covenant language ("curse") to illustrate a broader biblical principle that works in God's creation and applies to many situations, including health: the principles of cause and effect. Don't jump to conclusions: I am not saying for a moment that ill health is a curse from God. Again, the idea in that verse reflects the language of "blessings and curses" from the Old Testament.

But I am saying this: Much of the ill health we experience has a cause and effect component. More than half of the top ten chronic diseases in America have a lifestyle component—diseases like heart disease, stroke, diabetes, hypertension, some cancers, and others. That means we are doing things in our life that contribute, to some degree or another, to our own ill health. Yes, there are health issues that appear to be idiopathic—without a readily discernible cause or source (like genetics or other unknown causes). To that extent, we can say that *all* disease, and all ill health, has a cause and effect component. It's just that we don't know what all the causes are.

This chapter is not about idiopathic ill health—the kind we don't know the causes of. I am not a doctor or a medical researcher and am neither licensed nor qualified to play the role of one. Rather, this chapter is about the relationship of health to the things (causes) we *can* touch in our life. Even though Geneen Roth and I view God differently, she beautifully speaks to the relationship between God and health when describing what happens when we are wounded in life (the italics are hers):

> But right here, right now, in the center of this wound— *I've been abandoned and betrayed by who and what really matters and what I've got left is food*—is where the link between food and God exists. It marks the moment when we gave up on ourselves, on change, on life. It marks the place where we are afraid. It marks the feelings we won't allow ourselves to feel, and in so doing, keeps our lives constricted and dry and stale. In that isolated place, it is a short step to the conclusion that God—where goodness

and healing and love exist—abandoned us, betrayed us or is a supernatural version of our parents.[4]

In the above quote, we could easily substitute drugs, alcohol, shopping, sex, anger, workaholism, or whatever "crazy" is for us, in the place of "food." We do all kinds of things to ourselves because we have come to the conclusion, consciously or subconsciously, that God isn't there, that love isn't there, that something isn't there when we are down to nothing. And that makes God and health a very important connection.

God and Health

Although there is evidence that the landscape is changing, looking around Christendom you would not readily conclude that God and health are connected. If we open the umbrella to say that "health" includes physical, emotional, and spiritual concerns, then yes, the church is involved in connecting God and health. But I'm not going to let us get away with that kind of "everything is connected to health" defense. Primarily, the church addresses spiritual issues. Next come sermons, seminars, and classes that would fit in the emotional health category—topics like depression, marriage, child rearing, spiritual disciplines like prayer and worship, and other issues.

But when it comes to physical health, Christians have lagged far behind as a whole. Some churches now offer classes for women featuring aerobic exercises or yoga-type stretching and strengthening. I have even seen references to a church staff position called "Pastor of Health"—a paid staff member in a large church who coordinated the church's efforts to promote health among its members. And why not? We have "Pastor of Visitation" slots— someone to visit members once their health is so bad they get to the hospital. Why not a pastor-leader to help them avoid the hospital altogether? As they say, preventing is much less expensive than curing.

It is heartening to see some activity in Christendom around the subject of physical health, but we have a long way to go. From my observations as a pastor who has traveled and met Christians all over the United States, I can safely say that Christians are not appreciably healthier than non-Christians. By and large, we eat the same way (processed, packaged, fast foods), get just as little exercise, appear to suffer from the same chronic diseases, are just as overweight, and end up in the same doctors' offices and hospitals as non-Christians.

Historically, Christians have been famous for how we eat. Potluck suppers and dinner on the grounds have become synonymous with fellowship—as have donuts and coffee. Church gymnasiums and snack areas are filled with vending machines dispensing sugar-laden and trans-fat-filled products that have little connection with food. They are more packaged collections of chemicals, colorings, and preservatives. And we offer those products at church because they are familiar. And they are familiar because they are part of our lifestyle. Yet we don't often stop to ask, "Is there any connection—even in the most general sense—between those vending machines, the lifestyle they represent, and the health of the church?"

Many, if not most, of the prayer requests mentioned in Sunday school classes or small groups are concerning someone's health. And many times when we pray, we pray without a lot of faith. At the worst, we are not exactly sure what to believe about God and health, and at best we are not sure how to integrate God into our life as Christians who want to be healthy. To an outsider, it would appear that our relationship with God—the abundant life—doesn't apply to abundant health.

But here's how I believe it applies, in one word: stewardship. I believe we should add health to the list of things of which we are stewards in God's sight. When churches have stewardship campaigns, they are almost always about raising money. Or a "stewardship series" of messages from the pulpit is almost always about how to manage our money.

But is money all we are stewards of? Not at all. We are stewards of everything that comes from God (which is everything!): our time, our gifts and abilities, our relationships, the children God entrusts to us as parents, the gospel, the creation over which we were appointed caretakers in Eden—everything! And we are responsible for our health—physically, emotionally, and spiritually. We assume that Adam and Eve were not created with chronic diseases, so we rightly assume that their health was a gift from God to be cared for. He even prescribed a diet for them to eat and put them in a Garden where all their needs would be met (see Gen. 1:29). To include health as one of our biblical stewardship responsibilities seems clear to me. Jesus' famous Parable of the Talents (Matt. 25:14–30) was about managing money faithfully, but that certainly doesn't mean that money is our only area of responsibility as stewards.

I coauthored my own book on "God's Health Plan" over a decade ago.[5] But that doesn't mean I have stopped learning. Like God Himself, health in all its dimensions is an endless subject that touches our life in innumerable ways. I don't have all the answers to every health question, but I do have the answer to this one: How important should the study and pursuit of excellent health be in the life of every Christian? Hopefully, since you've read this far you already know my answer.

You and God and Health

Given the dominant role that health and health care play in our economy, the amount of information available to the public on this subject is staggering. It's hard to know where to begin. (I Googled "health" and got 1.24 billion hits. I rest my case.)

It is certainly not my goal in one chapter to convey what I, and many others, have written complete books about. Rather, my goal is to challenge you to include your personal health in the stewardship category of your life; to see it as something you are responsible before God to pursue and to maximize. The healthier you and I are, the happier we will be. The happier we are, the more productive we will be for the benefit of ourselves and our family. And the more healthy, happy, and productive we are in life, the more God is glorified.

Think of how a leader is viewed by others when they look upon the leaders' followers. If the followers are sickly, unhappy, and fruitless, one cannot help but wonder about the leader's concern or ability to care for them. But if the followers are robust, joyful, and fruitful, the leader is viewed entirely differently. Others who need help in their life will be attracted to the leader if they see his followers are well cared for. I'm obviously referring to how others view God based on the character and condition of God's followers.

This principle is illustrated in both the Old and New Testaments. In Zechariah 8:23, the prophet envisions a situation when the Jewish Messiah is reigning with righteousness from Jerusalem: "This is what the LORD Almighty says, 'In those days ten men from all languages and nations will take firm hold of one Jew by the hem of his robe and say, "Let us go with you, because we have heard that God is with you."'" When word gets out about the blessings the Messiah is bestowing on His people, others from all over the world will want to make their way to the throne of the Messiah so they too can participate in the blessings.

In the New Testament, Jesus told His disciples, "By this all men will know that you are my disciples, if you love one another" (John 13:35). Because it is not normal for people to love one another with sacrificial, unconditional love, when Jesus' disciples do that, it will stand out by contrast. People will say, "Look how they love one another!" They will wonder how, and why, such love is possible—and want to know the One who is the source of that love.

I believe the same impact hangs in the balance when it comes to our health. If the world looks at the Christian church and sees us to be no more healthy, happy, or fruitful than they themselves are, what motivation do they have for wanting to know our God? I realize that forgiveness of sin and inheriting eternal life are always the primary motivations for knowing God, but is that the only impact God wants to have on our life? It was Jesus himself who said, "The thief comes only to steal and kill and destroy; I have come that they may have life, and have it to the full" (John 10:10). The devil wants us to be unhappy, unhealthy, and fruitless, but Jesus wants us to live abundantly in every dimension of life.

The verse I quoted at the beginning of this chapter says it all. The apostle John wrote to those for whom he had spiritual oversight, "Dear friend, I pray that you may enjoy good health and that all may go well with you, even as your soul is getting along well" (3 John 2). "Good health"—physically, spiritually, emotionally— is what mankind was created to experience. Yes, it is a struggle to maintain good health in all those dimensions in the fallen world we live in. But it is our obligation not to let the discouragements and challenges of life keep us from pursuing the best.

If you are suffering from ill health today, do not read these words as a condemnation. All of us, like the countless cells in the human body, are in various stages of health, working to contribute good health to the body of Christ as a whole. If you are weak in any dimension of your life, take heart! Where there are causes you can impact to remedy their effects, purpose to do so. Where the causes are unknown, identify with the apostle Paul who was given grace and strength to triumph through his weaknesses (see 2 Cor. 12:7–10). God uses everything—strength and weakness—to display His love in our lives.

When we get down to nothing in other areas of life—job, money, relationships—if we have our health we have all God needs to get us on a new path. And because He is always up to something good in our lives, being on that path with Him is all we need.

11

The Mythical Get-Out-of-Pain-Free Card

(Suffering)

But he said to me, "My grace is sufficient for you, for my power is made perfect in weakness." Therefore I will boast all the more gladly about my weaknesses, so that Christ's power may rest on me.

2 Corinthians 12:9

My Story

When I experienced rejection at the Crystal Cathedral—the story I have related in this book—it was painful. But in every case, suffering has led to a greater experience of the depth of God's love and grace.

And I have to ask myself: Would I know as much of God's love and grace today if I had not suffered in the past? The answer is clearly no. Just like Job in the Old Testament, everyone who suffers—everyone who suffers in the context of a relationship with God, that is—has a clearer, deeper, wiser understanding of God after the suffering than before. The challenge is to remember that while going through the fire.

Is there anyone who knows God who would not want to know Him better? I have never met anyone who falls into that category, and it certainly doesn't include me. At this stage of my life, therefore, I have built into my spiritual worldview the fact that suffering is inevitable in this life. Some will suffer more than others—I can't explain that difference. But I do know that God's goal for my life is for Him and me to have a deep, abiding relationship with one another. And if suffering is something that can deepen that relationship, then so be it. I believe suffering falls into the "all things" that God causes to work together for good in the life of those who love Him (see Rom. 8:28). Therefore, suffering is a good thing.

Suffering is not meaningless, nor does its value end when the pain subsides. Indeed, the value of suffering continues in the postpain mode when our head is clear enough to reflect on God's faithfulness. God is going to use every season of suffering for good in my life, and in yours, to accomplish His purposes.

It's easy to feel like we're down to nothing when pain is all we can feel. When I felt like that in 2008, I had to continually remind myself that God was up to something good, that He was right there in the middle of the pain with me. He wants you to know that He is in the middle of your pain as well.

I was never a member of the military at any level, so I never went through "Basic"—the weeks-long regimen that every new recruit goes through. But I have heard it said that there's one phrase that allows new recruits to maintain their sanity in the midst of the mud, the pain, the cold, the being-yelled-at, and the lack of sleep: "You can do anything for six weeks." In other words, basic training is not the military—it is training *for* the military. And while an average day in the military, especially in combat zones, can be challenging, it is not usually as painful as basic training. (Unless you factor in the significant detail that you're being shot at with real bullets instead of with blanks.)

As painful as every branch's basic training is for new recruits, it is nothing like the additional training required for those in the services' elite squadrons: Navy SEALs, Army Rangers, Special Forces, Delta Force, and probably others secret to the public. Most people could not even qualify to enter the training for those units, much less endure the training after it started. Many drop out along the way because the suffering is too intense.

Take the Navy SEALs' Hell Week, for example: five straight days and nights of training except for four hours allowed for sleep. That's four hours for the entire five days, not four hours every day. Except for breaks for meals, and the four hours for sleep, the SEAL trainees are constantly moving, or should I say, constantly suffering. But there is a method to the madness. The SEAL trainers know that these soldiers are going to find themselves in the hardest, most pressure-packed combat situations in the world. They have to be able to function—especially to obey orders—even when their pain and fear levels are skyrocketing.

For much of the time during Hell Week, the SEAL trainees are in small teams. Most of the time—in the surf, sand, mud, or mountains—they have to carry a huge, three-hundred-pound log on their shoulders along with their other bulky gear. Occasionally, when the trainees are thoroughly convinced that this log has become part of their bodies, a trainer will give the team a set of instructions for a new challenge, but *purposefully omit any requirement to carry the log.* If the team leader is sharp enough in the midst of his mental fog and the confusion of the moment to catch the omission and move out without the log, the team is rewarded with a few minutes of rest. In other words, the goal is to see who's listening, who's alert, who's obeying orders—and who's not. In combat, alertness in spite of suffering can be the difference between life and death.

Suffering has the potential to do two things: dull our senses or heighten our senses. The combat metaphor is not used lightly if we take the Scriptures seriously—there is a spiritual battle going on all around us. And with any war, suffering is inevitable. All the more reason for us to stay alert, to keep our senses tuned, that we might hear from God, our spiritual Commander in Chief, with instructions on how to navigate the trouble we are in.

Just as lions on the Serengeti plains have learned to patiently watch the herds during the migration season to find those who are struggling or immature, so "your enemy the devil prowls around like a roaring lion looking for someone to devour." Peter's advice: "Be self-controlled and alert" (1 Peter 5:8). When we are experiencing pain and trouble, we are often lulled into a hopeless, "down-to-nothing" state of mind. And that makes us more vulnerable to the enemy of our soul who is "looking for someone" like us to devour.

What are we to look for? Not the presence of Satan, but the presence of God and His purpose in our suffering. He wants to craft a life message that the entire world can see and read, and part of that story will be written during periods of pain if we will be "clay in the potter's hand" and allow the next chapter to unfold.

Reasons We Suffer

The Bible is filled with examples of people who suffered for various reasons. But many people in our culture today have apparently not suffered much at all based on the following list. According to the Free Methodist *Light and Life* magazine, the following suggestions were turned in to the staff at the Bridger Wilderness Area (Wyoming) in 1996. Some people have a fairly narrow view of what true hardship is all about:

- Trails need to be wider so people can walk while holding hands.
- Trails need to be reconstructed. Please avoid building trails that go uphill.
- Too many bugs and leeches and spiders and spiderwebs. Please spray the wilderness to rid the areas of these pests.

- Please pave the trails so they can be snowplowed during the winter.
- Chairlifts need to be in some places so that we can get to wonderful views without having to hike to them.
- The coyotes made too much noise last night and kept me awake. Please eradicate these annoying animals.
- A small deer came into my camp and stole my jar of pickles. Is there a way I can get reimbursed? Please call...
- Reflectors need to be placed on trees every fifty feet so people can hike at night with flashlights.
- Escalators would help on steep hill sections.
- A McDonald's would be nice at the trailhead.
- The places where trails do not exist are not well-marked.
- Too many rocks in the mountains.[1]

Those hardships are not the kind we find in Scripture, nor the kind that most people have endured in their lives. In the broadest terms, we find at least three categories of suffering in the Bible.

First, people suffered for their faith. This is the most common kind of suffering described in the New Testament epistles. Christianity was spreading and churches were growing and Christians found themselves persecuted by others who saw their interests threatened by the rise of this new "religion." The apostles wrote often to the churches to encourage them in the midst of their hardships. The apostle Peter, writing to Christians scattered throughout Asia Minor, dedicated much of his first epistle to the subject of suffering for one's faith (see 1 Peter 1:6–7; 2:19–21, 23; 3:14, 17; 4:1, 12, 15–16, 19; 5:10). He gives explicit explanations for why they were suffering:

In this you greatly rejoice, though now for a little while you may have had to suffer grief in all kinds of trials. These have come so that your faith—of greater worth than gold, which perishes even though refined by fire—

may be proved genuine and may result in praise, glory and honor when Jesus Christ is revealed. (1 Peter 1:6–7)

In short, the proof of faith is found in the testing of faith. While there are many Christians in the world today who suffer for their faith, few in the American culture have—at least to the point of "shedding your blood" as the writer to the Hebrews says (Heb. 12:4). That day may come, but it is not the suffering that most experience today in America.

A second kind of suffering comes as a result of sin. This understanding came from the Old Testament covenant relationship between God and Israel. If Israel walked in God's ways, she would be blessed. If she rebelled against God, the blessings would be withheld and hardship would result (see Deut. 28)—even to "the third and fourth generation" (Exod. 20:5). It was this understanding that caused Jesus' disciples to ask about a man born blind, "Rabbi, who sinned, this man or his parents, that he was born blind?" (John 9:2). In this case, Jesus said, "Neither..."—but the disciples' question revealed the understanding of the Jews of that day.

But the New Testament does not discount the possibility of sin resulting in suffering in the life of a Christian. When Paul chastised the Christians at Corinth for their carnal abuse of the Lord's Supper (Communion) in the church, he said they should judge themselves and correct their attitudes and behavior lest God judge them himself. Paul connected the suffering of some in the church to their failure to examine and correct themselves: "That is why many among you are weak and sick, and a number of you have fallen asleep" (1 Cor. 11:30). Paul said that "many" Christians in that church were sick, and some had even died, as a result of their sin.

How common is that in our churches today? I don't know. There are certainly many Christians today who are sick—and Christians die every day. But it is beyond me to say that such illnesses or death are the result of sin. But I would say, given the precedent established in the New Testament, that they could be. The Christian's challenge is not to focus on the sickness or death, but on Paul's exhortation to godly living—not to live a carnal or sinful life that could invite hardship. Even though such suffering is a possibility, it is still not the kind of suffering with which most people readily identify today.

That leaves the third kind of suffering: the pain of living in a pain-full world. Every person on earth is subject to this kind of pain: Christian or not, holy or not, careful or not. There is no more clear evidence of the transition our world made from painless to painful than in Genesis 3. Before Adam and Eve disobeyed God, life in the Garden of Eden was painless. They had everything they needed, including fellowship with God Himself. But after their sin, pain entered their (and our) world: Eve would experience the pain of childbirth (see Gen. 3:16) and Adam the pain (toil) of eking out a living from the dust of the earth (vv. 17–19). The apostle Paul says that the "whole creation" groans to be free of the curse that was levied in Eden due to sin—free of the pain of living in a painful world (see Rom. 8:22–23).

This suffering comes in the forms that you and I know all too well: natural disasters, the crumbling of relationships and marriages, innocents who suffer due to the actions of others, freak accidents, unexplained illnesses, birth defects, mental and emotional breakdowns, wars, economic and financial hardships, hunger—and the list goes on. We live in a broken world, which means that we suffer the pain of this world's malfunctions. Just as the sun and the rains come to give life to all, so the world's short circuits find everyone at some point in their life.

Many people blame God, or at least criticize Him, for the fact that so many suffer, especially those who suffer innocently. "Either God is not powerful enough to fix the world and do away with suffering, or He's not loving enough. Either He is powerful enough and He doesn't care, or He cares but He's not powerful enough."

This is a classic argument against the existence of God that seems logical enough, but it completely ignores the biblical story. The Bible clearly explains how the world came to be as it is and how and when the world's dysfunctional state will be remedied—and how we are to live in the interim.

Since suffering in this life is a given—at least the third kind is—our focus should be on responding to suffering while doing everything we can to limit its reach in our lives and the lives of others—especially those who suffer innocently.

Responses to Suffering

If a Christian has some sense from God that his or her suffering is due to sin, the obvious remedy is to stop sinning! But in the other two cases—suffering for one's faith or suffering by virtue of living in this world—the response is the same: receive strength and grace from God so that, whether in strength or weakness, joy or pain, our life becomes a testament of faith in His good and perfect plan for our life.

When Jesus' disciples asked Him about the man who was born blind and Jesus said it was neither the man's or his parents' sins that caused the blindness, He said more: "Neither this man nor his parents sinned, . . . but this happened so that the work of God might be displayed in his life" (John 9:3). And what was the work of God? It was for Jesus to heal the man of his blindness, to reveal the power and compassion of God for one who was injured by being a resident of a painful world. And that's what Jesus did. Then the man gave clear and compelling testimony to God's goodness in his life when the religious leaders tried to detract from the great event by calling Jesus a sinner: "[The man] replied, 'Whether [Jesus] is a sinner or not, I don't know. One thing I do know. I was blind but now I see!'" (v. 25).

What does this mean for us? Three things: First, it seems *not* to mean that God's work is always to heal *all* those who are sick.

Sometimes Jesus healed *en masse* (see Matt. 4:24), other times he healed only an individual among many who were sick (as the lame man at the Pool of Bethesda; see John 5:1–11). That choice is up to God.

Second, it means that removing pain is not the only way glory is brought to God through our suffering. The apostle Paul is a good example. He suffered for a reason he did not explain, asking God three times to remove the source of his suffering. God's answer to Paul was no. Instead of taking suffering away from Paul, God gave him grace to endure it: "My grace is sufficient for you, for my power is made perfect in weakness" (2 Cor. 12:9). That decision resulted in glory to God as it gave Paul the opportunity to display Christ's power in his life.

We should take no small comfort in the fact that the great apostle Paul's first request (first three requests!) was not for grace to endure his pain but for the pain to be removed. Paul was human; we are human. No one likes to experience pain. But if God has a reason for the pain to remain for a season, or even permanently, that becomes a priority. God giving grace to endure pain and suffering likely brings more glory to God in the long term than if the pain is instantaneously removed. And that becomes a critical variable in the mix.

The founder of the Methodist branch of Christianity, John Wesley (1703–1791) had a perspective about his life in this world that encompassed everything—including suffering:

I am no longer my own, but thine.
Put me to what thou wilt, rank me with whom thou wilt.
Put me to doing, put me to suffering.
Let me be employed for thee or laid aside for thee,
Exalted for thee or brought low for thee.
Let me be full, let me be empty.
Let me have all things, let me have nothing.
I freely and heartily yield all things to thy pleasure and disposal.

And now, O glorious and blessed God, Father, Son and Holy Spirit,
Thou art mine, and I am thine.
So be it.
And the covenant, which I have made on earth,
Let it be ratified in heaven. Amen.[2]

Wesley's total surrender to God's will is amazing. How many
of us would say to God, "Put me to doing [or] put me to suffering"
without even clarifying, "Uh, Lord, I would definitely choose
doing over suffering if it's all the same to You." Wesley didn't care.
Either was fine with him—whatever pleased God and would result
in the most glory to His name.

Finally, it means that God's heart is one of compassion. The
argument of the critics—"God is either not loving enough or not
powerful enough to do away with suffering"—is answered in the
life of the man Jesus healed. God is both loving and powerful. He
is perfectly able to remove our suffering or use it to accomplish
something more important in our life and in this world.

If you are living with pain and it's nothing you can fix on your
own, consider imitating John Wesley's perspective—putting your
life in God's hands for His "pleasure and disposal." Pain and suffering can definitely be a down-to-nothing experience. But you
always have the work of God that He is doing in the midst of your
pain. Just as God walked with the three Hebrew men in Babylon's
fiery furnace (see Dan. 3:25), so He is with you in the furnace of
your affliction. And wherever God is, He is always up to
something.

PART III

WHAT GOD IS UP TO IN YOUR EMOTIONAL LIFE

Because we are emotional, passionate people, we think often about
Courage and Fear
Hope and Despair
Purpose and Confusion
Joy and Sadness
Forgiveness and Vengeance
And God is always providing ways to keep us emotionally strong.
Chapter 12 presents God as our ultimate source of security.
Chapter 13 helps us prepare for life's inevitable disappointments.
Chapter 14 proves that ultimate freedom is freedom from guilt.
Chapter 15 talks about joy as an ever-present possibility.
Chapter 16 shows why peace is the best kind of rest.

Nothing to Be Afraid Of

(Security)

For God did not give us a spirit of timidity, but a spirit of power, of love and of self-discipline.

2 Timothy 1:7

My Story

I held two positions related to the Crystal Cathedral and the Hour of Power broadcast. Those in charge of the Hour of Power stopped airing my sermons on the broadcast (sending a strong message about my future participation), and I ultimately resigned from being senior pastor of the church when they wouldn't allow me to preach on Sunday mornings. I repeat that detail here in order to make this point: being downsized, demoted, fired—call it what you will—can be intimidating. I used that word to mean it can make us doubt ourselves, make us feel less capable than before.

I had never been demoted from a position before, so didn't know quite what to expect in terms of my response to the experience. Even if you are in a position at or near the top of the organizational chart, there is still someone over you—in my case, the legal board of directors of the television ministry. Whether they are older or wiser is not the determinant when it comes to intimidation. Rather, it's their authority that matters. Even if we are stopped for a traffic violation by a policeman half our age, his uniform, badge, and gun spell a-u-t-h-o-r-i-t-y, and we automatically assume a defensive, intimidated posture.

When I was released from my hosting duties on the world-wide Hour of Power broadcast, I immediately began to doubt myself—which I shouldn't have done. We were receiving as many as 1,800 viewer communications a week in support of my remaining on the broadcast. As much as I appreciated that support, those in authority over me had found me no longer suitable for the job. What part of me did they not like? What had I done wrong? I did not dwell extensively on those questions, but they certainly crossed my mind. It's only natural for the "performance" part of our human nature to feel defensive and intimidated when someone says we have performed poorly.

Feeling intimidated by those who demoted me (they were members of my own immediate and extended family) represented an engraved invitation to timidity's cousin—fear—to make an entrance. As soon as we feel intimidated, we immediately grow fearful of the future. I feared losing everything I thought I had gained through years of (what I thought was) faithful service: reputation, responsibility, income, potential for future employment, and all the rest. After all, who would be interested in my services in the future? There are only two ways to approach the future: with faith or fear. And because faith does not come naturally, fear is our fallback position, our default when the Reset Button is hit on our life.

Fortunately, I did not remain intimidated by what had happened, or fearful of the future, for very long. But neither will I say I didn't experience both, because I did. I have been a Christian long enough to recognize natural attitudes when they enter my heart and know not to let them fester. But fear and intimidation are very real, very human responses to life's challenging moments. They didn't immobilize me, but they gave me pause.

When I thought I was down to nothing as a result of others
saying, "You don't measure up," I was given a gift from God: the
opportunity to remember that timidity and fear are not from God

W hen coalition forces invaded Iraq in the Gulf War of 1991 (because Iraq had invaded Kuwait), Iraq retaliated the next day by launching eight Scud missiles against Israel—and continued the missile attacks throughout the six weeks of the war. While there were a number of deaths in Israel associated with the missile attacks, postwar research showed the majority of the deaths were not directly related to missile explosions. The majority of deaths were due to heart failure brought on by fear, stress, and insecurity. It wasn't being hit by a missile carrying an explosive, biological, or chemical warhead that killed most people—it was the *thought* of it happening.

Because the suspicion of biological and chemical weapons in Iraq was a premise for the invasion by coalition forces, Israeli officials had prepared citizens for the possibility of such attacks. Israelis received gas masks and atropine syringes and were instructed to create a sealed room in their homes. The anticipation of being attacked by biological or chemical agents and dying a slow, agonizing death was sky-high when the missiles landed.

When the first missile attack proved to be less dramatic than anticipated, levels of stress declined significantly. (The United States and the Netherlands furnished antimissile systems to help defend Israel against the attacks.) As people's fear and anxiety subsided, mortality rates declined as well until they quickly fell back to nonwar levels. Though there were seventeen more attacks after the first one, mortality rates never rose above normal, nonwar rates. The missiles themselves killed very few people. Fear of the missiles killed many more.[1]

Fear, timidity, and intimidation are powerful agents against healthy living. They can immobilize, paralyze, and jeopardize what might otherwise be a productive life. While fear can be useful as a protective response—fear of getting hurt keeps us from doing foolish things—it plays far too large a role in most people's lives.

Where Fear Didn't Come From

The verse I quoted at the beginning of this chapter—2 Timothy 1:7—is often quoted among Christians as a way to say that we should not be fearful in general: "For God did not give us a spirit of timidity [fear]..." But we need to step back and see if that's what the apostle Paul meant when he wrote these words to his young pastoral protégé, Timothy.

The Greek word *deilia* can be translated as fear, cowardice, or timidity (or intimidation). The context of its use dictates the English word we should use to translate it. "Fear" works as an umbrella term—some modern translations of the Bible use "fear" in 2 Timothy 1:7. Others use "timidity" based on the context— and I tend to think this is a better choice. It all has to do with who Timothy was, what he was called to do, and what Paul was communicating to him when he wrote.

Timothy was a young man compared to Paul, recruited by the apostle to join him and Silas on Paul's second missionary journey (see Acts 16:1–5). In spite of his youth, Timothy was greatly esteemed by the apostle who mentioned him in his letters more often than any other worker (see Phil. 2:19–22). So valuable and faithful was Timothy that, years later, Paul assigned him the task of being his apostolic representative to the church at Ephesus (see 1 Tim. 1:3). The two letters Paul wrote to Timothy (1 and 2 Timothy) are Paul's instructions to Timothy on how to build up the church at Ephesus and safeguard its purity from those who would seek to tear it down or use it for their own advantage. Part of Timothy's responsibilities was to teach sound doctrine and refute false teachers, oversee the orderly life of the church, and appoint leaders (elders and deacons).

That was a lot to pile on the plate of a young man—especially when it came to refuting false teachers and taking a stand on matters of doctrinal purity against those who might have established themselves as authorities in the church at Ephesus. (There's that word "authority" again—remember it from my opening story, the role it plays in intimidation and fear?) When we get to the opening of Paul's second letter to Timothy—where the verse about "fear" occurs—there is evidence that Timothy was manifesting a degree of timidity/intimidation/fear (choose your word) that was going to undermine his role as Paul's apostolic representative.

It helps to read 2 Timothy 1:6–12 together to get the context for understanding verse 7:

> verse 6: Timothy needs to stir up his spiritual gift of leadership; for some reason (fear? intimidation?) the fire of his gift was almost extinguished.
>
> verse 7: A reminder: God gives us power, love, and self-control. You have no reason to be fearful or intimidated in the presence of those older and more established.
>
> verses 8–10: Don't be ashamed or intimidated to represent Christ. He is the one who has called you to your ministry.
>
> verses 11–12: I also suffer in my ministry, but I suffer for Christ to whom I have entrusted my life. I am not ashamed to represent Him in any setting to which He calls me.

So, from that context, I conclude that Timothy was being talked down to by some at Ephesus who had established themselves as spiritual authorities in the church, but who were teaching falsely and leading people astray. So Paul writes his young representative and urges him, "Don't be intimidated by them! Don't be timid or fearful! Fulfill God's calling for your life with the power, love, and self-control God has given you. The timidity and intimidation and fear you are feeling is not from Him!"

In these words we probably find the difference between Paul's and Timothy's personalities. We see in the New Testament that the apostle Paul was intimidated by no one. Even before he became a Christian, he was a bold, Type-A personality who would not be refused. Timothy, on the other hand, was likely not as strong as Paul from a personality perspective and needed to be reminded to rely on God's supernatural power when he began to feel timid or fearful.

Just like the Israelis who suffered heart attacks and died because of being fearful of the threat of Iraqi biological and chemical missile attacks, so the thought of being confronted, accosted, put down, humiliated, embarrassed, or accused can give us a spiritual heart attack (if not a physical one). Fear and intimidation are not from God—especially when we are doing what God has called us to do, as Timothy was.

That's the primary application of 2 Timothy 1:7: Don't be made to feel intimidated or fearful when you are walking in God's will and others accuse you of not doing so. Listen to them? Of course. Consider what they have to say? Absolutely. But if you have to agree to disagree, then you may have to part ways (just as Paul and his dear friend Barnabas did over an issue in Acts 15:36–41). But you walk away in submission to God, not in fear of man. "For God did not give us a spirit of timidity . . ."

Where Fear Came From

It is so important in life to understand our gifting and calling from God. For that understanding becomes our defense against fear and intimidation. That's easy to see from the story where fear and timidity first surface in the human experience.

Adam and Eve were called by God to have dominion over the earth—the creation and all its creatures (see Gen. 1:28). That was their calling, their task, their assignment. And within that domain, they had authority. They were in charge in the Garden of Eden. They had been put there by God as His representatives, bearing His image, to be His "managers" of all creation. They had no reason to fear anything or anyone. In the words of 2 Timothy 1:7, they had power (authority), love (a loving relationship with God and each other), and self-discipline (the ability to choose the right things to do—like not eating of the "tree of the knowledge of good and evil" [Gen. 2:17]—in exercising their calling of dominion over earth). What was there to fear?

But you know the story: Satan, God's antagonist, entered the Garden and challenged God's instructions, tempting Adam and Eve to disobey God and eat from the prohibited tree—which they did. As soon as they disobeyed God, their eyes were opened to the reality of evil, and everything changed. There was something new in the Garden: fear.

The next time God visited the Garden of Eden, Adam and Eve "hid from the LORD God among the trees of the garden" (Gen. 3:8). They were fearful—intimidated—by their own sinfulness in the presence of a holy God. So they hid from Him. They had no more power, fear had replaced love, and their self-discipline had been compromised. That's what happens when fear comes into our lives.

As the God-appointed authority in the Garden of Eden, Adam had the authority to resist Satan's temptations, even kick him out of the Garden. Adam was in charge. The Garden was his domain; he had no reason to yield his authority to Satan. But he did and exchanged power, love, and self-discipline for fear and intimidation. That's what Paul meant when he told Timothy that "God did not give us a spirit of timidity." In other words, fear and intimidation are not from God. Those are things we allow ourselves to get sucked into, just like Adam and Eve got sucked into disobeying God. As long as we are doing what God has called us to do—power, love, self-discipline—we have no reason to fear or be intimidated.

Back to Timothy for a moment: Timothy was the authority in the church at Ephesus just like Adam and Eve were the authorities in the Garden of Eden. It was Timothy's job, as the representative of the apostle Paul, to exercise apostolic authority in Paul's place with love and self-discipline. But he was wavering, just like Adam wavered. So Paul wrote him to say, "Stand firm! Don't be fearful or intimidated! You are exactly where you are supposed to be, doing what you are supposed to do."

Refusing Fear

I opened this chapter with my own confession of feelings of fear and intimidation upon being demoted from my previous position, and I need to clarify something: Even though we may feel that we are right where God wants us, as I did, that doesn't mean we should "stand firm" and refuse to submit to the authority of those over us when it comes to decisions that affect our life. When I accepted the position from which I eventually resigned, I did so in submission to the authority of those who extended the invitation. When they decided to rescind the invitation a few years later, it would have been inappropriate for me to refuse to leave and create a scene that would have brought reproach upon the name of Christ. So I left.

But here's the point I'm making: It would have been wrong for me to have left under a cloud of fear or intimidation as if I had done something wrong. Instead, it became my purpose to continue to exercise "power, love, and self-discipline" in the midst of a negative experience that had the potential to reflect poorly on me. I believed then, and continue to believe today, that God's calling is alive and well in my life and that I have nothing to fear about the future. God makes the assignments in my life, not man. And if He allows me to be moved from one place of service to another in His kingdom, I am fine with that. And so should you be if the same thing happens in your life.

When things happen in our lives that tempt us to think poorly of ourselves—we are fired from a job, divorced by a spouse, estranged from a friend, criticized by ourselves over a personal failure—we have to do two things:

1. Examine ourselves (see 1 Cor. 11:31). We have to make sure we have not created a reason for fear and intimidation to come in—like Adam did. If we have, we must make

things right and reestablish our moral and spiritual authority out of which love and self-discipline flow. We cannot
live with a compromised conscience and expect to have
power, love, and self-discipline.

2. Refuse fear (see 2 Tim. 1:7). If you are standing in moral
and spiritual authority before God, you have no reason to
fear or be intimidated by anyone. If God changes your place
in life, so be it. You can accept that change with the full confidence that it is God's doing, not man's. And you can know
that God is up to something new and good in your life.

There was a commercial on television a few years back that
showed a young girl standing in a beautiful meadow. The camera
panned across to another part of the field where stood a giant African rhinoceros. Suddenly the rhino began to race straight for the
little girl who remained unmoved, as calm and serene as before. As
the rhinoceros got closer to the little girl, these words appeared
on the screen: "Trust is not being afraid..." At the very last
moment, the rhinoceros stopped its charge and the little girl reached
out and petted the massive animal on its horn. The last words then
appeared on the screen: "...even when you are vulnerable."

It is impossible to live a life untouched by fear. There will continue to be situations in which we are tempted to yield our power,
love, and self-discipline to people or forces that would take it away.
But that doesn't mean we have to yield and live a fearful, intimidated life. Living a fearless life doesn't mean living untouched by
fear. It means trusting in God even in the moments when we are
most vulnerable.

If you have lost your power, love, and self-discipline lately and
have exchanged it for a spirit of fear or intimidation, fear not—you
are not down to nothing. You have the call of God on your life.
You have what God wants to do through you. And you have the
gift of God given to you if you will fan it back into flame. When
you do, you'll discover that God is up to something in your life.

13

What Goes Up Must Come Down

(Disappointment)

And hope does not disappoint us, because God has poured out his love into our hearts by the Holy Spirit, whom he has given us.

Romans 5:5

My Story

Baseball players position themselves beneath high fly balls because they know that what goes up must come down.

Stock traders position themselves to trade against a rising market because they know that what goes up must come down.

And the wise among us will position ourselves in life to not be crushed by the falling circumstances in which we previously trusted—because we know that what comes up must come down.

Not everything comes down of course. God's love, the loyalty of a spouse or friend—those and a few other of life's experiences rarely disappoint. But for the most part, life can be counted on to hand out a fair share of disappointments. And we need to be ready for them.

I confess to not expecting to be disappointed in my experience at the Crystal Cathedral. And whatever disappointment I felt, I chalk up to my own naiveté and unrealistic approach. As the saying goes, "If things seem too good to be true, they probably are." (Again, heavenly realities excepted—they are as good as promised.) And things seemed wonderful for two years. I was working among people I loved (and still do love), doing the work I was called to do. It never crossed my mind, given how the opportunity developed over a long period of preparation, that I wasn't in my "last" ministry. I thought I was there for life and was very happy with that expectation.

One of the main things I learned as I evaluated my disappointment in having to leave the Crystal Cathedral was being careful about the object of my disappointment. For starters, I was not disappointed with God. I have known Him long enough to know that God is always good and faithful and purposeful. I know that His reasons are above reproach. I have never found myself questioning God's reasons for anything that might touch His character.

It was much easier to be disappointed in people—those whose decisions impacted my life. But in hindsight, I've had to guard against making them the easy object of my disappointment. What did I think of them—that they were perfect, that they would never do anything with which I might disagree? If so, such an expectation or opinion was of my own doing, not theirs. I know they were doing what they thought was best, that they were not out to intentionally harm me. So I gradually looked for other objects.

And I found the only one that is reasonable: I was disappointed in life. I have learned from Eliphaz in the Old Testament that "man is born to trouble as surely as sparks fly upward" (Job 5:7). Disappointment is the stuff of life, and it is no sin to be disappointed when things don't work out. But I have also learned that even when life's blessings fly away like sparks from a fire, they come back down in new and different blessings. Which means that we are never down to nothing.

The English mathematician Sir Isaac Newton said it much more scientifically in 1687 in *Principia*, but gravity is basically the force that gives weight to objects. It's easy for us nonscientists to say, "The apple falls to the ground from the tree because it weighs five ounces." Okay, but *why* does it weigh five ounces? Why does it weigh anything? Gravity is a mysterious force that no one seems quite able to explain since Newton did the heavy lifting on the subject in the seventeenth century. Though I did discover recently that the whole notion of gravity is being challenged by a well-respected scientist.[1] No scientist can do away with gravity, of course, but perhaps they'll be able to better explain the force that keeps us in our seat in a new way.

Gravity affects everything on earth. Without the application of external force, what goes up must come down. Rockets without enough power to escape earth's gravity field will fall back down. Rockets *with* enough force to escape earth's gravity field will not. They will make it to the weightlessness of space. Metaphorically, we could say that all of life is about gravity: We stand up as babies after we're born, then we fall down when we die. As far as I know, everything in life that goes up comes down.

Search for "gravity" in the Bible, and you won't find it. No surprise there. But you will find a spiritual sort of gravity described in Ecclesiastes 3:1–8, the theme of that passage being, "There is a time for everything, and a season for every activity under heaven" (v. 1). Note the go up/build up and go down/tear down juxtapositions in the rest of the passage (vv. 2–8):

> a time to be born and a time to die,
> a time to plant and a time to uproot,
> a time to kill and a time to heal,
> a time to tear down and a time to build,
> a time to weep and a time to laugh,
> a time to mourn and a time to dance,

a time to scatter stones and a time to gather them,

a time to embrace and a time to refrain,

a time to search and a time to give up,

a time to keep and a time to throw away,

a time to tear and a time to mend,

a time to be silent and a time to speak,

a time to love and a time to hate,

a time for war and a time for peace.

Regardless of the area of life, things go up/good/abundantly at certain times and then go down/bad/poorly at other times. There is a season for everything. This chapter is about how we manage our expectations and hope during the down/bad/poorly times of life—specifically, the feelings of disappointment that inevitably accrue.

Disappointment is not a sin, nor is it as serious as anger or depression or bitterness—feelings that sometimes develop when our expectations aren't met. Disappointment is exactly what the word suggests: an appointment that wasn't kept or met. There is actually a piece of land on the coast of Washington state, Cape Disappointment, named by a fur trader in 1788 who labeled the cape based on how he felt when he was there. British fur trader John Meares was sailing south along the coast of (what is now) Washington state, looking for the legendary River of the West—what is now the Columbia River that drains into the Pacific. The mouth of the Columbia was just south of Meares's location—if he had sailed around a particular cape he would have encountered it. But, disappointed that he hadn't found the river, he turned back north—but not before giving the cape a name that mirrored his disappointment.

Fortunately, we don't name things we are near every time an appointment or expectation goes unmet in life. If we did, by this time most of the streets, buildings, and houses in the world would be named "Something-or-other Disappointment." We are disappointed often in life—evidence of the changing times and seasons spoken of in Ecclesiastes and the up-and-down nature of spiritual and emotional gravity.

Defining Disappointment

Someone once said, "Don't have any expectations, and you'll never have any disappointments." From a lexical point of view, I suppose that's true since *The American Heritage Dictionary* defines disappointment as "to fail to satisfy the hope, desire, or expectation of." So if we don't have any hopes, desires, or expectations, we'll never be disappointed. But neither will we live a very passionate, expectant, or forward-thinking life. After all, expectations are all focused on the future in one way or another. To have no vision for the future and what it might bring would be to live life in neutral—to live a life that takes whatever comes instead of a life that tries to create that which is fruitful and satisfying.

There are all kinds of reasons that we experience disappointment in life. Occasionally we are disappointed with ourselves when we have set standards and levels of performance we don't meet— like Peter when he denied knowing Jesus Christ three times in one night and then grieved over his behavior (see Matt. 26). But more often we are disappointed with others. We expect certain things from people based on our relationship with them or their spoken or unspoken level of commitment to us. And the higher the expectation, the greater our disappointment.

I don't know if there has ever been a group of people with greater reason to be disappointed than the followers of William Miller in 1844. A series of revivals in America's northeast had resulted in a great many new believers who were theologically unsophisticated. Miller was one of them, and he spent countless hours studying the doctrine of the Second Coming of Christ. In 1818 he concluded that Christ would return to earth in 1843 or 1844. He began teaching and preaching about his studies and conclusions and gained an eager following. Ultimately, he set October

22, 1844, as the day of Christ's return to earth. An economic crisis in the country in 1839 caused many to believe the end was near. Newspapers ran prophetic charts on their pages, so great was the enthusiasm whipped up by circumstances and Miller's teachings. New England was filled with people looking for Christ to return on October 22, 1844.

When that day arrived, commerce stopped in many towns as people gathered in churches and on mountaintops to await the arrival of Christ. And they were still there at the end of the day, thoroughly disappointed. Indeed, that day has been remembered in history as "The Great Disappointment."[2]

Somehow, in all his study, William Miller failed to take account of Matthew 24:36, 42 where Jesus says flatly that no one—not even Him—knows the day of His own return. Sometimes disappointment is entirely unnecessary and our own fault. The more due diligence we do, reading the fine print and asking questions in life, the greater the possibility that we won't be disappointed. Life is a *caveat emptor* ("buyer beware") experience.

But there are other times when we do our due diligence and can completely justify our high expectations. In those instances we are faced with one of life's difficult moments that calls on us for maturity and reasonableness. Consider what the disciples of Jesus felt after His crucifixion. The Messiah they believed had come to restore the kingdom of God in Israel and liberate the Jews from Roman oppression had Himself been put to death. What kind of a divine Messiah allows Himself to be killed by those He came to defeat? They thought they had been mistaken at best or duped at worst.

Typical of those with downcast hearts were two disciples who had been in Jerusalem for Passover and the crucifixion and were returning to their village a few miles away with "faces downcast" (Luke 24:17). The resurrected Christ joined them as they walked on the road to Emmaus and, in short, gave them the information they needed to understand the calamitous events of the last three days in Jerusalem. After Jesus left them, "They got up and returned at once to Jerusalem. . . . [and] told what had happened on the way" (vv. 33–35). Their disappointment had been entirely erased because they gained new information and insight.

But sometimes nothing can erase our disappointment; there is not a happy ending in spite of our best efforts. We lose a job or a spouse, a hoped-for medical procedure doesn't produce results, financial relief we need doesn't materialize—any number of things can happen that leave us genuinely disappointed and discouraged. In those situations we are forced to embrace life as it is—filled with times and seasons. There are times to be exhilarated and times to be disappointed. There is no guarantee in life that we will be spared our share of the disappointing times.

In those times, it falls to us to call disappointment what it is. Radio humorist and author Garrison Keillor once said, "Sometimes you just have to look reality in the face and deny it!" That gets a good laugh of course, but it's not good advice for healthy living. Denying disappointment is to give permission for it to become something worse: discouragement, depression, resentment, or anger. Far better to call disappointment what it is and try to remedy its cause if possible: recognize our inappropriate expectations, gather more information, or other responses. If it's not possible to deflate the disappointment, then we have to accept it as a season in life that God has allowed and look to the future.

Defending Against Disappointment

So many city dwellers were moving to rural areas in the 1990s, seeking a slower pace of life, that *USA Today* ran a piece on how disappointed many of them were with their new surroundings. Many of them found the rural life a bit more bucolic and slow than they had hoped for: dusty, unpaved roads, lack of utilities, smelly animal operations near their property, no curbside trash pickup, and slow-responding emergency services. A county commissioner of Larimer County, Colorado, dealt with so many disappointed new residents that he wrote a small booklet called "The Code of the West: The Realities of Rural Living." In the booklet he spelled out exactly how life in the rural West is lived. His goal was not to keep people away but to educate them about what to expect.[3]

Outside of common sense—due diligence and realistic expectations—I know of no way to defend oneself against disappointment. It's a fact of life, plain and simple. But I do know how to keep disappointment from becoming something negative—how to allow disappointment to play its assigned role in the process of growing up before we grow old. The formula for defending against the negative potential of disappointment is found in Romans 5:1–5. The key is in verse 5, the last sentence, but reading it in context helps:

> Therefore, since we have been justified through faith, we have peace with God through our Lord Jesus Christ, through whom we have gained access by faith into this grace in which we now stand. And we rejoice in the hope of the glory of God. Not only so, but we also rejoice in our sufferings, because we know that suffering produces perseverance; perseverance, character; and character, hope. And hope does not disappoint us, because God has poured out his love into our hearts by the Holy Spirit, whom he has given us.

First, having peace with God means that all of life's other disappointments are but pinpricks in the grand scheme of things. It doesn't mean they aren't important—it means they are *relatively* important. Not being able to find peace with God would classify as a *major* disappointment in life. But we can have that through Jesus Christ.

And because of that, Paul says, "we can rejoice in our sufferings." I believe we're justified in substituting the word "disappointments" for "sufferings," since some disappointments definitively cause us to suffer: "we can rejoice in our disappointments." Why? Because...

- disappointments produce perseverance,
- perseverance produces character,
- and character produces hope.
- *And hope does not disappoint.*

So, if we follow the positive progression, we begin with a disappointment but we end with no disappointment because we have "worked the system." We have developed perseverance, which is a godly character trait, which gives us renewed hope—and *hope does not disappoint.*

See what happens? When we are disappointed, our focus is on the person or the event that created our disappointment. But in time—hopefully sooner rather than later—our focus changes to the hope we have in God. And such hope, meaning God Himself, never disappoints. So our focus and attention goes through a transformation. We take our eyes off the circumstances we're in and put our eyes on God. Our hope in Him—His plan, His strength, His grace, His understanding, and His purposes—is what fills our heart, leaving no room for disappointment.

In such a transformation, disappointment is not denied. It is recognized, given a name, and allowed to exist. But it is not allowed to dominate our thinking. Instead we persevere through our disappointment and see our character find its true north by hoping in the person of God himself. And then, as Paul wrote, "We rejoice in the hope of the glory of God." It is possible to move from disappointment to rejoicing purely by moving past the disappointment and putting our eyes on God Himself who is ready to remind us that life's disappointments do not define us.

I have shared with you in this book a serious disappointment I went through in my own life, and I know that you have likely experienced disappointments just as deep. Sometimes they leave us feeling as if we can't move forward, as if we are down to nothing. But if we persevere through them and let our hope in God become our focus, we will have put ourselves in the perfect place to discover what He is up to in our life.

Yes, there are times and seasons in life. What goes up must come down. But the disappointing times can become hopeful times when we hope in God.

14

The Greatest Feeling in the World

(Freedom from Guilt)

Then I acknowledged my sin to you
and did not cover up my iniquity.
I said, "I will confess
my transgressions to the LORD"—
and you forgave
the guilt of my sin. *Selah*

Psalm 32:5

My Story

I have had many great feelings in my life—wonderful feelings. The innocent, trusting arms of one of my children when they were small, wrapped around my neck. And their young-adult arms doing the same thing today. Or the unconditionally loving arms of my wife in her embrace. Or the thrill of finally getting a giant blue marlin out of the Pacific and next to the boat after an hours-long tug-of-war. Or the humbling pleasure of seeing a resistant soul become a repentant saint by giving his heart to Christ.

You have your own list, I'm sure. Pleasure, like beauty, is ultimately in the eyes of the beholder. But there is one pleasure that exceeds all others in my book, and I suspect it does in yours—the pleasure of freedom from guilt. This is the flip side of the forgiveness coin: the relief of forgiveness on one side, the freedom from guilt on the other. One is a sense of gratitude, the other a sense of exhilaration. One makes me sorry I ever sinned, the other makes never want to sin again.

If only a sinless life was possible. I have sinned plenty in my life—wittingly and unwittingly—doing those things I ought not to have done and leaving undone those things I ought to have done, as the Anglican Book of Common Prayer *puts it in the "General Confession." But as much as I have sinned, I have been forgiven the exact same amount. I don't know of any sin for which I should have sought forgiveness that I haven't, either from God or man. That's not a boast—simply an awareness of the dangers of living with guilt. The times I have been slow or resistant to seek forgiveness, whether from God or man, have been like a graduate course in misery. The longer I live, the longer I want to live guilt-free.*

Coming through a protracted period of difficulty like I did for four months in 2008 can create a subjective fog through which one sees guilt or innocence. There were so many meetings, discussions, opinions, points and counterpoints—did I remain guiltless through all of that? Did I say anything that was harsh or unkind? Was I disrespectful to any in authority over me, either familial or organizational? Even if on the outside I maintained decorum, did I harbor any resentment or bitterness toward anyone?

I tried to remain sensitive throughout the process and not make a difficult situation worse by offending in word or deed. And by the time it was all over—the first week of November— I was able to walk away without the burden of guilt for anything I had done or said. Like everyone does, I wrestled with "Should I have . . . ?" and "Could I have . . . ?" but was never convicted that I should have done anything differently. The late Dr. Norman Vincent Peale once quoted to me the words of the great Reformer Martin Luther, saying, "You can't stop the birds from flying around your head, but you can stop them from building a nest in your hair." The birds were flying fast and furious for four months, but I managed to stay nest-free (as far as I know) throughout the process.

When I was alone, did I have thoughts that ran the gamut about the participants? And did I vent occasionally to my wife in the privacy of our relationship? Of course—those were the birds flying overhead. But I can honestly say that the birds weren't allowed to land. More often than not, I would end up laughing out loud, by myself or with my wife, in a "What are you gonna do?" manner. Sometimes the perplexities of life's situations are so confusing that we have to laugh or cry. And thankfully, most often I found the ability to laugh—not at anyone, but at the mystery of life.

The only thing worse than being down to nothing is to look up and find that you are not alone—that guilt is your faithful tormentor. How much better to live a guilt-free life so you'll be ready to embrace the "something" that God is up to in your life.

There's a trend afoot in our culture that troubles me: the conditional ("if" or "might"), blanket apology. I don't know when this language was first used, but it now seems to be boilerplate terminology for the public relations officers of celebrities—anyone whose words or actions are captured and disseminated by the mainstream media.

Here are the troubling words: "I want to apologize to anyone who might have been offended by what I did/said." Have you heard this? Whenever I hear it, I think one of two things: Either the person has no education or experience with the dynamics of actual guilt, confession, sorrow, and supplication, or they really aren't sorry at all—they don't think they did anything wrong, but they want us, the "offendees," to think they are sorry. This kind of postoffense confession has about as much gravitas to it as if the same person, first thing every morning, sent out a tweet, a Facebook status update, an e-mail, and a text message to the whole world that said, "I want to apologize to everyone for anything I might do today that offends anyone. I'm getting this out of the way now so you don't need to hassle me with it later today if I mess up."

The prime minister of New Zealand used the conditional, blanket apology in May 2010 when he made a joke implying that a particular tribe of natives was cannibalistic. A Fox News commentator employed this strategy when apologizing for a remark about an actor. A popular singer did the same when (sort of) apologizing for remarks he made in private about another music star. A CBS reporter used the "if she is offended" apology after reporting that a 2010 female Supreme Court nominee is gay. After a "wardrobe malfunction" on national television during the 2004 Super Bowl, the female singer involved apologized to "anyone offended."[1]

I'll put away my critical lens lest I become too focused on the specks in others' eyes and not the log in my own (see Matt. 7:3–5). And I will be the first to admit that the realization, acknowledging, and confession of sin (or hurtful words or actions) is tricky business. What was the deed in question? How should I feel? Who was offended or wounded? To whom should I apologize? What should I say? What is the difference between apologizing and asking forgiveness? And most importantly, how do I know when things are settled? How should I feel? Where does my guilt go?

If the people making the conditional-blanket apologies are not asking these questions today, it is likely due to the problem identified by psychiatrist Karl Menninger in his 1973 book, *Whatever Became of Sin?*[2] Nearly four decades ago, he noted, from the point of view of people and their problems, that "sin" was becoming an outmoded concept. He proved to be ahead of his time. Our post-Christian culture does not think broadly in terms of sin, guilt, repentance, atonement, or reparation. But the failure to acknowledge these realities does not make the effects of sin go away—especially the effect of guilt.

The Bible doesn't answer all the questions I listed in so many words, but there are enough examples of people who erred for us to gather a clear sense of what causes guilt, how to deal with it, and what should be the effect.

Grappling with Guilt

I'm going to use the best-known example of a celebrity in the Bible who sinned—his steps and missteps—as a framework: King David's dual sins of adultery and accessory to murder, both of which he attempted to cover up.

The story is well-known and is recorded in 2 Samuel 11–12. Summary: David had ascended to the throne in Jerusalem as the king of Israel. He was in a position of power and authority, revered as the mighty warrior who had dispatched the giant Goliath while a teenager and armies of enemies as a young adult. Now the king, he had sent his armies out to do battle with the Ammonites. Jerusalem was quiet without the army, and David found himself on the roof of his palace late at night. From his vantage point, he spied a beautiful woman named Bathsheba bathing in a nearby house. Using his executive powers, he sent for her and had sexual relations with her.

Later, when the woman discovered she was pregnant and informed the king of her condition, David made arrangements to have her husband, Uriah, sent back to Jerusalem to recuperate. David assumed Uriah would be intimate with his wife, thus allowing the pregnancy for which David was responsible to be assigned to the soldier. But Uriah was so loyal to his king and fellow soldiers that he refused himself any comfort while in Jerusalem, including sleeping with his wife. So David sent him back to the army but arranged to have him placed in a dangerous position so he would be killed in a battle—and this plan succeeded.

So David is now guilty of adultery (against his own wives and against Uriah and Bathsheba), guilty of trickery and deceit (attempting to make Uriah the responsible party in Bathsheba's pregnancy), and guilt of being an accomplice to murder (he didn't "pull the trigger," but he arranged for it to happen). And what did David do about his sins and his guilt? He covered his sins and suffered with his guilt for almost a year until after the baby was born. (He also married Uriah's widow and brought her into his palace as one of his wives.)

There were seven "penitential" psalms used by the early Christian church: Psalms 6, 32, 38, 51, 102, 130, and 143. "Penitential" means they convey the words and actions of a penitent man—someone who is laboring under difficult circumstances to include the guilt of sin. All but Psalms 102 and 130 were written by David—he was apparently quite familiar with this subject—and Psalm 51 is explicitly connected in the text to David's sin with Bathsheba. Consider the descriptions from the psalms of the person who is living with guilt:

- When I kept silent [about my sin], my bones wasted away through my groaning all day long. For day and night your hand was heavy upon me; my strength was sapped as in the heat of summer. (Psalm 32:3–4)
- O LORD, do not rebuke me in your anger or discipline me in your wrath. For your arrows have pierced me, and your hand has come down upon me. Because of your wrath there is no health in my body; my bones have no soundness because of my sin. My guilt has overwhelmed me like a burden too heavy to bear. My wounds fester and are loathsome because of my sinful folly. I am bowed down and brought very low; all day long I go about mourning. My back is filled with searing pain; there is no health in my body. I am feeble and utterly crushed; I groan in anguish of heart. (Psalm 38:1–8)

- Cleanse me with hyssop, and I will be clean; wash me, and I will be whiter than snow. Let me hear joy and gladness; let the bones you have crushed rejoice. Hide your face from my sins and blot out all my iniquity. (Psalm 51:7–9)
- Out of the depths I cry to you, O LORD; O Lord, hear my voice. Let your ears be attentive to my cry for mercy. If you, O LORD, kept a record of sins, O Lord, who could stand? (Psalm 130:1–3)

All these words were penned by David—not the words of a man enjoying the pleasures of life but the words of a man living in agony, crushed by despair, longing for release and forgiveness.

So it was a blessing to David when God sent a prophet named Nathan to call David out about his sin. Nathan told David a fictional story of a rich man who stole the lone lamb of a poor man to feed a visiting traveler. David, thinking it was an actual crime in his kingdom, "burned with anger against the man" (2 Sam. 12:5) and declared that the man deserved to die and must pay four times the value of the lamb to the poor man. And Nathan said to the king, "You are the man!" (v. 7).

David had outed himself and was undone.

Finding Freedom

Once David knew that his multiple sins with regard to Bathsheba were known, he did the right thing. That is to say, he did not issue a conditional, blanket apology to anyone "he may have offended." Nor did he use words like "mistake" or "accident" or blame the beauty of Bathsheba for entrapping him. David called sin "sin," using first-person pronouns: "Then David said to Nathan, 'I have sinned against the LORD'" (v. 13).

We don't have explicit evidence that Psalm 32 was written in connection with David's Bathsheba experience. If not, it certainly refers to another season of sin in David's life, recording his confession in plain terms: "Then I acknowledged my sin to you and did not cover up my iniquity. I said, 'I will confess my transgressions to the LORD'" (Psalm 32:5a).

And in Psalm 51, which is connected directly to David's sin with Bathsheba, he wrote,

> Have mercy on me, O God,
> according to your unfailing love;
> according to your great compassion
> blot out my transgressions.
> Wash away all my iniquity
> and cleanse me from my sin.
>
> For I know my transgressions,
> and my sin is always before me.
> Against you, you only, have I sinned
> and done what is evil in your sight,
> so that you are proved right when you speak
> and justified when you judge.
>
> *Psalm 51:1–4*

Words and actions reveal what people believe about their guilt, that is, about their wrongful choices. The meaning of the New Testament word "confession" is "to speak the same as; to agree." The Greek word is *homologeo*, which is a compound word made of *homou* (the same) and *logos* (word; something said). When we confess our sins to God or to another person in order to seek their forgiveness, we are saying the same thing about our sin that they say. If God calls our actions sin, that is what we must call them. We feel guilty because we have sinned, not because we made a mistake. Whether the act was premeditated (as in David's case) or not, it is the act that is in question. Whatever God says about it, we must say.

Note to whom David directed his confession: "Against you [God], you only, have I sinned." What about Bathsheba and

Uriah? David certainly sinned against them; they certainly deserved his apology. Obviously, Uriah was deceased so David couldn't seek his forgiveness. But what about Bathsheba? Did David apologize to her?

We don't know. But what we know about his "against you only" words was that this was David's admission and recognition that all sin is ultimately against God. David knew he had sinned against Bathsheba, but his words are a way of saying, "If I don't confess my sins to You, Lord, confession to others would be incomplete." David's words are a figure of speech—hyperbole—where he exaggerates a situation to make a point. (Like Jesus' seeming implication that we must hate our family members if we are going to follow Him. He obviously didn't mean "hate"—it was hyperbolic language, recognizing that following Jesus takes precedence over every other relationship in life. See Luke 14:26–27.)

And David found the freedom he was seeking: "And you forgave the guilt of my sin" (Ps. 32:5). If we read what David requested in Psalm 51, we can know what he ultimately received from God:

> Cleanse me with hyssop, and I will be clean;
> wash me, and I will be whiter than snow.
> Let me hear joy and gladness;
> let the bones you have crushed rejoice.
> Hide your face from my sins
> and blot out all my iniquity.
>
> Create in me a pure heart, O God,
> and renew a steadfast spirit within me.
> Do not cast me from your presence
> or take your Holy Spirit from me.
> Restore to me the joy of your salvation
> and grant me a willing spirit, to sustain me.
> *Psalm 51:7–12*

All we have to do is compare words like "joy of your salvation" to the horrific descriptions in the penitential psalms to realize the freedom David found. And it was all because he got honest about his sin and called it what God calls it. And because he came to God with a "broken spirit; a broken and contrite heart." The next time you hear someone make a conditional, blanket public apology, look for a "broken spirit; a broken and contrite heart." Those are signs that the guilt of sin has done its job—leading sinners to repentance.

The New Testament tells a similar story about sin and guilt. A "broken and contrite heart" is referred to as "godly sorrow" in 2 Corinthians 7:10–11. And 1 John 1:9 says, "If we confess our sins, he is faithful and just and will forgive us our sins and purify us from all unrighteousness." The invitation to flee the prison of guilt has been sent. The prison door has been flung open, waiting for us to walk through.

The banner headline on the August 2, 2000, edition of the *Chicago Tribune* read, "Guilty Plea Sets Inmate Free." The inmate had been sentenced to prison eight years earlier after being found guilty of a crime. The state's attorney's office cut a deal with him: Admit your guilt, and your time served will satisfy your sentence. Many people read the headline cynically: "Another criminal gets a plea bargain and goes free." But one resident, Lee Eclov, read it differently. He wrote, "Freedom is not in a plea of innocence, but in the admission of guilt."[3]

Anyone who has committed a "crime" against God or man or both can find freedom—not with a protestation of innocence, not with a conditional, blanket apology, but with an admission of guilt. In the words of radio humorist and author Garrison Keillor, "Guilt is the gift that keeps on giving"—until we respond. Then it gives us freedom.

If guilt over some act—no matter how large or how small, how recent or how distant—has made you feel like you're down to nothing, remember you are not. You can replace guilt with freedom by standing on God's promise to forgive. And once free, you'll see that God is up to something in your life.

15

How to Re-Joice

(Joy)

For the kingdom of God is not a matter of eating and drinking, but of righteousness, peace and joy in the Holy Spirit.

Romans 14:17

My Story

By the end of November 2008, the source of my ministerial joy since 1981 had been removed from my life. But I was about to get an education in "joy."

I had enjoyed more than twenty wonderful years as founder and pastor of Rancho Capistrano Community Church in San Juan Capistrano, California, as well as starting the school and conference center associated with the church. It was everything I love to do: teaching, preaching, counseling, "starting things" and seeing them prosper, and weeping and rejoicing with dear friends and church members as they journeyed through life. My wife, Donna, came into my life and shared most of those years with me and my children—it was a wonderful season of life!

When we left that church to go to the Crystal Cathedral, I anticipated more of the same only in a larger and different venue. And for the most part it was. I loved the people, the church, the television broadcast, the preaching—I felt I was continuing to fill the shoes God had custom-designed for me to wear in my life. And when I was asked to assume the role of senior pastor in 2006 as well as host the Hour of Power broadcast, it was, to me, God's confirmation that we were exactly where we were supposed to be. I felt blessed (daily happiness) and joyful (long-term, deep-seated contentedness) in what I was doing.

But three years later, it was all gone. What I had labored at since 1981 (actually, since 1976 when I joined the Crystal Cathedral in a ministry staff position after graduating from college) was no longer a part of my life. While there were many negative aspects of that experience, there were many positive ones as well. One of the most helpful was the opportunity to separate what brought me vocational joy and happiness from the venue in which it occurred. The simple fact that I had enjoyed equal measures of joy in two different local church settings was an indication that my joy was not based on geography or constituency. What brought me joy was the content (sharing God's truth), response (seeing people's lives touched), challenges (solving problems, overcoming obstacles), and entrepreneurial nature of ministry (the excitement of new possibilities). In other words, the source of my joy and happiness in life is tied to Christ in my life, not my life in any given organization or location.

Yes, that's a simple, basic belief of the Christian faith. But I dare say I'm not the only Christian who has needed, and appreciated, a reminder. It's easy to get settled into a routine, a paycheck, a schedule, and the ability to create joy on a cause-effect basis: If I do this in that place, I'll be happy. But on December 1, 2008, God sent me back to Joy School to be reminded of what I believed—and to give me an opportunity to prove it.

By November 2009—one year later—I had graduated from Joy School (though I'm sure there will be refresher *courses!). I was thrilled to be doing something I had never dreamed of doing, with a new group of people, in a different part of the country, and in a new venue. And I was loving every minute of it—and still am. During that year my book,* Leaning into God When Life Is Pushing You Away *(perfect timing, right?) was published. I had become chairman of a national media company that purchased two existing television networks (American Life TV and Family Net) and a Sirius radio station. My new signature television show* Everyday Life *aired for the first time on American Life TV. And best of all, Donna and I celebrated our twenty-fifth wedding anniversary.*

Two thousand nine turned out to be a blessed year because God went before me and opened doors and opportunities to continue doing the things that bring me joy: telling people about Him, encouraging them to trust Him, and directing them to the truth of His Word. And I relearned the lesson that joy is not in where or what we do as much as it is in Who we know.

I thought I was down to nothing in November 2008. But God was up to something—reminding me that my joy is in Him above all else.

Something called the World Values Survey has been administered in countries around the world since 1981 under the auspices of the University of Michigan. It measures a number of sociological, religious, political, and moral dimensions of the world's population by nation. The part of the huge survey most often quoted in the press is the "Happiness Survey"—a ranking of the happiest nations in the world. In 2008, the happiest nation in the world was Denmark, followed by Puerto Rico, Colombia, Iceland, N. Ireland, Republic of Ireland, Switzerland, Netherlands, Canada, and Austria. The United States, the world's wealthiest nation, ranked 16th out of 97 countries surveyed, while our British cousins ranked 21st.[1]

The happiness quotient is apparently a hot topic. Lots of people want to know how happy we all are (or aren't) and rightfully so in this stressful day and age. In 2006, a researcher at Britain's University of Leicester used responses from 80,000 subjects worldwide to create a happiness survey. Denmark, again, came out on top followed by Switzerland and Austria. He found that a nation's happiness quotient was most closely tied to levels of health, with prosperity and education being the next most important factors.[2]

The New Economics Foundation (England) took a slightly different tack in 2009, seeking to link happiness levels to a nation's ecological footprint (how much of its "fair share" of world resources it consumes) and life expectancy. The winner? Costa Rica. In fact, out of the 143 countries surveyed, nine of the top ten happiest were Latin American nations. The U.S., of course, didn't fare so well based on the ecology measure, ranking 114th.

That kind of happiness index—linking happiness to other measures of prosperity—was profiled in a 2009 book titled *Agenda for a New Economy*, authored by David Korten, chairman of the Positive Futures Network. He follows other researchers who say that the post-Industrial Age measurement of a country's prosperity, GDP (Gross Domestic Product), is no longer an adequate measure of a nation's well-being. He supports the use of a measurement called the Human Development Index (HDI), a variation of which is already in use by 150 nations in the world. The HDI incorporates other measures besides gross domestic production, such as health, education, and standard of living.[3]

What makes nations happy is, of course, correlated with what makes individuals happy. And that has attracted the attention of two well-known lecturers in Harvard University's psychology department. In 2006, Tal Ben-Shahar taught a course titled "Positive Psychology," attended by 855 Harvard students—the most popular class in the spring semester. The next year he published his ideas in a best-selling book, *Happier: Learn the Secrets of Daily Joy and Last-ing Fulfillment*. Apropos for the title, he says happiness is a func-tion of two variables: short-term pleasures ("daily joy") and long-term meaningfulness ("lasting fulfillment"). (We'll see shortly that, purposefully or not, Ben-Shahar was thinking biblically.)

Ben-Shahar's colleague, Daniel Gilbert, published his take on happiness in 2006 in a book called *Stumbling on Happiness*, in which he said humans are woefully inept at using their imagination to predict what will make them happy in the future. Our consumer culture is based on the notion that the purchase of XYZ product, get-ting married, having children, or getting a certain job will make us happy—and it does for a while, but not permanently. There are bet-ter ways of planning to be happy, he says, such as taking the advice of people who have been there and done that. Experience counts, apparently, when it comes to choosing paths to happiness.

In a 2008 article, researchers at the University of British Columbia published research that said people who give some of their money away to others and to charity are happier than people who spend it all on themselves.[4] As we move toward a biblical per-spective on happiness, that finding shouldn't surprise us—nor should this: Many, many studies have found a direct correlation between religious commitment and happiness.[5] And if you want to discover exactly how happy you are, you can actually take a "test" developed by two psychologists at England's Oxford University. You may not be happy when you get the results, but no one said finding happiness was risk-free.[6]

Happiness and Joy

In his book *Dangers, Toils & Snares*, John Ortberg uses a family example to set the stage for the rest of this chapter:

> When we take our children to the shrine of the Golden
> Arches, they always lust for the meal that comes with a

cheap little prize, a combination christened, in a moment of marketing genius, the Happy Meal. You're not just buying fries, McNuggets, and a dinosaur stamp; you're buying happiness. Their advertisements have convinced my children they have a little McDonald's-shaped vacuum in their souls: "Our hearts are restless till they find their rest in a happy meal."

I try to buy off the kids sometimes. I tell them to order only the food and I'll give them a quarter to buy a little toy on their own. But the cry goes up, "I want a Happy Meal." All over the restaurant, people crane their necks to look at the tight-fisted, penny-pinching cheapskate of a parent who would deny a child the meal of great joy.

The problem with the Happy Meal is that the happy wears off, and they need a new fix. No child discovers lasting happiness in just one: "Remember that Happy Meal? What great joy I found there!"

Happy Meals bring happiness only to McDonald's. You ever wonder why Ronald McDonald wears that grin? Twenty billion Happy Meals, that's why.

When you get older, you don't get any smarter; your happy meals just get more expensive.[7]

The fact that "happy wears off" is a good way to distinguish it from joy, biblically speaking. Happiness is for today, maybe tomorrow, but joy is forever. There may be some exceptions to that categorization, but it seems to me to be a fair way to break down the use of the words in Scripture. The distinction between short-term pleasure and long-term meaningfulness (noted above in the discussion of Ben-Shahar's book) is a biblical one—and one that bears remembering. To get the two confused is to invite a severe degree of confusion and disappointment. We're on solid biblical ground, I think, to say that short-term pleasure equates with happiness while long-term meaningfulness relates to joy. Both are important in life, but one is ultimately more important.

Generally speaking, the Old Testament was focused on happiness while the New Testament is focused on joy. For example, the phrase, "Blessed is the [person]" occurs thirty-eight times in the Old Testament and the four Gospels. (The word "blessed" is often translated "happy.") Think of Psalm 1—"Blessed is the man who does not walk…"—and Jesus' Beatitudes in Matthew 5—"Blessed are the poor in spirit…" But it only occurs three times in the New Testament epistles, and one of those three is a quotation of an Old Testament verse. Contrasted with the scarcity of "blessed/happy" in the New Testament is the family of "joy" words (noun and verb forms). They occur some sixty-seven times in the New Testament epistles. On the basis of word counts alone, joy seems to replace happy as the dominant theme when moving from the Old Testament to the New.

Why? Because the locus of life changed. In the Old Testament, Israel was given an earthly kingdom in which to live in the land of Canaan. To survive in a strange land surrounded by hostile neighbors, Israel would need God's blessings in abundance—and He promised just that. The best list of how God intended to bless (make happy) Israel is in Deuteronomy 28: "All these blessings will come upon you and accompany you if you obey the LORD your God" (v. 2). And the blessings God details would make anyone happy: They would have large families and their crops, harvests, and livestock would be abundant. All their enemies would be defeated. All their endeavors would be successful. All the nations on earth would fear them because of how God prospered them. God would cause rain to come on their crops causing them to grow in wealth. They would lend their wealth to the nations around them and borrow from none. They would always be at the top of the ladder, never at the bottom (vv. 3–14).

The focus in the Old Testament was on temporal happiness in the Promised Land, and God promised blessings to ensure Israel's happiness (as long as they obeyed Him and kept His commands). Israel failed to keep God's commands and the blessings stopped—they ended up in captivity for seventy years in Babylon (approximately 600–630 BC). So when Jesus came on the scene six centuries later, even though He used the language of "blessing" in the Beatitudes, the blessings were no longer about physical happiness (crops, children, and wealth) but about spiritual happiness (meekness, righteousness, mercy, purity, peace).

The apostles, in their epistles, employed the Greek word *chara* (joy, delight) and the verb *chairo* (be glad, rejoice) to express the possibility of joy in the midst of any kind of circumstance. Why? Because the focus had shifted from material happiness on earth to eternal joy in heaven. The church doesn't have a homeland on earth in need of blessed crops and animals and businesses. It's home is in heaven. And Jesus promised His disciples that, just as the world persecuted Him, it would persecute them. So they needed something deeper than a Happy Meal happiness that was here today and gone tomorrow. They needed the eternal food Jesus ate: "My food...is to do the will of him who sent me and to finish his work" (John 4:34). They needed a reason to be joyful now and forever, regardless of what circumstances befell them as they followed Christ's leading throughout the earth.

If life gives you a Happy Meal every day, all the better. But if it doesn't, your supply of joy will see you through.

Understanding Joy

Paul exemplified that kind of joy when he wrote his epistle to the Philippians, often called the Epistle of Joy. Here was Paul, a prisoner in a Roman cell, mentioning "joy" and "rejoice" fourteen different times in a short letter of four chapters. It wasn't necessary for Paul to be in a certain place doing a certain thing with a certain level of comfort for him to experience joy. He found joy wherever he was, even in jail.

Not only was he in jail, but others were taking advantage of his confinement, trying to usurp his position as an apostle. His response? "But what does it matter? The important thing is that in every way, whether from false motives or true, Christ is preached. And because of this I rejoice" (Phil. 1:18). His key phrase is this: "Rejoice in the Lord!" (Phil. 3:1) Not, "Rejoice in your job, your wealth, your comfort, your circumstances, or your place in the world." Those things might bring happiness for a time, but it is only "joy in the Lord" that brings happiness forever.

The great British apologist and author C. S. Lewis wrote an entire book about joy called *Surprised by Joy*.[8] An atheist well into his adult years, he describes the intense longing he had felt all his life for something he came to call "Joy":

> ... it is that of an unsatisfied desire which is itself more desirable than any other satisfaction. I call it Joy, which is here a technical term and must be sharply distinguished both from Happiness and from Pleasure. Joy (in my sense) has indeed one characteristic, and one only, in common with them; the fact that anyone who has experienced it will want it again.... I doubt whether anyone who has tasted [Joy] would ever, if both [Joy and pleasure] were in his power, exchange it for all the pleasures in the world. But then Joy is never in our power and pleasure often is.[9]

Having longed for Joy all his life, he found it in his conversion, first to Christianity, then to Christ himself. And on the last page of the book, he points out something that seems, at first glance, surprising—that Joy is not an end in itself, but a means to the true end, Christ Himself. Because we so often mistake joy for happiness, we seek it in order to be happy in this life. In reality, joy comes not when we seek it, but when we seek the One who is our joy:

But I now know that the experience [of Joy], considered as a state of my own mind, had never had the kind of importance I once gave it. It was valuable only as a pointer to something other and outer.... When we are lost in the woods the sight of a signpost is a great matter. He who first sees it cries, "Look!" The whole party gathers round and stares. But when we have found the road and passing signposts every few miles, we shall not stop and stare. They will encourage us and we shall be grateful to the authority that set them up. But we shall not stop and stare, or not much; not on this road, though their pillars are of silver and their lettering of gold. "We would be at Jerusalem."[10]

You and I would be at Jerusalem as well, the heavenly city that is our homeland. Joy today, on earth, is but a signpost—a foretaste—that points us to Jesus Christ and His eternal kingdom where those who know Him are bound.

When we are down to nothing in this life, we may be tempted to lose our happiness for a moment. But what we shall never lose is our joy in the Lord. God's gifts are both happiness and joy, but only one is eternal. And God's promise is that our joy will be complete in Christ (see John 15:11). Whatever God is up to in our life, we will ultimately have reason to rejoice.

16

The Rest of Your Life

(Peace)

"Come to me, all you who are weary and burdened, and I will give you rest. Take my yoke upon you and learn from me, for I am gentle and humble in heart, and you will find rest for your souls. For my yoke is easy and my burden is light."

Matthew 11:28–30

My Story

I once heard that in the ancient world, in Bible days, the difference between being rich and poor was what one had in the cupboard. If you woke up on a given morning and had food for the day at the beginning of the day, you were considered rich. If you woke up and had to go out and earn food for that day before you or your family could eat, you were poor. I've never done the research to determine if that description is accurate, but I like it as a generalization because it illustrates the tension with which most of us live on a daily basis: the tension between peace of mind through faith and the obligation to work and provide for ourselves. We may not be one meal or one day away from poverty, but we might be one month or one year or a few years. The unrelenting obligation to work and provide is like a steady drip, drip, drip in our lives that doesn't go away. But when our ability to provide is suddenly taken away, our faith is called into play. As our income and resources evaporate, so does our peace.

That was my experience in November 2008. For the previous thirty-plus years I had provided for my family doing things I loved: pastoring, speaking, being a television host, and writing books. Because all those streams of income were tied together and interdependent, when I left the pastorate, my income took a serious hit. And so did my peace of mind.

I confess that finance is an area of stress for me. Not because of consumer indebtedness or mismanagement. It's more of a hyperconscientiousness about not getting into any kind of financial straits. I've never wanted to succumb to living on debt and beyond what the Lord has provided. So when my income was suddenly cut off, I immediately began creating scenarios in my mind of how we would manage—starting with cutting expenses. Since two of my children are grown and on their own and two others are almost on their own, my wife and I have few expenses related to them. But we live in an expensive part of the country—southern California—where the cost of living is several times higher than in other places. Would we need to sell our home? Begin to live on savings? How long could we make it before I would need to take whatever kind of job I could find in order to create an income stream going forward?

As you know by now, within a few months we had formed a new enterprise based on reshaping two existing television networks. From that enterprise, income should be created for my wife and me to live on, relieving some of the financial pressure I feel. But these are new entrepreneurial ventures. So there is a continual sense of unrest about the future.

And that's what this experience has helped me to relearn: spiritual rest and peace in life is not about the presence or absence of anything material, especially money. I have known too many people who have more than enough money—enough so you would think they wouldn't have a care in the world—to know that the presence of money is not the secret to living a restful life.

We are called to a life of healthy tension—one foot in the kingdom of heaven and one foot in this world. Half our heart knows God is a Father who provides for His children, while the other half knows we are responsible to "work out [our] salvation with fear and trembling" (Phil. 2:12). Half our brain says, "Money isn't important," while the other half says, "We need money to purchase food and shelter." Half our emotions want to rest in the peace and security of Christ while the other half feels anxious about providing for our family.

When we get down to nothing—especially when "nothing" means no money—we are called to drill down deeper into the mystery of God's sovereignty and our responsibility. Which is one reason He allows us to get in these situations—so we will grow to be more like Christ who lived the perfect balance.

Few sporting events in the world can compare with the Tour de France bicycle race held every July in France. For twenty-three days—twenty-one days of racing broken up by two rest days—nearly two hundred professional riders drag themselves more than 2,200 miles from the top of France to the bottom and back again, crossing the final finish line on the Avenue des Champs-Élysées in Paris. Simply to ride a bike over that distance in twenty-one days would be a Herculean accomplishment. But to do it riding at top speeds, crossing the Alps and Pyrenees mountain chains, being buffeted by high winds, higher temperatures, and howling mountain rainstorms, all the while leaving a portion of one's flesh pasted on the asphalt as a result of crashes—it's no wonder that a certain percentage of the riders who start do not finish.

As the race wears on, Tour de France riders dream of only two things: food and sleep. Burning up six thousand calories a day on their bikes, recovery—deep, unbroken rest—becomes more and more critical. But when oozing skin abrasions stick to the bed-sheets and sore muscles cry out with every toss and turn, unbroken sleep becomes less and less likely. The more the riders need to rest, the more elusive that rest becomes.

To try to solve that problem, Dr. Allen Lim, a sports scientist hired by Team RadioShack (the team of Lance Armstrong, the most famous Tour de France rider of all time), tracks the team members' sleep patterns each night during the race. The riders wear a soft cloth headband at night while they sleep, the headband containing a sensor that transmits brain waves to a monitor. By studying the sleep patterns of the riders, he gains insights into exactly how rested they really are. Lying in bed for seven hours is not the same as resting for seven hours or sleeping for seven hours.

Everything Dr. Lim does falls under the heading of one of the most important components in endurance sports: recovery. If an athlete's body does not recover from a serious exertion—and recover within an optimum time window, using proper protocols like nutrition, massage, cooling, and sleep—there will be a negative impact on long-term performance. The effects of poor recovery are cumulative day after day. Poor recovery after one day's exertion makes the next day's performance suffer—and on and on over the life of a three-week event like the Tour de France.

The Tour de Life

Three weeks is a long time to live with extreme stress. But what about a lifetime? Stress to human beings is like water to a fish—we live in it continually so we don't really know any different. We are so used to stress that to be "stressed out" seems normal. We are so used to living with worry and anxiety that we think it's normal.

In 1967, two psychiatrists—Drs. Thomas Holmes and Richard Rahe—studied the medical records of five thousand patients to look for correlations between stress and physical illness. They discovered a correlation based on forty-three different life events experienced by the five thousand subjects. They constructed a self-administering test based on their findings: the Social Readjustment Rating Scale (SRRS), which has come to be known more commonly as the Holmes-Rahe Stress Scale (see pages 163–164). The idea is to identify the stressor events you have experienced within the last year and add up the points ("units") associated with each. The guidelines published by the doctors suggested a total score of 300+ indicates a person at risk of stress-induced illness; a score of 150–229 reduces the risk of illness by 30 percent; and a score of <150 indicates only a slight risk of illness.[1]

As I look over the list of forty-three life events, I see a number of them that were present from July of 2008 to a year later, most having to do with the significant vocational changes I experienced. But here's what else I recognized about the list: the forty-three events represent the "stuff" of life! Yes, there are some big events on the list, but we experience them all the time—many of them within a twelve-month period. Even vacation (third from the bottom) is listed as a mild stressor, which is why we so often hear people say, "I need a vacation to recover from my vacation!" (I encourage you to calculate your own score on the Holmes-Rahe scale. Disclaimer: I am not a doctor and this is not a book on medical illness. Computing your score will simply get you in touch with how many stressors we live with every day without realizing it.)

We are contestants in the Tour de Life—pedaling like mad, crashing without time to heal before getting back in the race, no time for full recovery, and experiencing the cumulative wearing down of our physical, spiritual, and emotional immune systems. If we substitute the word "unrest" for "stress," we can transition our

Holmes-Rahe Stress Scale

Life Event	Life Change Units
Death of a spouse	100
Divorce	73
Marital separation	65
Imprisonment	63
Death of a close family member	63
Personal injury or illness	53
Marriage	50
Dismissal from work	47
Retirement	45
Marital reconciliation	45
Change in health of family member	44
Pregnancy	40
Sexual difficulties	39
Gain a new family member	39
Business readjustment	39
Change in financial state	38
Death of a close friend	37
Change to different line of work	36
Change in frequency of arguments	35
Major mortgage	32
Foreclosure of mortgage or loan	30
Trouble with in-laws	29
Child leaving home	29
Change in responsibilities at work	29
Outstanding personal achievement	28
Spouse starts or stops work	26
Begin or end school	26
Change in living conditions	25
Revision of personal habits	24

(continued)

Holmes-Rahe Stress Scale (*cont.*)

Life Event	Life Change Units
Trouble with boss	23
Change in working hours or conditions	20
Change in schools	20
Change in residence	20
Change in recreation	19
Change in church activities	19
Change in social activities	18
Minor mortgage or loan	17
Change in sleeping habits	16
Change in number of family reunions	15
Change in eating habits	15
Vacation	13
Christmas	12
Minor violation of law	11
Your Total:	

discussion to biblical terms. The word "stress" only occurs once in the Bible in the sense used in this chapter (pressure, unrest; see Jer. 19:9), so I'll use the terms "unrest" and "rest" as more biblically familiar terms, as well as the word "peace"—even more biblically familiar than "rest."

Rest: Now and Then

The average person—at least the average American or citizen of any other industrialized, developed nation—is drastically in need of rest. That doesn't mean we're in need of a vacation or of doing nothing. A certain level of stress is healthy for human beings. Just as muscle fibers are made larger by first tearing them down through exertion, so we are made stronger and more mature as we do two things: create lives (to the degree possible) that have normal, healthy amounts of stress and develop strategies for managing or deflecting the unusual, occasional high loads of stress we experience. We are not going to be able to avoid the death of loved ones, for instance. But we can create a life system that allows us to absorb such stressful events in a "soft" rather than a "hard" way. When stress hits us "hard," it breaks us; when it hits us "soft," it's because we embrace it and accept it and incorporate it into the flow of life so we come out stronger rather than weaker.

The Bible talks about two dimensions of peace and rest, and one flows naturally from the other. One is eternal rest and peace, and the other is peace and rest now. We need both: rest and peace now and then. Here is what I find ironic about these two dimensions of rest: many people who have established a relationship with God through Jesus Christ sleep like a baby at night in terms of their eternal state of mind. They don't lose a wink of sleep over the fact that if they die before they wake they'll open their eyes in heaven and be there for all eternity. But those same people—the ones who trust God's promises about getting them to heaven when they die—toss and turn all night when it comes to trusting God with a problem in their marriage, or a financial crisis, or a wayward child, or a parent who needs long-term care.

Considering the logistics of both events—eternal versus temporal—doesn't it seem we ought to be a bit more stressed about getting to heaven when we die than about paying the overdue water bill? From our perspective, getting to heaven is infinitely more complicated and unlikely than working out a payment plan with a utility company or coming up with the cash to pay the bill. And yet we stress over the smaller matters more than the larger.

When it comes to eternal rest—getting to heaven—we have no alternative except to take God at His word. We've not seen heaven, we've not seen God, we have no idea how the mystery of sacrifice and redemption to pay for our sins actually works.... But we trust that God does; we take Him at His word and don't worry about it. If God says our faith in Jesus Christ will result in the gift of eternal life, we rest in that. And the simple fact is, if we are willing to trust God for that level of complexity in our life, we surely ought to be able to trust Him with lesser matters like the forty-three items on the Stress Scale above (plus the hundreds more that happened in your life and mine this week that didn't even make the scale!).

An entire chapter of the Bible—Hebrews 4—is devoted to the subject of eternal rest. The author of Hebrews uses an analogy to talk about eternal rest—the experience of the Israelites moving out of slavery in Egypt into the rest God promised would be theirs in the Promised Land of Canaan. And the whole argument boils down to one idea: faith, or belief. He reminds them that an entire genera- tion of Israelites—those who failed to believe God at Kadesh Barnea (see Num. 13–14)—"were not able to enter [the Promised Land], because of their unbelief" (Heb. 3:19). And he exhorts his readers to be careful not to fall short of entering God's eternal rest the way the Israelites fell short of entering their temporal rest (see Heb. 4:1).

So all that is required to be free of stress about eternity is to believe God's promises like John 3:16: "For God so loved the world that he gave his one and only Son, that whoever believes in him shall not perish but have eternal life." Or Romans 5:1, which even mentions the eternal peace with God we gain through believ- ing in Christ: "Therefore, since we have been justified through faith, we have peace with God through our Lord Jesus Christ."

I said earlier that one dimension of peace and rest flows from the other. When we have our eternal affairs settled with God, we ought to be able to trust God with the rest and peace we need while traveling to eternity. Think about it: Which is more important— what is going to happen to you for the rest of eternity or what is going to happen in the next few days, weeks, months, or years? If you said "eternity," you are right. It is far more important to get one's eternal destiny settled.

But with that stress-inducer out of the way, we have to turn to our ability to manage the daily stress of life. We can't prevent all of life's stressful events, but we can create a soft spot on which they can land, limiting the damage. Peace "now" has the same basis as peace "then": Jesus.

The apostle Paul put it most simply when he wrote, "For [Christ] himself is our peace" (Eph. 2:14). The same Jesus Christ who made it possible for us to have peace with God becomes our peace and rest in the midst of life's trials: "Come to me, all you who are weary and burdened, and I will give you rest. Take my yoke upon you and learn from me, for I am gentle and humble in heart, and you will find rest for your souls. For my yoke is easy and my burden is light" (Matt. 11:28–30).

Think of it this way: Where in the four Gospel accounts of the life of Christ do you have a record of Him running or sweating or stressing or wringing His hands—the stuff we do when we're behind the eight ball of life? I know what you're going to say. The night He was in the Garden of Gethsemane—yes, Jesus was definitely stressed that night, so much so that He perspired drops of blood (see Luke 22:44). Given that He knew He was about to be crucified on a Roman cross, we can understand.

I'm talking more about the everyday affairs of life. We just don't get the impression that Jesus lived a stressed-out life—the kind of life Peter lived. Peter is us—fretting, arguing, running, weeping and wailing over things he wished he hadn't done or said. But not Jesus. He had such a confidence that His life was in God's hands that He didn't lose His peace. And to share that peace and rest with us, He invites us to "come unto Him ... and learn from Him." We will find "rest for our souls" by yoking ourselves with Jesus, whose "yoke is easy and [whose] burden is light."

Don't Pray for Peace

When we're stressed and have lost our peace, our human tendency is to pray, "Lord, give me peace and rest." But that's not what the New Testament says to do. It says to pray, but not for peace. Instead we are to turn over to God, in prayer, the items on the Stress Scale that are creating stress in our life: "in everything, by prayer and petition, with thanksgiving, present your requests to God" (Phil. 4:6). "Father, I trust you to show me a new job ... to help me make peace with my boss ... to help me serve my spouse and children when I'm exhausted ... to show me a caregiver for my aging mother ..."

And then, "the peace of God, which transcends all understanding, will guard your hearts and your minds in Christ Jesus" (v. 7). We don't pray for peace, but peace is what we get. We give God all the stress-inducers in our life, and He gives us peace in return. "Peace" is actually the realization from Him that He, having given us His own Son (peace then), "will ... also, along with him, graciously give us all things" (peace now; Rom. 8:32).

Then, instead of rehearsing in our mind the items on the Stress Scale, we meditate on "whatever is true, whatever is noble, whatever is right, whatever is pure, whatever is lovely, whatever is admirable"—anything that is "excellent or praiseworthy," we think on those things. And because God is the epitome of all those things, when we stay focused on Him, "the God of peace will be with you" (Phil. 4:8–9).

When you are left with nothing in your life except stress, God wants to show you what He is up to by allowing you to feel as you do. He wants you to turn to Him for peace and rest, for now and then.

PART IV

WHAT GOD IS UP TO IN KNOWING AND TRUSTING HIM

Because we live in space and time, every person has
A past to make peace with
A present to make choices in
A future to make plans for
And God wants us to trust Him in all three dimensions of life.
Chapter 17 explains why knowing God is easier than you think.
Chapter 18 reminds us that God is ultimately in control of everything.
Chapter 19 talks about how God has a purpose in everything.
Chapter 20 says that God is the best person to trust in life.
Chapter 21 encourages us to remember there is always hope.
Chapter 22 assures us about how God views our past.
Chapter 23 reminds us that we can trust God with the future.
Chapter 24 talks about how to live in the presence of the future.

17

It's Not as Hard as You Think

(Knowing God)

Now this is eternal life: that they may know you, the only true God, and Jesus Christ, whom you have sent.

John 17:3

My Story

The late Russian dissident and author Aleksandr Solzhenitsyn (1918–2008) suffered terribly during his internment in the Russian gulag (prison), immortalized in the three volumes of his epic The Gulag Archipelago, 1918–1956. *It was in his prison experience that Solzhenitsyn gained knowledge of himself and of God that he desperately needed in his life—so much so that he wrote the shocking words, "Bless you, prison, for having been in my life!"*

Anyone who has suffered and survived, if he or she is honest, will say the same about their experience, counterintuitive as it may seem. That's why I can say with all gratitude, "Bless you, Crystal Cathedral, for having been in my life!" Not for a moment would I compare the pain of my experience with Solzhenitsyn's, but the degree of suffering is not the point. Rather, God works in each of our lives with the same purpose regardless of the circumstance: to help us know more of Him and more of ourselves.

When I reflect upon my experience of losing a ministry in which I thought I would spend the rest of my life, I realize just how shallow is our knowledge of God and of ourselves. Because we are created in God's image, we are infinite beings—created for immortality and eternity. That means instead of gradually learning "everything," we gradually learn just how much we don't know. Based on the authoritative nature of our opinions and pronouncements in moments of crisis, we give the opinion of knowing God and knowing ourselves well. But every time I close the door on one of those experiences and look back, I realize how much better my hindsight was than my foresight.

I learned new things about myself—not all of it worth sharing—and had other things confirmed, things I had learned before. And I learned new things about God—His character and His ways. I know even better now why the Bible says our thoughts and ways are not God's thoughts and ways, that His ways and thoughts are as high above us as the heavens are above the earth (see Isa. 55:8–9). If you had asked me in January 2008 what God's "thoughts and ways" were about my life, my ministry, and my future, I would have said, "I believe God plans for me to lead the Crystal Cathedral and its related ministries into greater fruitfulness than in 2007." Wrong! Those were not God's plans for my life. God's plans were as far from my thinking as the heavens are above the earth. Yet it was His plans, not my proposed plans, that came to pass.

I don't feel bad or inadequate for not anticipating God's plans ahead of time—that's not what we're called to do. During the Old Testament era, God did tell His plans to "his servants the prophets" (Amos 3:7). But God has not obligated himself to reveal His plans to us. We are called to know God, not His plans. And that means whatever plans God puts in motion, we can respond positively to them because we know the character of the "Planner."

My greatest point of gratitude is that in July 2008 I knew God at least well enough not to panic, not to do something I would have regretted, when changes in my life began to materialize. I knew that God does not allow random or capricious changes to happen in our lives. I knew Him well enough to know that all of history is filtered through the grid of His benevolence and permission. That did not mean I knew the outcome of what surfaced in July—but it meant that I knew Someone who did. And I am learning, slowly but surely, that is always enough.

Usually when we are down to nothing in our life, we are down to no information or answers. But if we know God, that's the same as knowing where the answers lie. Though we have no answers at the moment, we have God and what He knows. Knowing God means knowing that He is always up to something.

Say you woke up one morning with this thought in your mind: "I would really like to get to know President Obama." That being a worthy goal, you devise a strategy. First, you read everything that others have written about the president: books, opinion pieces dealing with the man rather than his policies, magazine articles—everything you can find. The result of that effort is to accumulate an outline of facts about him: dates, names, places, education, work history, achievements and such that are pertinent to his chronological life.

Since material written about him is secondhand, you turn to the books he has written himself—in this case, there are several. So you read *Dreams from My Father: A Story of Race and Inheritance* and *The Audacity of Hope: Thoughts on Reclaiming the American Dream*. Now you have drilled down to a deeper level; you are learning about the man in his own voice. And you also read many of his speeches.

Armed with a head full of facts and figures about the president, and an introduction to his thought as found in his own writings, you are ready for the final step: spending time with the president himself. In the early decades of our nation it was not hard to meet the country's chief executive. There was no fence around the White House and no Secret Service agents acting as gatekeepers. Anyone could enter the White House and, very often, gain access to the president to voice a concern. But try that today and you won't get very far. For an average citizen, it is next to impossible to gain access to the president at the citizen's request. But there is one circumstance under which you could show up at the White House and be ushered in immediately. And that circumstance is if the president wants to know you.

In the case of the president, or any other dignitary or celebrity to whom access is closely guarded, the issue is not whether we want to know them, but whether they want to know us. If they do, access is granted for as long as they are willing. When they decide the interview or meeting is finished, it is finished. But even then it doesn't mean that we will learn the answers to all of our questions about the president. He may talk to us in guarded terms and give only "official" answers, speaking as the president. Or the ideal might happen: he might loosen his tie, put his feet up on the coffee table, and enter wholly into the conversation, sharing things about his personal life, dreams, ambitions, and so on. Again, that is up to him. Not only does he determine *if* we will get to know him at all, he determines the *degree* of intimacy that will characterize our visit.

We can think of knowing God in similar terms. First, we can read the innumerable books that people have written about God, from which we would learn lots of facts and figures (from the authors' perspective). With that background, we might then turn to the book written by God himself, the Bible. Even though the Bible was penned during approximately fifteen hundred years by forty-odd different writers, it is explicit in its statements that the words are God's (see 2 Tim. 3:16; 2 Peter 1:20–21). The prophets of the Old Testament viewed themselves as God's mouthpieces: "Thus sayeth the Lord!" Reading the Bible gives us a consistent and thorough introduction to the character of God—who He is and what He has done in human history.

But knowing about God, even reading His book, is not the same as knowing God Himself—having a personal relationship with Him. And just as in the case of the president of the United States, that will only happen if God opens the door and invites us in and allows us to know Him "face-to-face." And that is exactly what He has done—to a degree. God does not tell us everything about Himself. Deuteronomy 29:29 says, "The secret things belong to the LORD our God, but the things revealed belong to us and to our children forever, that we may follow all the words of this law."

There are "secret things" that only God knows, and there are things "revealed to us" that belong to us—things God *wants* us to know about Him. And we would not know any of it if God had not taken the initiative to seek us out.

Theologians refer to the "irruption" of God into human history. Volcanoes "erupt"—they explode from within the earth. That's not what God did. He "irrupted"—broke into our realm from outside—in order to bridge the chasm that existed between us and Him. Such a chasm did not exist "in the beginning." In Genesis we have the image of God coming down to the Garden of Eden to be with His two human creatures (see Gen. 3:8). But sin created a gulf between God and man—and the entire Bible is the story of God bridging that gap, reestablishing fellowship with those He created in His own image, making it possible for us to know Him again.

What would have been our eternal condition if God had not taken the initiative to reach out to us and invited us to know Him? We would have been "alienated from God," "without hope and without God in the world" (Col. 1:21; Eph. 2:12). God put in motion a plan to give us hope and Himself, to reveal Himself to us so we might be drawn to His beauty, love, and forgiveness so we might choose differently than Adam and Eve chose—to be close to Him and know Him deeply.

The invitation to intimacy was engraved in the person of God's own Son, Jesus of Nazareth. Sending Jesus to humankind was God's ultimate act of self-revelation: "The Word [Jesus Christ] became flesh and made his dwelling among us. We have seen his glory, the glory of the One and Only, who came from the Father, full of grace and truth" (John 1:14). It could have been that Jesus coming into the world was equivalent to us meeting the president face-to-face in the Oval Office of the White House—a formal, official, nonrevelatory meeting. But to make sure that wasn't the impression we received, Jesus went about telling people, "Follow Me. Let's hang out, let's be friends, let's establish a relationship together. I want to know you, and I want you to know Me" (my paraphrase). He couldn't have described His intent to reunite people with the God who wants to know them any better than when He said, "For the Son of Man came to seek and to save what was lost" (Luke 19:10). People don't usually seek out people they have no desire to know. In fact the opposite is true: Jesus seeking us—looking for us as one would look for a single lost sheep who is separated from the flock and then rejoicing when it is found—is a perfect picture of the heart of God (see Luke 15:3–7). He wants to know us in the worst way.

The best example of Jesus' taking the initiative may be in Matthew 11:28–30:

"Come to me, all you who are weary and burdened, and I will give you rest. Take my yoke upon you and learn from me, for I am gentle and humble in heart, and you will find rest for your souls. For my yoke is easy and my burden is light."

God invites us to himself to teach us about Him and His kingdom. Does that sound like a God who is standoffish, who has His arms crossed and a scowl on His face, who wears a black three-piece suit and never loosens his tie or rolls up His sleeves to make us feel more at ease in His presence? No, not at all. It sounds like a God who wants to be known by those He created and loves.

No One Knows God, But Anyone Can

Perhaps the saddest reality in the world today is how many people have confused knowing about God with knowing God Himself. The Bible says that no one is born knowing God (see John 7:28–29; 1 Cor. 1:21; Gal. 4:8–9; 1 Thess. 4:5; 1 John 3:1). The people who have come to know God throughout history have made a conscious decision to accept His overtures to us as expressed in Jesus' words, "Come to me..."

The Bible also says whether a person knows God or not will be evident in his or her life:

- "They claim to know God, but by their actions they deny him" (Titus 1:16).
- "Whoever does not love does not know God, because God is love" (1 John 4:8).
- "We know that we have come to know him if we obey his commands. The man who says, 'I know him,' but does not do what he commands is a liar, and the truth is not in him" (1 John 2:3–4).

It is not up to us as fallible people to judge who knows God and who doesn't. We can only take people at their word and by their actions. Only God knows for sure who knows Him and who doesn't. But this is true: there is a special bond between God and those who know Him: "I am the good shepherd; I know my sheep and my sheep know me—just as the Father knows me and I know the Father—and I lay down my life for the sheep" (John 10:14–15).

The good news (the gospel) is that it is possible for anyone to know God through Jesus Christ. Watch for the change in these words spoken by Jesus (italics added):

- "You *do not know* [God]..." (John 7:28).
- "Though *you do not know* him..." (John 8:55).
- Then...
- "From now on, *you do know* him and have seen him" (John 14:7b).
- "The world cannot accept him, because it neither sees him nor knows him. But *you know him*, for he lives with you and will be in you" (John 14:17b).

That's quite a change in language. It highlights the fact that coming to know God—Father, Son, and Spirit—is a time-and-space event. Yesterday I didn't know Him, but today I do.

So what happened to make that possible? Faith. Belief. Trust. Acceptance. Embrace. The most common biblical word is faith or belief. When we believe that God really means it when He says, "Come to me..."—and we act on that belief—we enter into God's kingdom through a spiritual rebirth and begin a knowing relationship with Him. There is no other way to know God—no works, no acts of penance, no good intentions, no trying harder. It's simply a matter of honoring God by taking Him at His Word. As the most well-known verse in the Bible says, "Whoever believes in him..." (John 3:16).

Again, the presidential example: you could enjoy five minutes with the president, five hours, or five days. The longer you spent with him, the better you would know him. And the same is true in knowing God—our goal is to know Him better and better, as Paul prayed for the Christians in Ephesus: "I keep asking that the God of our Lord Jesus Christ, the glorious Father, may give you the

Spirit of wisdom and revelation, so that you may *know him better*"
(Eph. 1:17, italics added).

But you can't know Him better if you don't know Him at all.

No One Knows Himself or Herself, But Anyone Can

John Calvin, the great theologian of the Protestant Reformation,
wrote many treatises and commentaries on the Bible and theology.
But he is best remembered for his *Institutes of the Christian Religion*, his mammoth summary of Christian theology first published
in 1536. In chapter one ("The Knowledge of God and of Ourselves
Mutually Connected—The Nature of the Connection"), Calvin
dove into the heart of the Christian religion: knowledge of God
and knowledge of self.

But Calvin identified a problem: because Creator and creatures are tied together in so many ways, "it is not easy to determine
which of the two precedes and gives birth to the other."[1] That is,
do we need to know ourselves before we can know God, or know
God before we can know ourselves? After much theological discussion, he concludes,

> On the other hand, it is evident that man never attains to a
> true self-knowledge until he has previously contemplated
> the face of God, and come down after such contemplation
> to look into himself.... But though the knowledge of God
> and the knowledge of ourselves are bound together by a
> mutual tie, due arrangement requires that we treat of the
> former in the first place, and then descend to the latter.[2]

Calvin concludes that it is only by knowing God first that
we come to a true self-knowledge. And therein lies the flip side of
the "knowing God" coin: finally, finally, coming to know who we
are as individuals. The world is filled with people who are the lost
sheep Jesus talked about finding—people who desperately want to

know who they are and why they exist in this world. The absence of that knowledge can be secretly debilitating and crippling.

And it is obvious that people are looking. Modern society is the mirror image of the efforts of Solomon in his glory years to discover his identity in every corner of his huge kingdom—except in the place where it existed: *coram Deo*—Latin for "in the face, or presence, of God." After much painful and fruitless searching, he finally arrived at that conclusion (see Eccl. 12:13–14). We would be wise not to repeat his flawed strategy to find meaning in life. Rather, if we will set aside our self-discovery and engage in God-discovery, we will find that in Him is knowledge of self, reflected back to us.

Too often we think that, in relationships, our goal is to learn about the other person—and we do accomplish that. But the greatest benefit of relationships is that we learn about ourselves. Others are a mirror—a backboard, a sounding board—from which we get reflections and feedback about ourselves. If our only source of reflection and feedback is from other human beings—people who are similar to us—it can result in the blind leading the blind. Not that we can't learn from others—we definitely can and should. But when it comes to learning what we need to know—how to be a whole, satisfied, fruitful human being—we're out of luck if we only look on the horizontal plane because there are no such people on earth. As Romans 3:23 says, "For all have sinned and fall short of the glory of God."

Therefore we can't start with humans and learn how to know God; we have to start with God and learn how to be human. Why? Because we are created in God's image. By looking into His face—*coram Deo*—we will find reflected back to us who He created us to be. As perfect God and perfect human being, Jesus is the one in whose presence we should live. By becoming comfortable in His presence, He makes us comfortable in our own.

At the gate of the White House, regardless of how boldly you presented your needs and your credentials, you're not getting in unless the president has said he wants to see you. I know without a doubt that God wants to see you. You have even been told to "approach the throne of grace with confidence" (Heb. 4:16) in order to spend time with Him. Bold confidence in yourself won't get you in to see the president, but bold confidence in Christ will get you in to see God.

In the seasons of life when you are down to nothing, remember that God wants to see you and know you. Once you are in His presence, there is no limit to the things He can put in motion. That's just who He is—always up to something.

18

Who's in Charge Here?

(Sovereignty)

When I am afraid, I will trust in you.
In God, whose word I praise,
in God I trust; I will not be afraid.
What can mortal man do to me?

Psalm 56:3–4

My Story

The Crystal Cathedral and its related ministries, plus the Hour of Power *television ministry, have historically been huge operations. The financial numbers associated with these organizations are counted in the many tens of millions of dollars—and that doesn't include the value of the capital assets: land, buildings, equipment, inventories, and others.*

I mention this at all because of a subtle infection that can grow within churches as large as the Crystal Cathedral: a feeling that "we're in charge." Let me say up front that I don't know that this sense of autonomy was any more present at the Crystal Cathedral than at any other church. I only know that as money, size, staff, and influence grow, feelings of power grow. And it takes a conscious effort on the part of all involved not to believe one's own press releases about "success" in ministry.

My experience at the Crystal Cathedral reminded me of who is really in charge in our lives: God. What I wanted to happen didn't happen, and I was powerless to change things. And neither have the expectations of those in leadership come to pass (as of this writing) after my departure. It is a sober reminder that man makes his plans, but God orders his steps (see Prov. 16:9). Every time we think we are in charge in life, God has ways of showing us that we are not. We are continually reminded of our need to humble ourselves before Him, to seek His guidance and wisdom, to be submissive to how He changes our plans, to pray for "success" and allow God to write the definition of that word as He sees fit. As I begin a new season in my own life, I have fresh reasons to daily ensure that I acknowledge God's sovereign and providential control.

Sometimes we get the feeling that nobody is in charge, that our life is the equivalent of a steel ball ricocheting from pillar to post in the pinball game of life. And regardless of what we have in terms of possessions, relationships, or opportunities, we begin to feel like we're down to nothing because we have lost control. When I felt that way after others' control and decisions changed my life, I realized I had the only thing I really needed: God in charge.

A young woman brought her fiancé home to meet her parents. The plan was for the father to spend some time alone with the young man to find out more about his plans for the future. So the father invited the young man into his study and, after some small talk, got right to the point: "So what are your plans for the future?"

"I am a Bible scholar," the young man replied.

"A Bible scholar," the father said. "That's admirable, but how do you plan to provide the kind of living situation for my daughter that she deserves and likely expects?"

"I will study, and God will provide for us," the confident young man replied.

"And can you afford to buy a beautiful engagement ring to demonstrate your love for her?"

"I plan to focus on my studies and trust that God will provide."

"And children?" the father asked. "If you all have children, how will you support them?"

"Don't worry, sir, God will provide," came the reply.

The conversation continued like this for a half hour—every question by the father resulting in the young man's insistence that God would provide. Later, as the husband and wife were preparing for bed, the wife asked, "So how did your conversation go?"

The father answered: "He has no job and no plans, but the good news is he thinks I'm God."

I don't know the source of that story, but as a father, I laugh whenever I come across it. So my thanks to whomever attribution is due—it provides a humorous way for me to identify what Christians *don't* (or shouldn't) mean when they talk about God being in charge: the idea that because God is The Boss, He will do everything in life and we don't have to do anything.

Rather, what we mean by God being in charge is that He is in control of the world and economy He created. And the economy He created is that we have a part and He has a part. For us to do nothing and rely on God's executive powers to do everything is to misunderstand the "system" God put in place. Even before man sinned and broke his relationship with God, he had responsibilities: to tend the Garden of Eden. There's no doubt his responsibilities got harder after his relationship with God was disrupted by sin (see Genesis 3:16–19). But they definitely didn't go away.

I love the illustration of man's part and God's part found in the book of Nehemiah. The exiled Israelites had been given permission by the Persian king to return to Jerusalem and rebuild their city and their temple. It fell to Nehemiah to rebuild the wall around the city, which he did in a Herculean example of managerial efficiency. But the task was hindered by hostile people who had moved into the vacated area during the Jews' seventy years of captivity. So Nehemiah had to rebuild a wall while defending his builders and their city from attack. To that end, Nehemiah wrote:

> From that day on, half of my men did the work, while the other half were equipped with spears, shields, bows and armor. The officers posted themselves behind all the people of Judah who were building the wall. Those who carried materials did their work with one hand and held a weapon in the other, and each of the builders wore his sword at his side as he worked. (Nehemiah 4:16–18a)

God did His part by returning His people to their homeland after seventy years, but Nehemiah knew it was up them to rebuild the wall, which they did with a trowel in one hand and a sword in the other. God may be in charge in this world, but He gives us responsibilities and assignments as well that we are expected to carry out using the talents, gifts, and resources He has given us. And sometimes those responsibilities include going head-to-head with forces arrayed against us.

The Bible is full of information about God's control over the affairs of humanity—and about how we are to live in light of that fact.

The Evidence

In his missionary travels throughout the Mediterranean, the apostle Paul found himself in Athens (in modern-day Greece). While there he made his way to the Areopagus, the rocky hill in Athens where temples to the Greek pantheon of gods sat, the Parthenon being the best-preserved for today's visitors. On the Areopagus, it was the custom for Greek philosophers to gather and debate. Paul, as he did everywhere, was preaching the gospel to any who would listen and the philosophers said, "What is this babbler trying to say? ... He seems to be advocating foreign gods" (Acts 17:18).

As Paul gained the attention of the philosophers on the hill, he requested permission to speak to them. Contained in his remarks is one of the clearest statements in the Bible of God's "in-chargeness" in the affairs of the world. Remember as you read his words: Paul was standing in the midst of temples and altars dedicated to the panoply of man-made deities invented by the Greeks—there was even an altar with the inscription, "To an Unknown God." They had gods they hadn't even named yet, but worshipped them nonetheless. Paul spoke to them about a personal God who created the world and everything in it:

> The God who made the world and everything in it is the Lord of heaven and earth and does not live in temples built by hands. And he is not served by human hands, as if he needed anything, because he himself gives all men life and breath and everything else. From one man he made every nation of men, that they should inhabit the whole earth; and he determined the times set for them and the exact places where they should live. God did this so that men would seek him and perhaps reach out for him and find him, though he is not far from each one of us. (Acts 17:24–27)

Paul's God does not depend upon humans for His existence— their temples and services. He needs nothing from humanity, yet gives everything to humankind: "life and breath and everything else."

That is an amazing declaration of Scripture—that God moves nations and peoples around, establishing borders and boundaries, that they might accomplish His purposes and plans, all of which are for the good of those who know Him.

This is hard for us to grasp, I know—I struggle with the practical implications of this as much as anyone. All we see from our vantage point in the world is the wars, the invasions, the genocides, the rising and falling of leaders, the occasional birth and death of nations, the dissolution of empires into nation states—they all seem to be purely the result of human choices and actions. Yet Paul is saying that the hand of God is behind everything at the local and global level.

Think of the nation of Israel, for instance. Certain parts of the Christian church find great significance in the fact that Israel was restored to nationhood in 1948. They see the hand of God at work fulfilling ancient prophecies, keeping ancient promises to His covenant people to gather them from the four corners of the world and restore them to their Promised Land. At the heart of Israel's insistence on her right to live in her homeland are these promises, much to the consternation of her Arab neighbors. It's difficult to argue with those who see significance in this nation-building activity given Israel's history. The ten northern tribes of Israel were carried into captivity by Assyria, never to return to Israel, and the two southern tribes were carried into captivity to Babylon, returning to Israel after seventy years (though many Jews stayed in Babylon, not returning). They lived in the land for several centuries, through the period of Christ and the early church, until the Roman legions under Titus destroyed Jerusalem and dispersed the Jews in AD 70—and they have wandered the world as strangers and aliens ever since.

Until 1948, that is, when by United Nations' decree the Zionist movement led Jews out of Europe and Russia after World War II to settle in Palestine, the modern name given to the Holy Land after World War I. And Jews have been streaming back to their homeland from all over the world ever since. There has never been a more unlikely movement of peoples on earth than the return of Jews to Israel—nearly six million to date. The most persecuted race of people in the history of the world is once again alive and well in her homeland with a Gross Domestic Product of some $200 billion.

The fact that this regathering of Israel was foretold by her prophets more than two thousand years ago—not to mention the age-old antagonism between Israel and her Arab neighbors that continues from the time of Isaac and Ishmael—gives even skeptics reason to consider God's control of the affairs of the earth and its peoples. Regardless of which side of the Jewish-Palestinian debate you are on, something completely unlikely and seemingly impossible has happened. But for the God who is in charge, all things are possible (see Matt. 19:26).

But God is not just in charge of the affairs of nations. After all, what are nations except collections of individuals? For God to accomplish something at a national level, some individual(s) need to make decisions and take steps. So God is just as involved with us personally as He is with nations.

The classic statement of this reality is Jesus' own words, "And even the very hairs of your head are all numbered" (Matt. 10:30). Jesus said this in the context of sending out His disciples to preach the good news of the kingdom of God. They should not fear those who would oppose them because God's care for them extended to the very hairs of their head. A metaphor, of course, but the point is easy to understand.

And there is the well-known passage in Psalm 139 that says, "All the days ordained for me were written in your book before one of them came to be" (v. 16). David had been marveling at the completeness of God's involvement in his life and suddenly realized that God had been planning and orchestrating his life from before David was born.

But let's be honest: just because the Bible uses these word images to talk about God's overarching superintendence of our life … does that make it so? Well, every person has to come to grips with this issue—how much of the Bible do we believe? How many of the metaphors and word pictures are just that—or are they pictures that represent truth just as doctrinal as the words about salvation, like John 3:16?

The Bible answers that question itself, saying that, "All Scripture is God-breathed and is useful for teaching, rebuking, correcting and training in righteousness" (2 Tim. 3:16). It also says that "no prophecy of Scripture" is the result of an individual's private opinion; the Scriptures did not have their "origin in the will of man, but men spoke from God as they were carried along by the Holy Spirit" (2 Peter 1:20–21). So I choose to take the Bible at its word. I choose to believe that God watches the sparrows, the hairs on my head, the kings of nations, and nations themselves and orchestrates them all according to His perfect wisdom and will.

The Exercise

Count Basie and "Lips" Page were two legends in the world of jazz from a previous era. The two men were together in Kansas City and were supposed to go out one evening, except Count Basie did not have his wardrobe with him. The two men being about the same size, Page told his friend Basie he could wear one of his suits. That worked for Basie because he knew Page to be a stylish dresser and knew he would be well attired. Basie agreed to the arrangement but would reveal later, "I didn't know what I was getting myself into."

Everywhere they went that night—restaurants, clubs, wherever—Page was at Basie's elbow cautioning him about soiling his suit: "Don't lean on that," or "Hey man, that chair is kinda dirty," or "Be careful where you sit, man." Basie said it was one of the most unenjoyable evenings he had ever spent, saying, "I never was so glad to get back home and take off a suit."[1]

I cite that story to compare "Lips" Page with God and us with Count Basie. Page owned the suit so he had a right to be concerned about how it was treated. But he made life miserable for his friend by micromanaging his every move. His generous offer should have been made with the understanding that generosity entails risk—he might have to have the suit cleaned or repaired if anything happened. But instead, both men had a miserable evening—one being picky and the other being picked on.

That is NOT how God chooses to exercise His control over the earth. God owns us and the whole world, but He turns us loose in His world to exercise our will to choose and act—just as Adam and Eve were free to make the choices they did in the Garden of Eden. God is not following us around, tapping us on the shoulder every time we are about to make a misstep in life. Somehow—and this I don't understand—God is able to allow us freedom in life while being sure that His purposes and plans are still accomplished. As I've already mentioned in this book, God causes all things to work together for good for those who are called according to His purpose—and one of His purposes is to conform us to the image of Jesus Christ for all eternity (see Rom. 8:28–29).

And I have no idea how God does that. But I'm comfortable with not knowing. The more I witness the hand and heart of God at work in my life—the story I'm telling in this book is a prime example—the more settled I become in the biblical truth that God is in charge of everything, that I don't have to worry about anything. He loves me and turns me loose in His earthly sandbox to build and enjoy my life consistent with the guidelines for happiness and safety He has given in His Word. And I have yet to find the edges of that sandbox—the place where He says, "Don't do that—you're going to make a mess of it!" He takes my messes and my successes and brings them all together for His glory and for my good.

William Carey (1761–1834), the father of the modern missionary movement, labored for forty years in India without once returning to his home in England. A brilliant man, he translated parts of the Bible into more than a dozen Indian languages—with pen and paper, one foreign word at a time. One day after he had been at his work for twenty years, a fire raged through his printing offices and warehouse. All his equipment, along with the manuscripts he had worked on for twenty years, were destroyed in a matter of hours. And he had no Xerox copies, no copies backed up on a computer hard drive—nothing. It was all gone.

When he wrote with this news to his pastor friend in England, Andrew Murray, he said, "The ground must be labored over again, but we are not discouraged.... We have all been supported under the affliction, and preserved from discouragement." He said that in the previous Lord's Day meeting he had preached from Psalm 46:10—"Be still, and know that I am God"—communicating these two points:

1. God has a sovereign right to dispose of us as he pleases.
2. We ought to acquiesce in all that God does with us and to us.

When we are down to nothing, we do have to remember what is true: God is God, and we're not. God, not us, is in charge. When He allows our circumstances to make us wonder where He is in our lives, here's the answer: He is right where He has always been, causing all things to work together for good. We have to remember to do our part while He does His. Because He never sleeps or slumbers, we know that He is always doing His part in our life—always up to something.

19

Cancel Your Accident Insurance

(Purpose)

In him we were also chosen, having been predestined according to the plan of him who works out everything in confor-
mity with the purpose of his will, in order that we, who were
the first to hope in Christ, might be for the praise of his glory.

Ephesians 1:11–12

My Story

*Many people don't know this, but the Crystal Cathedral is
part of a Christian denomination called the Reformed Church
in America (RCA). While the church is known as the Crystal
Cathedral, the official name of the church when my father
founded it was, and still is, Garden Grove Community
Church—Garden Grove being the small community just south
of Anaheim, California, now swallowed up by the greater Los
Angeles metropolitan area.*

*What is common now—omitting denominational refer-
ences from the name of a church—was less common when my
father omitted reference to the RCA from the name of his
church. But he was born and bred in the Dutch Reformed tradition, as was I. The RCA is the oldest non-Anglican Protes-*

tant denomination in continuous existence in America. Its roots in America extend back to 1628 when the first Dutch Reformed congregation was established in New Amsterdam (now New York City). That congregation continues to exist today at the corner of Fifth Avenue and Twenty-ninth Street in New York City under the name Marble Collegiate Church.

The Schuller heritage, being Dutch, influenced my father's decisions to attend two RCA-affiliated schools, Hope College and Western Theological Seminary. After seminary he was ordained as a minister in the RCA and founded Garden Grove Community Church as part of the RCA in 1955. Besides adhering to the historic, orthodox creeds of the Christian faith (the Apostles' Creed, the Nicene Creed, the Athanasian Creed), the RCA also subscribes to the later confessions and creeds that grew out of the Protestant Reformation (began in 1517): the Belgic Confession, the Heidelberg Catechism, the Canons of Dort, and the Belhar Confession. That is a serious Reformed heritage that I grew up in!

Why this history lesson? Because of how the history and theology of the RCA shaped my own life and thinking—and how it impacted the events of 2008. Protestant churches (denominations) that have roots in the Protestant Reformation share a strong commitment to the sovereignty of God in the affairs of humanity. Yes, man chooses, decides, and acts in life—we are not puppets on strings—but all of man's human volition falls under the umbrella of God's sovereignty. It is God's will that is done on earth as it is in heaven. Practically speaking, I like this expression of the interaction of God's sovereignty and man's will: "We get up in the morning energetically and work as if everything depends on us. But we go to bed at the end of the day peacefully knowing that everything depends on God."

Growing up in this theological environment, I learned early on, and later confirmed by my own biblical study and *experience, that a commitment to the sovereignty of God has an overriding practical implication: there are no accidents with God! From our human perspective, life is filled with accidents and seemingly arbitrary or random events—especially when they result from a negative motivation in a person. But from God's perspective, none of those exist. God sees the past, present, and future as one. He knows every event that has or will take place and ordains it for His loving and good purposes. He is not the author of contrary, negative, or evil events, but He allows them for His own purposes. Indeed, He uses them to accomplish His sovereign plans and purposes.*

So during the summer of 2008, as I did what I felt was my responsibility as a human being—to work hard to resolve the conflicts that had arisen in our church—my Reformed, biblical heritage kept whispering in my ear: remember, Robert, there are no accidents with God. It was still agonizing. I still lost sleep. I still hurt over those events. But not ultimately. Ultimately I know that God is sovereign in all the affairs of men—even in the affairs of what seems at times to be the most intractable and complicated institution on earth, His church!

When I thought I was down to nothing, another thing I realized I had never lost was my conviction regarding the sovereignty of God (for which I am grateful to my Reformed heritage). If God allows big changes, big events, in our life, they are not accidents. Those changes and events are often the first sign we have, that God is up to something new.

To clarify the title of this chapter, I am not encouraging you to cancel your accident insurance—or any other insurance policies you have. In California, as in most other states I assume, it is against the law not to have "auto" insurance, which, for all practical purposes, is accident insurance. And with the recent passage of the Health Care and Education Reconciliation Act of 2010, it has become against the law not to have health insurance of some kind.

Even though there is no stronger believer in God's sovereignty than I, I carry insurance policies to protect my family against financial calamity brought on by unplanned events. The Bible calls on us to be wise and responsible as well as faithful. The Bible promotes saving (see Prov. 6:6–8; 13:22) and counting the costs in life (Luke 14:28–33), both of which are a form of insurance against seen and unforeseen events. But because modern events can be so expensive to resolve, insurance spreads the risk out among a larger pool of contributors. You may live an accident-free life, but your monthly insurance premiums ensure you will be protected if not.

The question could be raised whether insurance is an attempt to negate or deflect the effects of something God may have intended to happen in His sovereign will—and therefore an attempt to change or resist the will of God. That is a question that allows for no resolution with which the human mind will ever be comfortable. It is an infinite and fruitless process to speculate on the what-ifs in life—the places where man's volition intersects with the sovereignty of God. We are called to formulate our understanding on what we know God has revealed, not what He hasn't. And the Bible has revealed two things clearly: God is sovereign, and man is responsible (see Rom. 9:1–29). We are called to act responsibly, in faith, and trust God with every outcome.

Somewhere in her monumental book, *The Tapestry: The Life and Times of Francis and Edith Schaeffer*, Edith Schaeffer used an illustration that stuck with me. Being Presbyterians themselves, the Schaeffers (as reflected in their many books) lived their lives under the umbrella of God's sovereignty. Yet their lives were filled with more twists and turns than the narrow mountain roads in Switzerland where they lived and ministered for decades. To read the accounts of their ministry at L'Abri (The Shelter) in Switzerland is to read page after page of ministry, family, financial, personal, and relational "accidents"—events no one planned on but were "normal" for anyone living by faith as missionaries to intellectual and countercultural young people in the 1960s and beyond.

Edith Schaeffer said that life is like a giant tapestry hanging on the wall of a medieval European castle. On the front of the tapestry an image of great beauty is presented in intricate detail, created by the warp and weft threads passing over each other in a carefully orchestrated arrangement. A beautiful tapestry can look like an immovable painting, so precise is the completed image. But in truth, every tiny part of a tapestry is a thread of a unique size, material, and color—tens of thousands of them in a given tapestry. While every thread is separate and seemingly meaningless on its own, together, in the hands of a master weaver, the separate threads become a unified picture. Looking on the backside of a tapestry presents a totally different picture—threads are stretched to connect with others, threads are tied off in knots, and the whole thing can look indecipherable—a mess to the untrained eye.

And that's the way life looks at times to us—threads going off in different directions, threads stopped, new threads started, like the back of a tapestry. And mostly we see the back of the tapestry of our life, not the front. But the view of our tapestry from heaven is different. God sees the beautiful version of our life where all the "messes" on the backside of the tapestry have a purpose and a reason. When we learn to see life with God's eyes—and granted, that often happens in retrospect—we begin to appreciate the art and craft invested in our life by God. There is a beauty and symmetry that we find it hard to see when we're in the midst of one of life's "accidents."

And that is the walk of faith—living by faith, not by sight (see 2 Cor. 5:7). The walk of faith is believing that every thread has a purpose, that every knot is holding something critical in its proper place, that the picture God is constructing has a beauty He can see and which we will see in due course when we gain the perspective of time and wisdom—and ultimately the perspective of eternity.

God's Purpose for Your Life

One of the most famous of the historic Reformed confessions of Christian belief is known as the *Westminster Standards*. Its three parts are "The Confession of Faith," "The Larger Catechism," and "The Shorter Catechism." The answer to Question 1 of The Shorter Catechism is famous for its brevity and focus:

> Q1. What is the chief end of man?
> A1. Man's chief end is to glorify God, and to enjoy him forever.

That short answer is thought to be the best statement of the purpose of human beings ever penned outside the Bible. And it certainly fits nicely with the clearest statement in the Bible concerning the purpose of God for those who belong to Him: "For those God foreknew he also predestined to be conformed to the likeness of his Son, that he might be the firstborn among many brothers" (Rom. 8:29). Amazing! God's ultimate purpose for my life is to become like Jesus Christ.

What does it mean to enjoy God forever? The psalmist David took a stab at the idea in Psalm 16:11. He expressed confidence (v. 10) that the grave would not be the end of his life, that God would not abandon him to decay in the earth. He then stated his conviction boldly: "You have made known to me the path of life; you will fill me with joy in your presence, with eternal pleasures at your right hand." *Eternal pleasures at God's right hand*. We know what earthly pleasures are, and we can extrapolate those feelings using our human imagination to get closer to eternal pleasures. But doing our best probably leaves us far short of understanding.

A better way is to eavesdrop on a conversation Jesus had with God the Father on the night He was arrested and condemned to die. From Jesus' conversational prayer with His Father, look at the phrases He used and imagine what kind of relationship they had:

> Glorify your Son, that your Son may glorify you.... I have brought you glory on earth by completing the work you gave me to do. And now, Father, glorify me in your presence with the glory I had with you before the world began.... For I gave [my disciples] the words you gave me and they accepted them.... All I have is yours, and all you have is mine.... Holy Father, protect [my disciples]...so that they may be one as we are one....I am coming to you now.... Father, just as you are in me and I am in you. May they also be in us....I have given them the glory that you gave me, that they may be one as we are one: I in them and you in me.... [Y]ou loved me before the creation of the world." (John 17:1–24)

The kind of intimacy and love ("pleasure") enjoyed by Jesus and His heavenly Father is hard to comprehend. Unity, intimacy, love, agreement, harmony, glory—divine pleasure in a divine relationship. But here's what's important for us: it is God's purpose for us to be conformed to the image of Jesus. If that is the kind of relationship with God that the "firstborn" Son of God enjoys, surely we (the "many brothers" [and sisters!]) of Romans 8:29 can expect it as well.

But you may have noticed: the word "purpose" is not in verse 29. So how do we know this is God's purpose for us? Because Paul uses that word in Romans 8:28, the preceding verse (and second only to John 3:16, perhaps the most beloved verse in the Bible): "And we know that in all things God works for the good of those who love him, who have been called according to his purpose." There in those two verses are the cross and the crown, the problems and the pleasure, the pain and the gain for the person who belongs to God.

In the second half of Romans 8, Paul has been contrasting our present suffering with our future glory. And Romans 8:28–29 are the culmination of a chain of thoughts. First, he writes that we have hope in the midst of our troubles—being down to nothing—because our hope is in God (vv. 24–25). Then he says God's Holy Spirit prays within us when we don't even know how to pray, interceding "for the saints *in accordance with God's will*" (vv. 26–27; italics added). There it is—the sovereign, accident-preventing will of God! Even when we are suffering, the Holy Spirit intercedes for us to God the Father that we might persevere in God's will.

Then come our two focus verses—verses 28–29—that explain how God is at work in all those difficult circumstances to work them together for good "according to His purpose"—which is that we might be conformed to the image of the Son of God, Jesus Christ. Pastor and author Robert Morgan puts it this way: "In Christ, we have an ironclad, unfailing, all-encompassing, God-given guarantee that every single circumstance in life will sooner or later turn out well for those committed to Him."[1]

In other words, there are no accidents with God. God's purpose of you getting to heaven conformed to the image of Christ will not be thwarted. And He will use every single event ("all things") in your life as part of the process of accomplishing His purpose in your life.

The Biggest Little Word in the Bible

Pastor Morgan goes on to recount the events in the life of a friend of his. Dave was a pastor, married to a woman who had been a diabetic since age twenty-one, a condition that resulted in occasional health crises in her life. Near the end of 2002, she was in and out of the hospital several times, and one of her kidneys failed, forcing her onto dialysis. About that time, a difficult season in his church resulted in Dave losing his pastorate—the first time something like that had ever happened. Dave had no income and no job and a wife in a severe medical crisis. When they were down to nothing, God was up to something.

A member of their former church covered the monthly premium of their health insurance so Dave's wife could continue her treatments. Gifts of food and money began appearing. Another friend gave them his vacation condominium to live in which "just happened" to be near a hospital with an excellent kidney transplant hospital—exactly what they needed when Dave's wife's younger sister donated a kidney. After the transplant surgery and his wife's health recovered, God opened the door for a wonderful new church for Dave to pastor. Looking back, Dave saw the purpose of God at work: four months off work so he could shepherd his wife through her health crisis, gifts that sustained them during that period, then the resumption of their ministry.[2]

If there is a key word in Romans 8:28, it has to be "all"—what many have called the "biggest little word in Scripture." And this is how we know there are no accidents with God—because He uses "all things" in our lives for good, for conforming us to the eternal image of His Son, Jesus. If you will meditate for a moment on the power of that word "all," you will be convicted of "all" the things you have ever complained about or wished had never happened.

I identified with Pastor Dave's story—being thrust out of a fruitful ministry in a church he loved. But I'm glad that "losing your pastorate" is included in the "all things" in Romans 8:28. It means there is nothing—not one thing—that God does not intend to use in accomplishing His purpose for your life. Even if you are seemingly down to nothing, God is going to use that "nothingness" to accomplish His purpose in you.

Do you want to see God's purpose accomplished in your life, to become like Jesus? (Yes.) Then you must live like Jesus, who learned obedience through the things He suffered (see Heb. 5:8). It's all right to question the things that happen in our lives—the times when we get down to nothing. But only if we come to the same conclusion that Jesus came to concerning the will of God: "Father, if you are willing, take this cup from me; yet not my will, but yours be done" (Luke 22:42).

Can you think of anything in your life not covered by "all things"? (No.) Then even when you are down to nothing, you still have this: the promise of God that there are no accidents in life. Not even being down to nothing. Even that trying circumstance has a part to play. If you are down to nothing right now—physically, emotionally, financially, relationally—spend time meditating on Romans 8:29–30. And then thank God that His will includes being up to something new and good in your life.

20

You Have to Trust Somebody

(Trust)

When I am afraid,
I will trust in you.
In God, whose word I praise,
in God I trust; I will not be afraid.
What can mortal man do to me?

Psalm 56:3–4

My Story

It's the worst feeling in the world—feeling duped or deceived. And we've all been there at one time or another. There are different levels of broken trust, of course, from outright lies to the gradual realization that things aren't like they were supposed to be. I've experienced both in recent days, and the experiences have caused me to think again about the whole issue of trust.

The "gradual revelation" experience was the one I've described in these introductory stories. I entered into a relationship with my parents—who have run the Crystal Cathedral since its inception—and the legal board of the church and the television ministry. Everything was formalized legally, of course, so "trust" really wasn't an issue. This was not like buying a used car on a handshake from one's neighbor. (There were detailed contracts in place outlining my duties and responsibili-

ties and those of my father, the outgoing senior pastor; another contract with the Crystal Cathedral congregation, and another with the denomination. I had legal options with regard to the violation of those contracts that I chose not to exercise.)

Or was it? I think it was more like that for me. I knew the legal aspects had to be formalized and was fine with that. But coming to the Crystal Cathedral as pastor and host of the television ministry was like coming home. My parents founded the church and built it in their image for more than fifty years. We didn't sign legal papers in our family when we went about the multitude of arrangements and decisions that every family does. We acted on trust—as a family. Word given was word kept. And I returned to the Crystal Cathedral with that expectation.

"Expectation" is the operative word—I was probably at fault for having too "friendly" an expectation about what I was entering into. When my parents made the decision to drastically scale back my involvement with the ministries, I took it as a breach of trust. There were no operational reasons for my demotion—both the church and the Hour of Power *were prospering. Rather, as my father stated publicly, there was a lack of "shared vision." I thought I had been hired to cast a vision for the ministries for the future, so I was surprised that my vision was being resisted.*

Every time trust is broken, we feel like we're down to nothing—there is a vacuum now where confidence and trust once lived. But because God is trustworthy, we are never down to nothing. Even when human trust is broken, God is always up to something.

During his so-called "born-again period" (late seventies to early eighties) singer-songwriter Bob Dylan recorded three albums, *Slow Train Coming* being the first in 1979. The most

well-received song on that album—it won a Grammy in 1980—
was "Gotta Serve Somebody." It's a lengthy song—five and one-
half minutes—so I won't go through all the lyrics. But the first two
stanzas set the tone:

> You may be an ambassador to England or France
> You may like to gamble, you might like to dance
> You may be the heavyweight champion of the world
> You may be a socialite with a long string of pearls.
>
> But you're gonna have to serve somebody, yes indeed
> You're gonna have to serve somebody
> It may be the devil or it may be the Lord
> But you're gonna have to serve somebody.[1]

This may not be Dylan at his lyrical best, but the point is well
made: everybody serves somebody in life. And since Jesus had a
way of dividing humanity into two camps—those for Him or
against Him, those who love God or those who love "mammon"—
Dylan was on good ground in making the either/or division in his
song.

I cite this song in this chapter because I think we could substitute the word "trust" for "serve" and make a defendable point:
"You're gonna have to trust somebody." As Dylan wrote, you may
choose to trust the devil (or a person, a government, an institution,
money, power, status, or something else in this world) or you may
choose to trust the Lord—but you're gonna have to trust
somebody.

Trust is a bummer, isn't it? We have to extend, but we do so
knowing we're likely to be hurt. We have to exercise trust many
times every single day of our life. We trust that the grocery clerk is
ringing up our items correctly. We trust that a spouse who adds "I
love you" to his or her good-bye when we part really means it. We
trust that the policeman who pulls us over is a real policeman, not

an imposter out to do us harm. We trust that our teenager's plans for the evening are actually where he or she is going to be. We trust that our financial planner is actually investing our hard-earned and hard-saved funds and not embezzling them. And we trust that the prescription the doctor gives us will help us.

If we don't exercise trust, we stop living and functioning. Our whole society—our cultural conversation and interaction—is based on trust. It's an unspoken moral code among *most* of the people in *most* societies—emphasis on *most*. In my book *Leaning into God When Life Is Pushing You Away*, I told the story of Don Richardson, a missionary to the Sawi people in New Guinea— how they seemed to delight in the Bible story about a man named Judas who befriended Jesus for three years before betraying Him. Judas was a hero in their eyes! It turns out duplicity was a high value in the Sawi culture. They would catch a baby pig in the jungle, bring it home, and earn its trust by taking care of it, for the sole purpose of killing it and eating it as an adult—much easier than chasing an adult pig through the jungle. They would even do the same with humans, welcoming a stranger into the village and befriending him in order to later kill and eat him.[2]

Like I said—*most* cultures. I'm glad trust has not been completely replaced by deceit as a high value in American society and in most societies around the world. But even when we are expecting the best, the worst can happen. And one story in the Bible illustrates what can happen when naïve trust is exercised—and how it can hopefully be avoided.

The Prologue to Trust

The setting of Joshua 9 was the Promised Land of Canaan; Joshua had led the Israelites across the Jordan River, and the major Canaanite city of Jericho was destroyed. Before moving farther into the land to roust the inhabitants out of their promised homeland, Joshua conducted a covenant renewal ceremony with the people. He read to them all the laws of Moses, "the blessings and the curses" (see Deut. 27–28), to remind them of their total dependence on God for everything in their lives. It is ironic that Joshua himself became one of the first to forget to depend on God for something critical.

Many of the surrounding nations made war against the Israelites to prevent their entrance into Canaan. But the residents of one city, Gibeon, had a different plan: they sought to establish a covenant of peace with Israel. That would have been impossible, however, because Joshua had been commanded by God to drive out all the inhabitants of the land, not to make treaties of coexistence with any of them. So how would Gibeon (the leader of a group of four cities; see Josh. 9:17) arrange to make a treaty of peace with Joshua so he couldn't drive them out of the land? By duplicity and deceit.

A group of people from Gibeon—just a few miles from where the Israelites were camped—clothed themselves in ragged clothing, loaded their donkeys with old, cracked wineskins, and took with them dry, crusty bread. All this elaborate planning was to support the story they told Joshua when they met him: "We have come from a distant country; make a treaty with us. . . . This bread of ours was warm when we packed it at home on the day we left to come to you. But now see how dry and moldy it is. And these wineskins that we filled were new, but see how cracked they are. And our clothes and sandals are worn out by the very long journey" (vv. 6, 12–13).

They told a great story, saying they had heard of the power of Israel's God, and they wanted to submit themselves to Israel to be their servants. Joshua, to his credit, challenged their story: "But perhaps you live near us. How then can we make a treaty with you?" (v. 7). But the Gibeonites persisted and Joshua gave in— "Then Joshua made a treaty of peace with them to let them live, and the leaders of the assembly ratified it by oath" (v. 15). But tucked away in Joshua 9:14 is the mistake in their due diligence that would turn out to be a thorn in Israel's flesh: "The men of

Israel sampled their provisions *but did not inquire of the* LORD" (italics added).

Three days later, as their knowledge of their new homeland increased, Joshua and his leaders learned that the Gibeonites were not from a foreign country but were their neighbors. Immediately Joshua and his army set out for Gibeon, but they couldn't attack the deceivers because of the treaty they had signed. So they subjugated them, making them "woodcutters and water carriers for the entire community" (v. 21). The Gibeonites remained alive and got their wish to be servants (though perhaps in a different fashion than they had hoped for), and Joshua kept the terms of the treaty of peace by not killing them.

It was a rookie's mistake that Joshua made—limiting his due diligence about the strangers to the natural realm. He should have taken it to the next level and inquired of the Lord: "Lord, we want to obey You by not entering into covenants with pagan nations. Please open our eyes to see who these people really are, if they are who they claim to be. Help us not to be deceived. Help us not to put our trust in someone who will not honor it, thereby causing dishonor to Your name. Give us a sign, Lord, something that will let us move ahead with confidence."

(I confess to this being a mystery. I prayed diligently about taking on the senior pastor role of the Crystal Cathedral but still was not "protected" from the events that transpired. I believe God uses even our prayers and our most honorable intentions to work out His perfect plan in our life—even when the reverse of what we pray for happens.)

That ought to be the prologue to any "deal" we may be considering that has serious, long-term implications: marriage, a business partnership, a relationship, a job, an investment—actually, any decision we make ought to have prayer and the counsel of God as its prologue. We live in a world in which we see reports of breaches of trust in the news almost daily. Whether such breaches make the news or not, we know they happen. Statistically speaking, there's no reason we should be immune to people who are not trust-worthy. If we do not live with a divine shield of protection in this world, we can be deceived. Even with a divine shield of protection around us, we will still be deceived. But God will turn it into good.

Footnote to the story: Gibeon was an important city in Canaan, occupying a central and strategic position. When the king of Jerusalem heard how Joshua's armies destroyed Jericho and Ai, and how Gibeon had made a treaty with the invading Israelites, he gathered four other kings and their armies and attacked Gibeon. Normally, this would have been a favor to Israel—it would be one more Canaanite city that Joshua wouldn't have to attack himself. But since he had made a covenant with Gibeon, he was obligated to go and defend them against the coalition of five kings who were attacking.

The point is this: entering into improper relationships can create huge obligations in the future, obligations we will be spared if we are not deceived. That's good theological theory, but the execution isn't always that simple. Joshua failed to inquire of the Lord and incurred obligations that became like a millstone around his neck. Other times we may inquire of the Lord and still be taken in or deceived. But there is no question that our responsibility is to inquire—to ask the Lord to reveal anything we need to know. What He does or doesn't reveal is up to Him, and ours to act on in good faith.

The Epilogue to Trust

I love this illustration of total trust that appeared in the monthly magazine of the seminary I attended. Author Dale Bruner's words are so enjoyable that I'll quote him directly:

> The best parable of trust we have in our home is our cat, Clement of Alexandria. (He had a companion cat, Archbishop Thomas Cranmer, but a local coyote ate the archbishop recently.) When our cat goes outside, he lives

in terror. He looks around as though it's a jungle, and he is terrified. But when he comes in the house, he lies on the floor right between the kitchen and the dining room— where we walk most frequently—and falls asleep in total trust. [My wife] Kathy or I could squash Clement's head, but he trusts us.

Our cat lives in complete, total confidence with his human companions. (In this connection, I think the best animal synonym for faith is purring.) Every time I see Clement just lying there, I say to myself, *That's what Jesus wants me to do—to trust him.* The kind of trust the cat shows in us is the kind of trust the Lord Jesus Christ invites from us.[3]

Purring in the midst of feline contentment after negotiating the jungles of this life is a perfect metaphor for trust (see Ps. 131:1–2). And it's also the epilogue to trust. We perform our due diligence in this world, vetting those we meet and with whom we may want to establish some kind of temporary or permanent relationship. And we seek the Lord for His wisdom and guidance, going slowly and making ourselves available for any course correction He might offer. And then we rest; we trust; we purr in contentment that we've done all we can do and now we hand it over to Him. He is trustworthy—meaning worthy of trust. He is the one person we can trust without fail, regardless of what happens.

Jesus is no stranger to broken promises, don't forget. Two men He poured himself into for three years turned their back on Him when He needed them most. Peter denied three times in the space of minutes that he even knew who Jesus was on the night Jesus was arrested and arraigned in Jerusalem (see Matt. 26). Peter knew immediately what he had done and was heartbroken at his lack of faithfulness to the Lord he loved. And fortunately, he and Jesus restored their relationship shortly after the resurrection (see John 21), and Peter died as a martyr for Christ in Rome many years later.

The other major instance of betrayed trust is more famous and ended poorly. Judas Iscariot, the treasurer in the group of Jesus' twelve disciples, took a payoff from the religious leaders of the day to help them entrap Jesus when He was in Jerusalem for the Passover. The arrangement worked, and Jesus was arrested in the Garden of Gethsemane where He had gone to pray in anticipation of the ordeal He knew was coming. Like Peter, Judas felt remorse over what he had done, returning the money to those who hired him. But instead of trusting that somehow Jesus could forgive his trickery, he took his own life by hanging.

So Jesus knows what it feels like to trust two close friends and have His trust go unrewarded. The human part of His nature was no doubt hurt and wounded by these failures of his friends. But it is His very experience with the pain of failed trust that makes Him the epilogue, the last word, when our trust is not returned by others. The writer of the book of Hebrews in the New Testament makes explicit the fact that Jesus can help us because He has been through everything we have. If we are tempted to retaliate against those who have shown themselves not to be trustworthy, He can help because He was tempted with the same thoughts (see Heb. 2:18; 4:15). The result of His experience with our kind of disappointment is that we should "approach the throne of grace with confidence, so that we may receive mercy and find grace to help us in our time of need" (Heb. 4:16).

I love the way Psalm 4:4–5 pictures both the prologue and the epilogue to trust:

> In your anger do not sin;
> when you are on your beds,
> search your hearts and be silent. *Selah*
>
> Offer right sacrifices
> and trust in the LORD.

It's natural for anger to well up when our trust in another person leads to disappointment. But to keep that anger from turning sinful (see Eph. 4:26), there are things we can do: *Search* our hearts to see if there is any fault in us (see Ps. 139:23–24). Be *silent*; be slow to speak (see James 1:19). Offer the *sacrifice* of praise to God that He is in control (see Heb. 13:15). And *trust* in the Lord to direct your path (see Prov. 3:5–6).

In the final analysis, we should not be surprised when our trust is not honored. It is going to happen in this life, and we need to be prepared. That's the realism we find in Psalm 118:8–9:

> It is better to take refuge in the LORD
> than to trust in man.
> It is better to take refuge in the LORD
> than to trust in princes.

Trust puts us in a hard place because it is an expression of honor: "I trust you." And it encourages others to be and do their best. So we should always extend trust whenever possible. As the apostle Paul wrote, love "always trusts, always hopes" (1 Cor. 13:7). We trust with all our heart while protecting our heart at the same time with ultimate trust in the Lord. Even when others disappoint us, He never will.

If your trust was not honored by another and you think you are down to nothing, you are not. If your ultimate trust is in Jesus Christ, you will always have Him. He is trustworthy—and proves His trust over and over by always being up to something in our lives.

21

There Is a Good Reason to Hang On

(Hope)

And hope does not disappoint us, because God has poured out his love into our hearts by the Holy Spirit, whom he has given us.

Romans 5:5

My Story

Within a few months I went from being an out-of-work pastor to co-owner of a cable television network and the host of a new program on that network, Everyday Life. *Needless to say, my head and heart were spinning from the rush of change we were experiencing. We had moved from being down to nothing to seeing that God was up to something. During the weeks that we negotiated the purchase of the American Life Network (now Youtoo TV), I often thought of myself like the proverbial dog that runs madly alongside a car, barking loudly. What would I do if I actually caught the car?*

As any entrepreneur knows—or any parent or person who lives in a constantly changing environment knows—sometimes we make life up as we go along. It's like being thrust out on the dance floor in a major competition and having to make up the steps on the fly. You put one foot after the other, often not knowing where they'll land, all the time hoping not to trip yourself or your partner and land in a pile on the floor.

"Hoping not to trip." Hope was a key ingredient in the process I was going through at that time. I confess that my hope was tested during the summer of 2008 when I was negotiating with the Crystal Cathedral and Hour of Power about my future with those ministries. That is, I had no certainty or confidence about the outcome. I believed God was in control and my faith in Him was solid, but when it came to outcomes, I could only hope for what I wished to be true. Isn't that how the world, including us Christians, hopes much of the time— on the basis of personal desires and wishful expectations rather than out of certainty?

There's nothing wrong with that when it comes to the everyday affairs of life. The simple truth is, we don't always know what God's will is and so we are left to pray and hope based on our desires—all the while saying, "I hope this is Your will, Lord. But if not, may Your will be done." And I didn't know if I would remain as the pastor of the church and host of the Hour of Power or not. I hoped to, but I had no certainty of the outcome.

When it became clear that my expectations would not be met, I started hoping for something different—but with a radically different kind of hope. I began hoping that God would reveal a new direction, a new ministry, a new mission for my life. But my hope was not wishful thinking; it was certain. I began to realize that God had never promised I would stay in a certain ministry position all my life. I might have wished for that, but I had no certainty it would happen. But when it comes to believing my heavenly Father has a ministry and calling for me to fulfill . . . that was something of which I was certain. Once I resigned from my previous position, I was free to walk in the biblical hope—meaning biblical certainty—

that God was at work in my life to take me to my next appointment.

And hope was exercised in yet another way—one I cannot encourage anyone else to imitate based on my experience, but one I had complete confidence in at the time. And that confidence bore fruit and proved that my hope was well-grounded. I can only say that my certain hope was fueled by the Holy Spirit for that given situation.

When we negotiated the purchase of ALN from the previous owners, things moved rapidly—so rapidly that I had reached an agreement in principle to purchase the network before funding was in place. This is not necessarily unusual in entrepreneurial ventures. Contracts are often signed on the basis of good-faith pending and contingent on the successful arrangement of funding. But as a Christian, I was concerned about getting ahead of the Lord, about not presuming on His blessing in the form of funding for this new venture. A large amount of money was at stake here, money that had not been promised by anyone.

If I told you every conversation and discussion that had been held up to the point of agreeing to buy the network, you would not think it was enough to warrant "certainty" on my part that the deal would go through. I can only tell you that, in my heart and soul, God gave me confidence to know that He was in this deal and would provide. So we signed the purchase agreements not "hoping" (as in "wishing") God would provide, but hoping (as in being certain) that He would.

And He did. We bought a television network without funding in place on the basis of confidence in God's leading in that situation. There are some things like salvation and God's love and guidance that every Christian can be biblically certain about. But when it comes to individual matters—hoping to stay in a certain job, hoping to buy a new business—certain *hope only comes from hearing from God. And that is different in every circumstance in every believer's life. And it is dependent on cultivating a knowledge of God—who He is and how He works in our life.*

Becoming responsible to pay large sums of money when you have very little is an act of faith and biblical hope, not to be undertaken lightly. But I signed the papers confident that God was up to something new in my life. He was, and is— and has not failed to provide.

Hope is a huge biblical theme. From Genesis to Revelation, variations of the word hope occur 185 times. But that should come as no surprise. The Bible is certainly a mirror of humanity, and if hope appears often in Scripture, it's only because hope is a staple of the human life—and it certainly is.

Hope is all about the future, whether five minutes from now ("I hope I hit the ball in the fairway.") or fifty years ("I hope I can golf on my ninetieth birthday."). When you think about it, every use of the word hope is an emotional expectation about the future. And the future is something we know little or nothing about. We have desires and expectations, but no one can predict the future with 100 percent accuracy apart from biblical revelation.

When the word hope is used apart from its biblical meaning, it is an expression of desire or expectation or longing that is not based on foreknowledge or certainty. For instance, look at these sentences I selected at random from Internet news feeds:

- "I have launched a petition, and I hope you'll add your voice..."
- "I hope someone really cool [makes the movie]..."

- "I hope [the little girl that was burned] gets better soon..."
- "New Mexico hopes the new plant deal doesn't stink..."
- "US allies hope for continuity after McChrystal departure..."
- "I hope the tournament becomes a tradition..."

See the pattern? The focus is on the future, but a future without certainty. In every one of those quotes, the speaker or writer has absolutely no way of knowing whether what he or she hopes for will come to pass. And as I said in my introductory story, that's okay—there's no way we can know the future when it comes to the details of life.

But there is a problem if you are a Christian. We are inundated by the daily media with a definition of hope that is different from hope in the Bible. We even use the uncertain kind of hope in our own language in our cultural conversation. And again—that's okay—I'm not playing speech police here. But the problem comes when we are drenched in one meaning of the word hope and then read the word hope in the Bible and apply that same cultural meaning of uncertainty.

The best way I know to illustrate the difference in the two kinds of hope is to reprint the same quotes substituting biblical synonyms for the word hope and let you see the difference:

- "I've launched a petition and am *absolutely certain* you'll add your voice..."
- "I *have no doubt* that someone really cool [will make the movie]..."
- "I'm *totally sure* [the little girl that was burned] will get better soon..."
- "New Mexico *is completely sure* the new plant deal doesn't stink..."
- "U.S. allies *have no doubt* about continuity after McChrystal's departure..."
- "I'm *convinced* the tournament will become a tradition..."

Sometimes we hear people speak that way, don't we—using really certain-sounding words? But the truth is, using that kind of strong language is like the preacher who wrote in the margin of his sermon notes: "Weak point—pound pulpit here." That is, using strong, confident language doesn't change anything about the ability of the speakers to know the future.

In 2002, five-year-old Samantha Runnion was abducted, kicking and screaming, in plain view of her friend in their "safe neighborhood." In ten days she would have turned six years old. In a press conference held just hours after the abduction, while a huge mobilization was under way to look for the suspected abductor and Samantha, the Orange County, California, sheriff made this statement: "I can guarantee you that all the resources available to law enforcement and the county of Orange, the Orange County Sheriff's Department and the FBI, will be put forward to bring Samantha home before her birthday."[1] Samantha was found less than twenty-four hours later, her lifeless body lying by the side of a rural road. Her funeral was held a few days later at the Crystal Cathedral with more than six thousand people in attendance.

The sheriff made good on part of his promise—he found Samantha before her sixth birthday. Sadly, he was not able to return her to her parents alive. His passionate expression of hope gave hope to our community and fueled an outpouring of support, with many people mobilizing to help search for little Samantha. But we do not know the future. We can only pray and hope, while leaving the details of the future to God. (Within a week, the accused murderer was behind bars.)

When the New Testament uses forms of the word "hope" in contexts dealing with trust in God, it uses it to mean absolute confidence and certainty. (There are plenty of examples in the New Testament that mirror human, noncertain hope like Luke 23:8: "Herod...hoped to see [Jesus] perform some miracle.") That's why it's dangerous to bring the world's definition of hope to the Bible and forget that the word means something different when

God says it. We might read something that God intends to be understood as a certainty and interpret it as a contingency. Non-biblical hope means expectation, desire, or longing, but the Bible adds something absolutely critical: confidence, surety, and certainty.

For instance, Hebrews 11:1 says, "Now faith is being sure of what we hope for and certain of what we do not see." Being "sure and certain" is a far cry from "I hope it doesn't rain this Saturday." A canceled picnic is one thing—but what about when you are down to nothing? How much difference would it make to be "sure and certain" that God was doing something in your behalf? It could make the difference between hanging on and throwing in the towel. And that's a big difference.

The Biblical Reason to Have Certain Hope

I don't know if this story is true, but it makes a good point about the nature of biblical hope:

An elderly woman was diagnosed with a terminal illness and given only three months to live by her doctor. Having lived a full life, the doctor's diagnosis was easier for her to accept, and she began to get her affairs in order. She asked her pastor to come to her home to discuss arrangements for her funeral—hymns to be sung, favorite Scriptures to be read, and her desire to be buried with her well-worn Bible. "And there's one more thing," she said near the end of their conversation. "I want to be buried with a fork in my right hand." The pastor's dumbfounded look was her invitation to explain: "Throughout all my years of attending fellowship suppers at church, whenever the dishes were being cleared off the table someone would always say, 'Keep your fork.' It was a reminder to me that something even better was coming—a dessert like chocolate cake or hot apple pie with a scoop of ice cream. So when people see me in my casket with a fork in my hand, and they ask why, I want you to tell them: 'Keep your fork—the best is yet to come!'"

That dear saint didn't just hope, in a longing sort of way, to participate in the marriage supper of the Lamb (see Rev. 19:9). She was so sure she would participate in the resurrection of the saints that she packed her own fork!

That is exactly the kind of hope exhibited by the writers of the New Testament. They were so confident in the hope of the resurrection and in the promises of God that it colored their every thought and action. They could endure any circumstance because they knew what the final outcome of their life was going to be. They were very much like the guy who records a sports event off the television to watch later. When he gets home, instead of rewinding it to the beginning of the game, he plays the ending of the game first to see who won. If his team won, then he rewinds it and plays the whole game. He can endure any trying moments in the game because he knows his team wins in the end. If they suffer a momentary setback, even fall behind significantly in the score, it doesn't matter at all. He relaxes and enjoys the thrill of the game because he knows the final outcome.

So what is the source of this kind of hope—not only eternal hope but hope in the midst of our struggles in life now? Why should we be absolutely certain that God is at work in and through us even when our circumstances suggest the opposite? The answer is simple and profound at the same time: Jesus in you, the hope of glory. As with everything in the Christian experience, it all comes down to Jesus. Or, as the sign in front of the country church said, "Know Jesus? Know hope. No Jesus? No hope."

When the apostle Paul wrote his letter to the Colossians, he talked about "the mystery that has been kept hidden for ages and generations, but is now disclosed to the saints. To them God has chosen to make known among the Gentiles the glorious riches of this mystery, which is *Christ in you, the hope of glory*" (Col. 1:26–27; italics added). If we substitute the word "certainty" for "hope" in that last phrase, we get the biblical meaning: "Christ in you, the certainty of future glory." The "glory" Paul is writing about is the glory he mentions in Romans 8:30—the ultimate consummation of the Christian's relationship with God in heaven.

And how do we know heaven is our future destination? Because of Christ living in us. Jesus Christ is our hope. By the presence of the Holy Spirit, Jesus lives within the heart of every person who has placed their faith in Him. That's why Paul wrote that "hope does not disappoint us, because God has poured out his love into our hearts by the Holy Spirit, whom he has given us" (Rom. 5:5).

Think of all the times in life you have hoped for something and been disappointed. From childhood we were told by our parents, "Don't get your hopes up. It might not work out." But we got our hopes up anyway, and it didn't work out, and we were sorely disappointed. But that's life, right? We know not to get our hopes up, but we do it anyway—and suffer dashed hopes many times.

What if our parents had told us, "It's okay to get excited and hope for this because it's definitely going to happen"? It would have been an entirely different experience. We would live for days with the excited certainty that something was going to come true, almost experiencing the fulfillment of it before it ever happened. That's what the Bible means when it says, "Christ in you, the hope of glory." Paul said it another way in writing to Timothy: "Paul, an apostle of Christ Jesus by the command of God our Savior and of *Christ Jesus our hope*" (1 Tim. 1:1; italics added).

It boils down to this: if Jesus Christ is who the New Testament says He is—the Son of God, crucified yet raised from the dead to new life—then we can have hope because He is our hope. If He is not who the New Testament says He is, then we have no hope. As Paul wrote in 1 Corinthians 15, "And if Christ has not been raised [from the dead], our preaching is useless and so is your faith. . . . If only for this life we have hope in Christ, we are to be pitied more than all men" (vv. 14, 19).

Anyone who can say with certainty, "I know I will be raised from the dead one day to spend eternity in heaven" . . . that person can also believe with certainty that God will meet the needs of His children on our way to heaven. As Romans 8:32 says, "He who did not spare his own Son, but gave him up for us all—how will he not also, along with him, graciously give us all things?"

How to Have Hope

If someone you know well, someone you trust implicitly, makes you a promise, what do you do? You rest. You relax. You anticipate the fulfillment of the promise. You don't worry or fret or live with anxiety. You have known this person for years and he has never failed to keep his word to you. So you don't give the need that your friend has promised to meet another thought. You *believe*. You walk by faith. You make plans based on hope in the promise. You trust in the certainty of that which you expect your friend to do.

Well, Jesus is that person to you. As you just read, Jesus is your hope. And He is not only your hope for heaven, He is your hope for the help you need right now. God's goal for you is not to let you struggle and straggle through life only to have you fall through heaven's door by the skin of your teeth. I have already reminded you in this book that God's goal is to help you become like Jesus—a person who never went through a trial without complete confidence in God's goodness and deliverance. Jesus knew that God was trustworthy regardless of what might come. And that is the kind of person God is shaping us to become in this life— not just that we have a photo-finish entrance into heaven.

Jesus even knew that after his crucifixion God would raise Him from the dead on the third day. He told His disciples this before it ever happened—to their amazement (see Mark 9:30–32). This kind of faith was first demonstrated in the Old Testament by Abraham, whom God told to offer his only son, Isaac, as a sacrifice. This made little sense to Abraham since God had promised that Abraham would be the father of multitudes of descendants.

And if God took away his only son, how would there be any descendants? But Abraham moved ahead in faith believing that God would raise Isaac from the dead (see Heb. 11:19). Though God provided a ram as a substitute at the last minute, sparing Isaac from death, Abraham had laid his son on an altar and raised a knife over his body when God intervened and provided a substitute sacrifice. Now that is what I call hope! That is certainty that God will provide an answer when we are down to nothing in our experience.

But guess what? If we are going to have those moments of certainty in our life when we place our hope in God and His promises, we're going to have to experience situations in which it appears that all hope is lost. Why would you need to have hope except for the fact that you sometimes have no hope? And there is no time when you need hope more than when you are down to nothing.

If that's where you are, you must have Jesus to have certain hope. And when you have Him, you must believe that He is in you and is your hope of glory. Jesus is the only reason you need to hope—to know for a fact—that God is up to something in your life.

22

I'm Sorry, I Have No Recollection of That

(The Past)

I, even I, am he who blots out
your transgressions, for my own sake,
and remembers your sins no more.

Isaiah 43:25

My Story

In my ministry as a pastor—and even as a husband, father, and friend—I have often heard people express a desire to be able to forget something that happened: a word, an event, a look, an accusation, a betrayal, or some other painful memory that persists from the past. It's understandable to want to go back and pick up life "BP"—before the pain.

I confess to having those desires from time to time in my life. I'm no more a glutton for pain than the next guy, so I have no desire to revel in or relive memories that are painful to recall. That was especially true from November 2008 going forward. The months I've described in previous chapters were full of painful conversations, memories, speculations, and conclusions, and the memories are no less so. Who wouldn't want to take a pill and be free of a painful past?

I, for one, wouldn't. The more pain I experience in life, the more I realize the role pain plays—even the pain I may have caused myself or others. If given the opportunity to have every painful memory erased from my mind, I would decline. I have learned that memories—actually, the past events that memories represent—are something to be embraced because of what we can learn from them—because of the role they play in shaping our lives.

No one sets out to find pain in life just so they can benefit from it in some way. Pain has a way of finding us without our looking for it. I would never have orchestrated the events of the summer and fall of 2008. But now that they are memories of a closed chapter of my life, I don't try to squeeze those memories into a dark corner of my mind. I use them to remember the faithfulness of God to me, the love of friends, family, and associates, the lessons I learned that will make me wiser in the future, and the fact that life is a long and winding road. We do not know what is around every bend in the road, and painful memories from the past prepare us to be ready for what may suddenly appear.

While painful memories are sometimes the result of things said or done to us, I don't embrace those memories in order to meditate on or stew over how I may have been mistreated. Absolutely not. If I am ever wronged in life, my responsibility is to forgive immediately, to hold no grudges, to seek no revenge— period. At the same time, by remembering those events or words, I am reminded of the fragility of life. I am reminded that I too have on occasion been the cause of others' pain. I am motivated to live in a state of reconciliation with others, trusting that I can do unto others the same as I hope they will do unto me.

The pain of the past, if we will let it, can cause us to fall into each others' arms, grateful for what we have learned, grateful for the grace of God, grateful for the ties that bind us to one another.

Sometimes, when we are down to nothing, the past seems

*like all we have. And if the past was painful, it can seem like
we are all the more poor. But then we remember that the past
doesn't dictate the future in God's eyes, and it shouldn't in ours
either. Suddenly we realize that all we have is the present and
the future! Today and tomorrow are like a blank canvas on
which God—who is always up to something creative—is prepared to paint something beautiful.*

The setting is a chamber, a hearing room, in the senate's part
of the U.S. Capitol. We've seen this setting many times on
television: at a semicircular row of elevated desks at one end of the
room sit the senators, members of the committee that have called
the hearing, and their staff members sitting behind them. At a table
on the floor in front of the senators sits one or more witnesses,
often accompanied by attorneys. Behind the witness's table are
rows of seats filled by the press, the public, and other government
officials and employees.

The questioning begins:

SENATOR: "Mr. Smith, is it true that you...?"
WITNESS: (Covers the microphone with his hand, confers
    with his attorney, then replies.) "Senator, I have no
    recollection of that event."
SENATOR: "Mr. Smith, why did you say...?"
WITNESS: (Covers the microphone with his hand, confers
    with his attorney, then replies.) "Senator, to the best
    of my memory, I never said that."
SENATOR: "Mr. Smith, in the meeting on January 4, did
    you discuss...?"
WITNESS: (Covers the microphone with his hand, confers
    with his attorney, then replies.) "Senator, I don't
    recall discussing that subject."

And on it goes. Of course, most hearings are more productive than that, and most witnesses are more forthcoming. But we have all seen instances when a witness's memory, even while under oath, seems conveniently vacant of the exact facts or details that are being requested. I never know what to make of these kinds of replies. Is the witness being truthful? Has the witness blanked the events out of his memory? Is the witness playing a game of semantics as one former president did when he asked, "It depends on what the meaning of 'is' is"? I don't know. But I do know that most people prefer to forget the painful parts of their past and move on.

I have never experienced this personally, but I have read that before mandatory seat belt laws and shatterproof glass, if a person in a severe car accident went through the windshield, his or her face could be imbedded with tiny shards and slivers of glass. No matter how hard a surgeon worked to find and remove all the pieces, many would remain. The tiny slivers would be painless until such time as, months or years later, they worked their way to the surface of the facial skin. The pain of the slivers resurfacing would require their removal by a doctor—a potentially endless process of reliving the pain of a past event, one sliver of glass at a time.

Many people experience something similar in their life—experiencing the pain of a past event when something calls it unbidden to the surface. To avoid such pain, they live every day on the defensive; they live in a protective mode rather than an offensive mode. Instead of moving ahead with life, they are bound to things in the past. And because their pain—and the accompanying resentment, bitterness, shame, or embarrassment—rises so quickly to the surface, we can only assume that they live with those negative emotions on an ongoing basis. Rather than *dealing with* the resentment, bitterness, shame, embarrassment, anger, or other negative emotions when the event took place, they try to stuff those emotions down somewhere deep. And often they try to cover those emotions with hurtful behaviors: overeating, alcohol, drugs, promiscuity, materialism, or other defensive lifestyles. What they discover is that it takes an infinite amount of those lifestyles to cover a painful past—meaning, it's impossible. But they keep trying and become addicted to the process of insulating themselves against the past.

But we don't have the luxury of living life like an integrity-challenged witness in a senate hearing. We can't confer with an attorney and simply decide, on the spot, that we have no memory of a past event. In fact, the harder we try to rid ourselves of the past, the more deeply ingrained in our memory it becomes. How do we teach our young children to remember Mom's or Dad's phone number, or the 911 number, to use in an emergency? Or their home address to tell a policeman in case they're ever lost? We go over it and over it and over it—perhaps at the supper table every night—knowing that repetition is the doorway to memory.

Just so, every time we purpose to "forget" our past, our past is played across the stage of our mind afresh, creating new and deeper wrinkles in our gray matter. The way to be free of the past is not to try forgetting it, but to deal with it the way God does.

The Past Tense of God

I know—"God" is not a verb. Neither does God have a past. As we understand the eternal nature of God, He does not exist in time as we experience it. He has always existed and will always exist, and the millennia of planet earth's existence are like a parenthesis in the timeline of eternity. (There I go using "time" metaphors to describe eternity.)

We get this understanding about God from the Bible of course. Genesis 1:1 says, "In the beginning God created the heavens and the earth." We could also read it this way: "In the beginning of time, God created..." That same idea occurs in John 1:2–3, where the apostle writes, "[Christ] was with God in the beginning [of time]"—because the very next verse picks up the theme of creation: "Through [Christ] all things were made..."

In Isaiah 46:10 God says to the people of Israel, "I make known the end from the beginning, from ancient times, what is still to come." And three times in the book of Revelation, God is referred to as "the Alpha and the Omega," the one "who is, and who was, and who is to come," "the Beginning and the End," and "the First and the Last" (Rev. 1:8; 21:6; 22:13).

All these descriptive words are meant to convey the eternal nature of God, the one who is not bound or constricted by the limitations of time. That means God doesn't live in what we call the present tense. Rather, He lives in the past, present, and future tense all at once. He sees everything from the beginning to the end as one event. That's hard for us to conceive—imagine stepping back and viewing your entire life, from birth to death, as one giant panorama, cyclorama, or tapestry. You would be able to see at once things we struggle to figure out in our time-bound existence, such as how things in the past are connected to the present, and how the present is connected to the future.[1]

If such an all-encompassing perspective was possible, it might keep us from reliving the past in painful ways; we would have the advantage of seeing how the threads of our life tie together and produce meaning and beauty. But such is not possible. So the next best way for us to view life is to try to see it as God does. And this will require a bit of understanding.

The writers of the Old Testament used beautiful imagery to describe how God relates to the dark parts of our past—our sins, the parts we wish we could forget, or at least do over and do differently. The writers used human language to describe how God views our regrettable past. Being human, what other language would they use? Let's look at their words and think about the human dimension of them:

> as far as the east is from the west,
> so far has he removed our transgressions from us.
>
> *Psalm 103:12*

From the east to the west, in biblical times, was an infinity apart from one another. The writers had never seen a satellite photograph of the earth as a ball floating in space. The earth was flat to them—if one person went east and another went west they would never see one another again. And that's the image of us and our dark past. It's as if God stands us back to back with our sins and says, "Robert, you walk east. Robert's Sins, you walk west." And we would never meet again. That's how God views, from His perspective, you and the painful parts of your past. Not all your past—but the parts you would rather forget.

> Though your sins are like scarlet,
> they shall be as white as snow;
> though they are red as crimson,
> they shall be like wool.
>
> *Isaiah 1:18*

Here the idea is change. We could imagine dipping a pure white sheepskin into a vat of red dye to effect a complete change in the wool, but the image here is the opposite. Part of our past is the scarlet color of sin—like the "scarlet letter" that Hester Prynne had to wear after committing adultery in Nathaniel Hawthorne's nineteenth-century novel. Maybe this verse is why Hawthorne chose to make the cloth *A* she wore scarlet—a brilliant reminder of sin. But God says the brilliant red of our past is changed in His sight to the brilliant purity of perfection, of sinlessness.

> You have put all my sins behind your back.
>
> *Isaiah 38:17*

This may be the most human, and humorous, of all the images. What do we do with our children when we want to hide a toy or treat from them? We put the object behind our back so they can't see it. Or, as the saying goes, "Out of sight, out of mind." But God has no front or back or side. God is spirit, Jesus said, not a corporeal body (see John 4:24). But what happens to the object we hide from our child behind our back? We can't see it either! So, in this verse, God says that the forgettable parts of our past are not only hidden from us—they're hidden from Him as well.

> For I will forgive their wickedness
> and will remember their sins no more.
> *Jeremiah 31:34*

We're back to the senate hearing chamber with this one. Jeremiah suggests that if we say to God, "Do you remember that thing I did back then?" God would cover the microphone with His hand, confer with Jesus (the Advocate, or attorney; see 1 John 2:1), and say to us, "I'm sorry, but I have no recollection of that sin." I'm being facetious, but you get the point. Jeremiah is saying that God not only forgives, but He forgets the forgettable parts of our past.

> You will again have compassion on us;
> you will tread our sins underfoot
> and hurl all our iniquities into the depths of the sea.
> *Micah 7:19*

No one in Micah's day, Micah included, knew how deep the Mediterranean Sea was. They only knew that they didn't have a line long enough to reach the bottom no matter how much line they acquired. It could have been infinitely deep as far as they knew. The point was, anything lost in "the depths of the sea" was gone forever—irretrievable, lost, never to be seen or experienced again. And the same for being trod underfoot, just in a different way. A coin or a pearl dropped in a muddy marketplace, trampled under-foot by man and beast, was lost to the owner. That, Micah says, is the nature of God's compassion when He views the dark parts of our past.

But there's a problem: all these verses are metaphors, figures of speech. Therefore, we have to understand what they mean in order to understand how to view our past the same way God does.

The Past Tense of You

All the figures of speech (anthropomorphisms—assigning human characteristics to God) used in the verses above cannot mean what we hope they mean: that God forgets, can't see, can't find, changes, drowns, or looses the parts of our past that we want to forget. God knows everything, sees everything, "remembers" everything, and knows where everything is—including our sins and the forgettable parts of our life. So why does the Bible seem to say the opposite?

For this reason: all those verses were written to say that, *as far as we're concerned*, God has forgotten our past. In other words, once God forgives us and extends His compassion toward us concerning the forgettable parts of our past, it is as if they never happened *in terms of their effect on our relationship with Him.*

Does God remember every event, word, or act you wish He would forget? Yes.

Does His eternal memory of your past, present, and future change how He feels about you? No.

This is hard for us humans to grasp, but God does not let your past influence His present and future love for you. When it comes to how we feel about other people, just being in the same room with someone who has hurt us is sometimes difficult. But not for God. He really does feel toward you as if He has forgotten, lost, hidden, or changed your past.

In fact, God embraces your past for this reason: He gave up His own life, in His Son, Jesus Christ, to make sure your past did not become an obstacle between you and Him. What sense would it make for God to have sent Jesus into the world to die for your past, present, and future sins—and then forget the very things Jesus died for? When God watched His own Son die a grievous death for the sins of the world, He embraced His Son. And when He embraced His Son, He embraced all the sin that was laid on Him—our sin. As Isaiah wrote, "And the LORD has laid on him the iniquity of us all" (Isa. 53:6b).

God embraces your past because it is the reason His Son came into the world. It is the reason He wants to know you and have a relationship with you—not because you don't have a past but in spite of the past that you have! And therein lies the secret to how we are to relate to our own past tense: the same way God does.

God doesn't forget our past, and neither should we.

God finds meaning and purpose in our past, and so should we.

God brings healing from our past into our present, and so should we.

God embraces us and our past, and so should we.

God doesn't stuff our past out of sight and hide it, and neither should we.

Allow me to expand the text of one of the Bible's greatest promises about your past and your future: "'[In spite of your past] I know the plans I have for you,' declares the LORD, 'plans to prosper you and not to harm you, plans to give you hope and a future [in spite of your past]'" (Jer. 29:11). There's the connection between the past, present, and future that we need. God knows our past, yet has a future of hopeful plans for our life.

If your past has made you feel like you are down to nothing, remember the "something" of Jeremiah 29:11 that God is up to: a future of hope. He can say that because He sees the past, present, and future as one. And He wants you to trust Him with what He sees when your eyes get clouded by the past.

23

Living on a Need-to-Know Basis

(The Future)

"For I know the plans I have for you," declares the LORD, "plans to prosper you and not to harm you, plans to give you hope and a future."

Jeremiah 29:11

My Story

Regardless of how hard we work to create a specific future, sometimes it doesn't happen. You already know what did happen—the very positive future I anticipated was cut short after a little less than three years. And you know that I'm okay with that, as I've said many different ways throughout this book. I continue to find life lessons to be learned through this transitional experience, one of the most important being that we live on a "need-to-know" basis with God. I knew what I needed to know when I was transitioning into leadership of the Crystal Cathedral and the Hour of Power. *But I obviously didn't know everything. God gave me what I needed to know then, not everything I would have liked to know about the future.*

And the same is true now. The day I signed my resignation letter in November 2008 I didn't know what the future held. God has been faithful to open doors and provide direction since then, and I am excited about what has developed as a new venture and ministry through television. But the truth is, I'm holding the work I am now doing lightly. I don't know what the future of my new venture will be. I have learned that we should leave the future to God. My goal is to be faithful today and trust God's faithfulness for tomorrow.

When I thought I was down to nothing, I wasn't. Until God takes me home to heaven, I will always have the future in which God is always up to something good.

The Normandy invasion in 1944 by Allied forces seeking to defeat Germany—otherwise known as D-day—was the largest coordinated military movement in history. Thousands of ships and airplanes, hundreds of thousands of Allied troops, and fifty miles of French coastline made for a logistical nightmare. Trying to plan something that big would be bad enough—but try keeping it a secret! German spies and intelligence agents were everywhere, scanning the horizon for signs of an Allied invasion.

To limit the chance for invasion plans being revealed ("Loose lips sink ships," the military said), Allied planners instituted a "need-to-know" basis when it came to disseminating information. Lower-level commanders were given responsibilities and tasks to plan for without knowing the big picture. For as long as possible, they were told only what they needed to know to plan and prepare for their part of the overall operation. They knew what to do one day at a time, but did not know the details about the future.

That's the way life is in general. No one knows the future, so the wisest among us will not make concrete plans on the basis of things that may not come to pass. The September/October 2000 issue of *The Futurist* magazine contained an article listing some of the worst predictions of all time about the future. There were some real doozies—here's a sample that illustrates how dangerous it is to speak about the future before it gets here:

- "Inventions have long since reached their limit, and I see no hope for further developments." (Roman engineer Julius Sextus Frontinus, AD 100)
- "The abdomen, the chest, and the brain will forever be shut from the intrusion of the wise and humane surgeon." (John Eric Ericksen, surgeon to Queen Victoria, 1873)
- "It doesn't matter what he does, he will never amount to anything." (Albert Einstein's teacher speaking to Einstein's father, 1895)
- "It would appear we have reached the limits of what it is possible to achieve with computer technology." (Computer scientist John von Neumann, 1949)
- "The Japanese don't make anything the people in the US would want." (Secretary of State John Foster Dulles, 1954)
- "I predict the Internet... will go spectacularly supernova and in 1996 catastrophically collapse." (Computer scientist Bob Metcalfe, inventor of Ethernet, 1995)

These predictions remind me of something I heard once: "If you want to see God laugh, just tell Him your plans!"

Making blanket predictions about the future—even predictions based on intelligence and accurate data—is not wise. But there's a difference between not knowing the future yourself and knowing Someone who does. As the saying goes, "I don't know what the future holds, but I know Who holds the future." It's fine for us not to know the future as long as we know that God knows. In the previous chapter I explained the eternal nature of God—that He sees past, present, and future at once. Given that fact, He knows what our future holds before it ever takes place.

Our challenge is this: don't get so attached to the present that we fail to see what God wants to do in our future. Fortunately, the

Bible is full of examples of people who were completely comfort-able with their lives, never expecting God to step in and give them a totally different future.

I Never Would Have Imagined

Lots of people end up doing things in life they never could have imagined themselves doing—and happily so. They are examples of how it pays to live a flexible life and remain open to the possibili-ties. I cited Jeremiah 29:11 at the end of the previous chapter because it speaks to the need not to dwell in the past. But its empha-sis on the future is for every person to heed. The verse was spoken by Jeremiah, the prophet of God, during Israel's worst days— when they were under siege by the Babylonians and about to be carried into captivity. It was a promise intended to give Israel hope in the midst of her calamity. For all Israel knew, the nation was fin-ished. Her homeland was overrun, and her people carried off to distant lands. But God had other plans: "'For I know the plans I have for you,' declares the LORD, 'plans to prosper you and not to harm you, plans to give you hope and a future.'"

So God is not limited to the kind of future He can reveal: from bad to good, from good to better, maybe even from good to bad as He did for a temporary time in Israel's life. The point is to let God be God when it comes to the future—just as these biblical charac-ters did:

• Moses was wanted in Egypt for murdering a man, so he fled to the desert land of Midian at age forty where he worked as a shepherd for his father-in-law for forty more years. At age eighty he probably assumed the heat was off in Egypt and he could spend the rest of his days quietly in Midian. But then God appeared to him in a burning bush and gave him a new assignment—at age eighty: return to Egypt and lead the Hebrew slaves out of captiv-ity. Moses protested but found arguing with God to be fruitless. So he spent the last forty years of his life as a shepherd of former slaves rather than of sheep (see Exod. 2–3).

Lesson: Even if you're retirement age, don't assume the future can't change. As long as you're alive, God may have a new plan for you.

• Rahab was a pagan prostitute who lived in Jericho. When the Israelites gathered on the banks of the Jordan River to invade Canaan as their Promised Land, she helped two Israelite men as they were spying out the city. She had heard of the power of God to defeat the Egyptians in Egypt and decided it was safer to be on God's side—and so assisted the spies. As a return for her help, she and her family were saved by the Israelites when Jericho was destroyed. Though the Bible doesn't say how, Rahab's life changed radically: she became the great-grandmother of King David and an ancestress of Jesus Christ (see Ruth 4:18–21; Matthew 1:5).

Lesson: Even if you are not proud of your life today, God can give you a future you couldn't have imagined.

• David was a young teenaged boy, the youngest of eight brothers. While his brothers served in the Israelite army, David was relegated to running errands and helping his father, Jesse, at home. But when the prophet Samuel came to anoint one of Jesse's sons as the next king of Israel, he chose David. Many years of persecution from the current king passed before David assumed the throne. But God's future for David was ultimately fulfilled.

Lesson: Don't look at yourself as unqualified for anything. When God plans your future, He also plans what you'll need to realize it.

• Gideon was a farmer with no expectations of being a "mighty warrior." But that's exactly how God greeted him when Gideon was threshing his wheat, minding his own business. Gideon protested the call of God to lead Israel to defeat a neighboring army, claiming he was the least in his family, which was the weakest family in the tribe of Manasseh. God's answer: "I will be with you." (Judg. 6:16). And indeed God was with him, leading Gideon to defeat a massive enemy army with only three hundred soldiers. When God called Gideon "mighty warrior," he probably looked around as if to say, "Are you talking to me?"

Lesson: Don't create an inviolable identity for yourself that would cause you to resist or miss the future identity that God has planned for you.

• Mary and Joseph were a young couple in Nazareth engaged to be married, Joseph a carpenter and Mary a young teenaged girl. At first Mary had a hard time believing that her future was to be the earthly mother of the Son of God. And Joseph had an even harder time—he believed Mary had conceived as a result of promiscuity. But in time they adjusted their perceptions of themselves and their futures and believed that God was the reason for this radical change in their lives (see Luke 1). Think of how the future of the world might have been different if they had rejected the future God planned for them.

Lesson: People who change the world are just people like you who embrace the possibilities the future presents. Don't discount the likelihood of being a world changer in the future.

• Saul was a self-righteous Pharisee whose mission in life was to stamp out the growing Christian movement in Jerusalem and beyond. He believed Jesus of Nazareth was a messianic imposter who was rightly killed by crucifixion—until he met that same Jesus face-to-face in a blinding, postresurrection vision (see Acts 9). As Paul said in his own words (see Phil. 3), he fully embraced what became the most unlikely future of anyone in history: the chief representative on earth for the same Lord who had been his chief enemy.

Lesson: Don't exclude from your considerations things that seem completely impossible. Nothing is impossible for God.

How to Plan for the Future

In 1861, when Union and Confederate troops met on his property in the Shenandoah Valley of Virginia for the bloodiest battle in the civil war, farmer Wilmer McLean decided he wanted no part of such a conflict occurring on his farm in the future. So he sold his farm and moved to the most inconspicuous place he could find, an old house in a Virginia village called Appomattox Court House. It was just four years later, when General Ulysses S. Grant was pursuing the Confederate general Robert E. Lee through Virginia that McLean would encounter the war again. When Grant sent a message to Lee asking him to sign a truce agreement, the place where the two commanders met was in Wilmer McLean's living room![1]

Well, farmer McLean got part of his wish—not to have any more blood shed on his property. But his desire not to be part of the war just wasn't part of his future. So what does that say about planning? Should we even bother to try arranging the future or just "leave everything to God" and take what comes? The answer is: yes.

Planning for the future is human; it's what we do to make life happen. The Bible, one of the most human books ever written, supports that notion—but with a caveat—as expressed in Proverbs 16:9: "In his heart a man plans his course, but the LORD determines his steps." The mentality in the Old Testament, expressed in this verse, was to make plans and then stay flexible for God to either confirm or alter our steps. That makes perfect sense, doesn't it? It's the "let go and let God" part that becomes a challenge. What if we like where we are and what we're doing? The idea of giving that up and doing something different is not appealing at all.

But wait—if a friend could peer into the future and see that a change in your path would produce a situation that would make you even happier than your current place, wouldn't you be willing to make the change? Most people would. I know, Benjamin Franklin said, "A bird in the hand is better than two in the bush." In other words, be safe; don't give away a sure thing to go after something that isn't. That's good advice to use in the planning stages of our life. We should do our best not to make foolish plans, to reach for something that's way beyond our grasp.

But we're talking about God making the change. And God doesn't make mistakes. If circumstances force you to make a change you hadn't planned on, a change you don't want to make, keep God in the mix. If your life is committed to Him and you are trusting Him to work all things together for good (see Rom. 8:28), then His future for your life is the one you want to embrace.

There is one passage in the Bible that presents both sides of the future—human and divine—in eminently practical terms: James 4:13–17. James is the most "Old Testament-like" book in the New Testament, full of Jewish wisdom from a Christian perspective. James' exhortation is a fleshed-out version of Proverbs 16:9.

James presents a hypothetical scenario: A group of people are planning a year-long business venture in another city to make money—without any awareness of God's plans. But James challenges that humanistic approach to the future: "Why, you do not even know what will happen tomorrow. What is your life? You are a mist that appears for a little while and then vanishes" (v. 14). Instead he writes that this should have been their perspective (and ours): "Instead, you ought to say, 'If it is the Lord's will, we will live and do this or that'" (v. 15).

If it is the Lord's will. That's the key phrase for the person who looks at the future with a God-consciousness. We don't control the future—God does. Therefore we can make and carry out no plan that does not fit through the grid of God's overall will. Wherever you and I are today, we should think this way: "I am planning for the future, but allowing God to have the final say. I am comfortable with living my life on a need-to-know basis. I am comfortable with what I know today because I trust that God knows about the future and will do what is best for me."

Prior to 1995, the Northwestern University (near Chicago) football team had a horrible reputation—they had not had a winning season in twenty-four years. In fact, they set an NCAA record by losing thirty-four consecutive games between 1979 and 1982. But things changed in 1995 when their record was 10-2. They won the Big Ten Conference title, were ranked eighth in the nation, and went to the Rose Bowl. Coach Gary Barnett accumulated seventeen national coach-of-the-year awards.

The following spring, 1996, Coach Barnett knew he had to get his players' eyes off their victorious past season and get them focused on the future. So he called a team meeting during which he handed out award certificates to the many players who had made such an outstanding contribution to the 1995 season. He even made up a placard representing his own seventeen coach-of-the-year awards. The players cheered wildly for one another and for their coach as the awards were presented.

But after all the cheering had subsided, Coach Barnett took his placard and walked over to the side of the stage where a trash can sat with "1995" painted on the side. He took one last admiring look at his awards placard—then tossed it into the trash can. Silence and bewilderment filled the auditorium—until the players got the point. One by one, the star players from 1995 walked to the stage and dropped their award certificates into the trash can until it was filled with the laurels of the past.

Coach Barnett's silent message was heard loud and clear: the past is great while you're living it, but it has nothing to do with the future. Anyone who gets stuck in the past will not accomplish what the future has to offer.[2]

If you feel like you are down to nothing because a glorious past has been taken away from you . . . you are not. You have "hope and a future" because God is up to something in your life.

24

The Never-Ending Story

(Eternity)

Now this is eternal life: that they may know you, the only true God, and Jesus Christ, whom you have sent.

John 17:3

My Story

There are times in our lives when the minute hand, even the second hand, seems to be glued to the face of the clock—when pages in our daily calendar seem to be stuck together, unable to be turned. Time seems to stand still in those moments. And the degree of pain, or discomfort, or trouble we are experiencing just makes time that much stickier. If it's true that "time flies when you're having fun," it's all the more true that "time stands still when you're not."

Jury duty, lying in the dentist's chair, standing in line at the DMV, sitting in a rush-hour freeway parking lot—pick the place you'd rather not be and time stands still. Or maybe it's something more personal: an ICU ward after surgery, an attorney's office negotiating a divorce settlement, waiting to hear good news—any news—about your missing child, waiting for the phone to ring in response to the scores of résumés you've sent out, or trying to save a job you believed was God's will for your life.

That last one was where I was for four months—July through October 2008—four months that seemed like four years, or forty or four hundred years. No number is big enough during those times—they feel like forever. What allows us to survive some of those events is the expectation of closure. We know a dentist visit is going to be over in an hour. Jury duty will be over in a week or two. But the ICU? The search for a job? Trying to save a job? They are made all the worse because we don't know, as the Romans would say, the terminus ad quem *("the limit to which")—the last possible date of our experience. Not knowing that date makes us think, "This could go on forever."*

But is that true? No—we use the word "forever" as a figure of speech without stopping to compare our present circumstance with the actual "forever" of eternity. What seems to be eternal to us at the moment is just a blip on the screen of eternity, time wise. Of course, eternity knows no time—that's the point. So when we measure the hours, days, months, or years of a troubling circumstance in our life against eternity, it represents an immeasurably small fraction of our existence: 1/eternity, written as a fraction, gets smaller and smaller with every extension of our mind's ability to grasp what eternity means.

But God has placed us in time for the moment, and it is with time that we must reckon the affairs of our lives. So when I was going through my transition out of the Crystal Cathedral, it was all very real. It dragged and seemed it would never end. Though this thought never made events move faster, it was comforting to remember that, in the grand scope of eternity, who occupies the pulpit of the Crystal Cathedral is a very small matter. Likewise for who hosts the Hour of Power *television program—very small. God is at work to fulfill His purposes in the world, and He is the only irreplaceable member of the cast. The rest of us move on and off the stage according to the ebb and flow of our lives, and God's grand drama of redemption carries on.*

That is not to say our parts are unimportant—they aren't. But they are not as life defining as we think they are at any given moment. So we must live in two worlds at once: the world of time is the stage, but the world of eternity is the backdrop. One of the scenes in my part of God's drama involved pastoring the Crystal Cathedral for two years. It was a joy and a pleasure—and like all blessings in life, I am thankful to God for the experience.

In the future, when I feel like I am down to nothing, I will have this experience to remind me that I am part of something much bigger than myself: God's eternal plan of redemption. I will know that God is up to something eternal and using the times of my life to accomplish it. To be involved in what He is doing is something I will always have and for which I will always be grateful.

Nobody knows for sure how long the human race has been in existence, nor when the earth was formed. Estimates on the short side, formulated by the Irish bishop James Ussher (1581–1656), put the age of the earth at 6,014 years (as of 2010). By a literal interpretation of the chronologies in the Old Testament, he put the date of the creation on the evening preceding October 23, 4004 BC. While his work represented an incredible feat of scholarship for his day, modern Bible scholarship—not to mention findings from scientific-dating methods—suggests that a literal reading of the chronologies is not an accurate way to determine the beginning of time. On the long side, the sky is the limit—the age of the earth and its inhabitants is calculated in the millions of years and the universe in billions.

But compared to eternity, the numbers are irrelevant. Think of the largest number possible—compared to "forever," it means nothing. These are hard ideas around which to wrap our minds. Indeed, it took the mind of Albert Einstein to make sense of time, space, and matter with his theory of relativity. But we must try— otherwise we will fail to appreciate that which awaits us.

Think of the human body—no two are exactly the same size, but let's think in round numbers: it is estimated that the human body contains 100 trillion (100,000,000,000,000) cells. Thousands upon thousands of cells are dying and being created at every moment of our life. With that many cells present in the human body at any given time, any one of them might seem very insignificant. But none is—all have a significant role to play in the life of the body. And remember—a disease like cancer begins with just one rogue cell that somehow survives the body's immune system long enough to divide, multiply, and create a foothold, often resulting in death. Every cell makes an impact—even if it is just one out of 100 trillion.

But comparing one to 100 trillion still doesn't approach what it means to compare our lifetime on earth with eternity. Nor, like that one cell, does it mean our life is insignificant. God is the one who created time out of eternity and placed us in it. The biblical record suggests that, had sin not interrupted God's plans in the Garden of Eden, man would have lived forever on earth in a perfect world, enjoying a harmonious relationship with the Creator-God. But the intervention of sin did not cancel that eternal plan. Perfection has simply been moved forward to what the Bible calls "a new heaven and a new earth, the home of righteousness" (2 Peter 3:13; cf. Rev. 21:1).

We know what it is like to live in time, where things happen one after another. Even in eternity, we can expect for time to play a role just as it did in Eden. We will still do things consecutively, not "all at once." So there's nothing ungodly about time. It's just that it will be a lot longer in eternity than the years we are keeping track of here on this original earth. Indeed, time will be forever.

Our challenge now is this: not to confuse temporal time with eternal time, not to forget that a time is coming that will put our earthly time into the proper perspective.

Life as a Two-Timer

Every human being, biblically speaking, straddles two domains: earth time and eternity. In other words, eternity doesn't begin when we die. Think of it (generally) in terms of a baby: a baby doesn't begin to exist when it is born. It has already existed for nine months in its mother's womb. Birth represents only a change in its environment: from living internally to living externally, from being fed intravenously in the womb to taking nourishment by mouth on the outside. The baby began to live at conception and only its surroundings and ability to live independently of its mother changed.

So it is with eternal life—death doesn't usher us into eternity. Rather, it takes us into a new dimension of eternity. Jesus Himself gave us the best definition of eternal life we will find anywhere: "Now this is eternal life: that they may know you, the only true God, and Jesus Christ, whom you have sent" (John 17:3). All those who know God and His Son, Jesus Christ, are experiencing eternal life right now.

But it is not just those who know Christ who are living in light of eternity. For Christians, the entrance into eternal life is put in terms of births; for those who have not come to know God, it is put in terms of deaths. Everyone is born once, then some are "born again"—a new, or second birth, through faith in Christ (see John 3:3, 7). Everyone also dies once, but those who die apart from faith in God are said to experience a "second death" (Rev. 2:11; 20:6, 14; 21:8). So every human being lives as a two-timer: time on earth and time in eternity. The difference, biblically speaking, is the difference between eternal life and eternal death.

The idea of such a division in humanity is hard for many to come to grips with. But it should be no harder than the idea of the existence of God, of eternity, of a new heaven and new earth—all things our rational minds struggle to comprehend. But this is one thing I have no problem comprehending: that God's ways and thoughts are much different, much "higher," than mine. God himself said so through the prophet Isaiah, as I highlighted in Chapter 17 of this book. But it bears repeating on such a weighty topic:

> "For my thoughts are not your thoughts,
> neither are your ways my ways,"
> declares the LORD.
> "As the heavens are higher than the earth,
> so are my ways higher than your ways
> and my thoughts than your thoughts."
>
> *Isaiah 55:8–9*

If God is God (and He is), then we must let Him have the first and the final words on the beginning of life and the end of life as we know it on this earth—and what eternity will mean for the two divisions of souls into which all humanity is divided in Scripture. What I don't understand should never keep me from doing what the prophet Isaiah said just before he recorded God's own words: "Seek the LORD while he may be found; call on him while he is near" (Isa. 55:6).

Psalm 90:10 gives the Old Testament perspective on our time on earth and the words "may be found" and "near":

> The length of our days is seventy years—
> or eighty, if we have the strength;
> yet their span is but trouble and sorrow,
> for they quickly pass, and we fly away.

I believe Genesis 6:3 provides good reason for expecting a human life span of 120 years—the length of Moses' life (see Deut. 34:7). So combining both passages, we are given 70–120 years—there are no guarantees—in which to sort out the meaning of life and restore our relationship with the Creator-God. What makes it more challenging is the "trouble and sorrow" of those years and how quickly they pass before we "fly away." It is so easy to get distracted by the troubles and trials of life on this earth, so distracted that we lose sight of the big picture: Who made me? Why am I here? What is the meaning of life? What happens after I die?

Isaiah wrote that God is "near," that He "may be found." And Psalm 90 says there is "trouble and sorrow" that can cloud our awareness of His nearness. In the same vein, the apostle Paul wrote,

> We don't yet see things clearly. We're squinting in a fog, peering through a mist. But it won't be long before the weather clears and the sun shines bright! We'll see it all then, see it all as clearly as God sees us, knowing him directly just as he knows us!
>
> *1 Corinthians 13:12, The Message*

And Ecclesiastes 3:11 explains why we "squint" at all, why we bother to try to understand time and eternity:

> He has made everything beautiful in its time. He has also set eternity in the hearts of men; yet they cannot fathom what God has done from beginning to end.

Look at the last few words: "from beginning to end" is a perfect description of God's eternal nature. And man, created to be an immortal being, has a taste of eternity in his heart. But when he looks through the "trouble and sorrow" of this life, "squinting in a fog, peering through a mist," he can't quite figure out the whole idea of eternity. And too many people, for want of clarity here and now, refuse to believe in the eternal God at all. But Isaiah's words still ring true: God is "near" and "may be found" if we will take advantage of the ways He has revealed Himself to us.

The apostle Paul says, "For since the creation of the world God's invisible qualities—his eternal power and divine nature—have been clearly seen, being understood from what has been made, so that men are without excuse" (Rom. 1:20). And Jesus even said that our desire to know—our willingness to squint through the fog of this life—has something to do with how clear our vision of God becomes (see John 7:17).

Living as a two-timer is not easy. The Bible says we are citizens of heaven (see Phil. 3:20), yet we find ourselves residents of earth—a legal foot in each realm. Sometimes we get so enthralled with this temporal place in which we reside that we lose sight of our eternal home. Yet that is exactly what we must not do, especially on those days when we feel we are down to nothing. Not only is God always up to something, He is up to something eternal—preparing a new heaven and new earth for us then, and preparing us now to inhabit it forever.

On the very last page of the last volume of the seven-volume *The Chronicles of Narnia*, C. S. Lewis beautifully describes what it might be like to wake up in eternity one day—as Aslan, the lion and Christ-figure in the books reveals to the children that eternity lies before them:

> Then Aslan turned to them and said:
> "You do not yet look so happy as I mean you to be."
> Lucy said, "We're so afraid of being sent away, Aslan. And you have sent us back into our own world so often."
> "No fear of that," said Aslan. "Have you not guessed?"
> Their hearts leaped and a wild hope rose within them.
> "There was a real railway accident," said Aslan softly.
> "Your father and mother and all of you are—as you used

to call it in the Shadowlands—dead. The term is over: the holidays have begun. The dream is ended: this is the morning."

And as He spoke He no longer looked to them like a lion; but the things that began to happen after that were so great and beautiful that I cannot write them. And for us this is the end of all the stories, and we can most truly say that they all lived happily ever after. But for them it was only the beginning of the real story. All their life in this world and all their adventures in Narnia had only been the cover and the title page: now at last they were beginning Chapter One of the Great Story which no one on earth has read: which goes on forever: in which every chapter is better than the one before.[1]

You and I are part of the cover and the title page of God's never-ending story that goes on forever. It is my prayer for you that you will accept God's invitation to be part of a life that will be happier ever after. You will never again be down to nothing. Even in eternity, God will always be up to something.

Notes

1. God Is Always with Me

1. "Footprints in the Sand," accessed May 3, 2010, http://www.wowzone.com/fprints.htm.
2. Richard Alleyne, "Loneliness Increases Your Blood Pressure," *The Telegraph*, accessed March 19, 2010, http://www.telegraph.co.uk/health/healthnews/7473166/Loneliness-increases-your-blood-pressure.html.
3. Martin H. Manser (compiler), *The Westminster Collection of Christian Quotations: Over 6000 Quotations Arranged by Theme* (Louisville, KY: Westminster John Knox Press, 2001), 233.
4. C. H. Spurgeon, "The Education of Sons of God: No. 2722," accessed May 3, 2010, http://www.spurgeongems.org/vols46-48/chs2722.pdf.
5. Laura Parker, "Dropping Nets," Life Overseas, accessed March 19, 2010, http://www.lauraleighparker.com/?p=1009.
6. The Practice of the Presence of God, accessed March 19, 2010, http://www.practicegodspresence.com.
7. Mark Water (compiler), *The New Encyclopedia of Christian Quotations* (Grand Rapids: Baker Books, 2000), 621.

2. What You Can't Live Without

1. Robert A. Schuller, *Getting Through What You're Going Through—Comfort, Hope, and Encouragement from the Twenty-Third Psalm* (Nashville: Nelson Books, 1986), xvii.

2. Harry F. Harlow, "The Nature of Love," Classics in the History of Psychology, accessed May 14, 2010, http://psychclassics.asu.edu/Harlow/love.htm.

3. See Maia Szalavitz, "It's the Orphanages, Stupid!" Forbes.com, accessed May 14, 2010, http://www.forbes.com/2010/04/20/russia-orphanage-adopt-children-opinions-columnists-medialand.html.

4. Lauren Slater, "Monkey Love" in *The Boston Globe*, March 21, 2004. See http://www.boston.com/news/globe/ideas/articles/2004/03/21/monkey_love/ (accessed May 14, 2010).

3. Being Together Is Better

1. See http://ocgathering.blogspot.com and http://www.ocgathering.com.

2. Robert A. Schuller, *Leaning into God When Life Is Pushing You Away* (New York: FaithWords, 2009).

3. John Donne, *Devotions Upon Emergent Occasions*, Meditation XVII, accessed May 17, 2010, http://www.luminarium.org/sevenlit/donne/meditation17.php.

4. Robert D. Putnam, *Bowling Alone: The Collapse and Revival of American Community* (New York: Simon and Schuster, 2001).

5. Ibid., 355.

6. To quote the rendering of Romans 12:2 from the *J. B. Phillips New Testament*: "Don't let the world around you squeeze you into its own mould, but let God re-mould your minds from within."

7. C. S. Lewis, *The Four Loves* (New York: Houghton, Mifflin, Harcourt, 1991), 44.

8. Meg Daley Olmert, *Made for Each Other: The Biology of the Human-Animal Bond* (Cambridge, MA: Da Capo Press, 2009), 191. See also Jeffrey Kluger, "Study: A Dose of Oxytocin Increases the Cuddles," May 2, 2010, TIME.com, accessed May 17, 2010, http://www.time.com/time/health/article/0,8599,1986318.00.html.

4. You Are Your Own Best Friend

1. Leanne Payne, *The Broken Image: Restoring Personal Wholeness Through Healing Prayer* (Grand Rapids: Baker Books, 1981, 1996), 125.

2. Leanne Payne, *The Healing Presence: How God's Grace Can Work in You to Bring Healing in Your Broken Places and the Joy of Living in His Love* (Westchester, IL: Crossway Books, 1989), 52.
3. Shane Stanford, "Racing Past Illness and Bias Toward Love," April 2, 2010, CNN.com, accessed May 26, 2010, http://www.cnn.com/2010/OPINION/04/02/stanford.who.am.i/index.html.
4. Ibid.
5. William Shakespeare, *Hamlet*, Act 1, Scene 3, line 78.

5. How to Be Set Free

1. Ed Rowell, "Why Am I Angrier Than I Used to Be?" *Leadership Journal* (Summer 2000), 79–80.
2. The editors of PreachingToday.com, *More Perfect Illustrations for Every Topic and Occasion* (Wheaton, IL: Tyndale, 2003), 106.
3. Wess Stafford, "A Candle in the Darkness," May 7, 2010, Christianity Today.com, accessed July 2, 2010, http://www.christianitytoday.com/ct/2010/may/9.23.html.
4. Wess Stafford, "Wess Stafford Responds," *Christianity Today*, June 2010, p. 43.

7. You Are Totally Gifted

1. Luisa Kroll and Matthew Miller, "The World's Billionaires," March 10, 2010, Forbes.com, accessed May 28, 2010, http://www.forbes.com/2010/03/10/worlds-richest-people-slim-gates-buffett-billionaires-2010_land.html?boxes=HomepageSpecialStorySection.
2. "Buffett's Lasting Legacy: Immaterial Wealth," May 6, 2010, NPR.org, accessed May 28, 2010, http://www.npr.org/templates/story/story.php?storyId=126538348.

9. Nobody Has More Money than God

1. www.americanlifetv.com
2. I'll say more about the "new" ALN in subsequent chapters. But to see a sample of what's ahead, go to the ALN website (americanlifetv.com) and click on the "Watch Everyday Life" link on the right side of the page.

3. There is no evidence that the senator ever made the statement, but he has received credit it for it nonetheless ("A Billion Here, A Billion There..." The Dirksen Congressional Center, accessed June 14, 2010, http://www.dirksencenter.org/print_emd_billionhere.htm).

10. Living Old, Dying Young

1. I had the pleasure of authoring a book on health with my chiropractor, Dr. Douglas Di Siena: *Possibility Living: Add Years to Your Life and Life to Your Years with God's Health Plan* (New York: HarperSanFrancisco, 2000).
2. Geneen Roth, *Women Food and God* (New York: Scribner, 2010), 2.
3. The book I coauthored in 2000 (see note 1) was a few years ahead of its time in connecting health with all aspects of our lifestyle.
4. Roth, *Women Food and God*, 6.
5. See note 1.

11. The Mythical Get-Out-of-Pain-Free Card

1. Mike Neifert, *Light and Life* (February 1997), p. 27.
2. John Wesley, "Covenant Prayer," from *The United Methodist Hymnal*. Also available at http://en.wikipedia.org/wiki/Wesley_Covenant_Prayer (accessed August 2, 2010).

12. Nothing to Be Afraid Of

1. Paul Martin, *The Sickening Mind: Brain, Behaviour, Immunity and Disease* (New York: HarperCollins, 1997), 2–3.

13. What Goes Up Must Come Down

1. Dennis Overbye, "A Scientist Takes on Gravity," July 12, 2010, NYTimes.com, accessed July 30, 2010, http://www.nytimes.com/2010/07/13/science/13gravity.html?pagewanted=1&_r=2&sq=gravity&st=cse&scp=2.
2. Robert J. Morgan, *On This Day* (Nashville: Thomas Nelson Publishers, 1997), "October 22nd."

3. Patrick O'Driscoll, "Rural Areas Rustle Up Rules for City Slickers," *USA Today*, August 8, 1997, section A, page 4.

14. The Greatest Feeling in the World

1. Juli Weiner, "An Incomplete History of 'If Anyone Was Offended...' Apologies," May 13, 2010, VanityFair.com, accessed August 4, 2010, http://www.vanityfair.com/online/daily/2010/05/an-incomplete-history-of-if-anyone-was-offended-apologies.html.
2. Karl Menninger, *Whatever Became of Sin?* (New York: Hawthorn Books, 1973).
3. The editors of PreachingToday.com, *More Perfect Illustrations for Every Topic and Occasion* (Wheaton, IL: Tyndale, 2003), 50.

15. How to Re-Joice

1. "Denmark 'Happiest' Country in the World," last modified July 2, 2008, CNNhealth.com, accessed June 30, 2010, http://www.cnn.com/2008/HEALTH/07/02/nations.happiness/index.html.
2. "Denmark 'Happiest Place on Earth,'" last modified July 28, 2006, BBC News, accessed June 30, 2010, http://news.bbc.co.uk/2/hi/5224306.stm.
3. Tracy F. Rysavy, "Rethinking the GDP," *ACRES USA* magazine, Vol. 40, No. 4, April 2010, pp. 5, 80.
4. Elizabeth W. Dunn, Lara B. Aknin, Michael I. Norton (March 2008), "Spending Money on Others Promotes Happiness," *Science* 21: Vol. 319. no. 5870, pp. 1687–1688. (Accessed from Steve Wright, "Can Money Buy Happiness?" MeaningandHappiness.com, accessed June 30, 2010, http://www.meaningandhappiness.com/can-money-buy-happiness-spend-givingother-people/302.)
5. See Wikipedia article, "Happiness," accessed June 30, 2010, http://en.wikipedia.org/wiki/Happiness.
6. Steve Wright, "Oxford Happiness Questionnaire," MeaningandHappiness.com, accessed June 30, 2010, http://www.meaningandhappiness.com/oxford-happiness-questionnaire/214.

7. John Ortberg, *Dangers, Toils & Snares: Resisting the Hidden Temptations of Ministry* (Sisters, OR: Multnomah Publishers, 1994), 99–100.

8. C. S. Lewis, *Surprised by Joy: The Shape of My Early Life* (New York: Harcourt, Brace & World, Inc., 1955).

9. Ibid., 17–18.

10. Ibid., 238.

16. The Rest of Your Life

1. "Holmes and Rahe Stress Scale," Wikipedia, accessed July 12, 2010, http://en.wikipedia.org/wiki/Holmes_and_Rahe_stress_scale. In Chapter 10 of our book, *Possibility Living: Add Years to Your Life and Life to Your Years with God's Health Plan* (New York: HarperSanFrancisco, 2000), my coauthor, Dr. Douglas Di Siena, discusses the Holmes-Rahe Stress Scale and offers practical advice on alleviating harmful levels of stress.

17. It's Not as Hard as You Think

1. John Calvin, *Institutes of the Christian Religion.* Online version at http://www.ccel.org/ccel/calvin/institutes.iii.ii.html (accessed August 3, 2010).

2. Ibid.

18. Who's in Charge Here?

1. Patrick Kavanaugh and Barbara Kavanaugh, *Devotions from the World of Music* (Colorado Springs: Chariot Victor Publishing, 2000), 202.

19. Cancel Your Accident Insurance

1. Robert J. Morgan, *The Promise: How God Works All Things Together for Good* (Nashville: B&H Publishing Group, 2008), xviii.

2. Ibid., 191–92.

20. You Have to Trust Somebody

1. Words and music by Bob Dylan. © 1979 by Special Rider Music.
2. Robert Schuller with William Kruidenier, *Leaning into God When Life Is Pushing You Away* (New York: FaithWords, 2009), 181–82.
3. Dale Bruner, "Is Jesus Inclusive or Exclusive?" *Theology, News, and Notes* [of Fuller Theological Seminary] (October 1999), p. 3.

21. There Is a Good Reason to Hang On

1. "5-Year-Old Samantha Runnion Has Been Kidnapped in California," CNN Live Events/Special, July 16, 2002, CNN.com, http://www.studentnews.cnn.com/TRANSCRIPTS/0207/16/se.03.html.

22. I'm Sorry, I Have No Recollection of That

1. Current thought in quantum mechanics says there are at least two dimensions of time and maybe many more. Christian astrophysicist and apologist Hugh Ross talks about this extensively, helping us understand how time "works" and how we relate to it.

23. Living on a Need-to-Know Basis

1. James R. Edwards, *The Divine Intruder* (Colorado Springs: NavPress, 2000), 154.
2. Andrew Bagnato, "Good Guys Finish First (Sometimes)," *Chicago Tribune Magazine*, September 1, 1996, p. 15.

24. The Never-Ending Story

1. C. S. Lewis, *The Last Battle* (New York: HarperCollins, 1994), 210–11.